The Spirit of Entrepreneurship

Sharda S. Nandram · Karel J. Samsom

The Spirit of Entrepreneurship

Exploring the Essence of Entrepreneurship
Through Personal Stories

With 19 Figures and 25 Tables

 Springer

Dr. Sharda S. Nandram
Nyenrode Business Universiteit
Straatweg 25
3621 BG Breukelen
The Netherlands
s.nandram@nyenrode.nl

Professor Karel J. Samsom
70 S. Winooski Ave # 111
Burlington VT 05401
USA
ksamsom@mac.com

ISBN-10   3-540-34760-7 Springer Berlin Heidelberg New York
ISBN-13   978-3-540-34760-6 Springer Berlin Heidelberg New York

Cataloging-in-Publication Data
Library of Congress Control Number: 2006930740

Springer is a part of Springer Science+Business Media

springeronline.com

© Springer Berlin · Heidelberg 2006
Printed in Germany

Cover photo by John Waller, Uncage the Soul Productions, Portland, OR, USA

Hardcover-Design: WMXDesign GmbH, Heidelberg

SPIN 11768289   43/3153-5 4 3 2 1 0 – Printed on acid-free paper

Foreword

Ambition, perseverance, intuition, creativity, responsibility, but above all: passion. Those are the terms that help me describe entrepreneurship. Whether you are young or old, man or woman, minority or majority, healthy or disabled, it is the passion for building new ventures and finding new roads that characterizes the entrepreneur. You have to believe in yourself, your team, your product, your company and in your customers. You have to be pragmatic and rational in your approach. But it is the passion that makes you successful.

In my own entrepreneurial life, I have covered experiences from working on the grocery shop floor to building the family retail company out into Europe, then the US, then other parts of the world. After my retirement from the executive board of the retail company my grandfather started in 1887, Royal Ahold, I started a whole new exciting chapter in my entrepreneurial life by opening a shop and a restaurant in my new hometown of Hereford, England. The restaurant world is a new one that gives me fun and satisfaction by engaging in new and exciting challenges. Cooking is like entrepreneurship; it is only possible with... passion. Sometimes things get burned, but there is always a sense of fulfillment when things succeed in the way you want them to. It is through mistakes and setbacks that you can value your achievements.

I was invited by the researchers and the president of Nyenrode, my alma mater, to introduce The Spirit of Entrepreneurship and I am very pleased to do so. This study investigates the full range of entrepreneurial processes and behaviors and illustrates these with sixty diverse cases of entrepreneurs and entrepreneurial executives. Sixty very different individuals, who are connected not only through their education at Nyenrode, but above all through their spirit of enterprise. Reading their stories and putting them into perspective is a useful exercise and experience I recommend for future as well as established entrepreneurs.

For me, always taking a pragmatic and optimistic view towards business and towards life is key! Every multinational started at one time with one person having an entrepreneurial idea. Customers and markets may change, but the foundations of success remain the same. Understanding and innovating the business processes, targeting profitability, managing and trusting people, building lasting customer relationships and finally attending to social and environmental values. This book of personal stories will inspire new generations of entrepreneurs, who, with the right mindset, will listen to their heart, follow their passion as well as reason.

Dr. Albert Heijn
Entrepreneur, Retired Chairman and CEO of Royal Ahold

Preface

What motivated us to research and write yet another book about entrepreneurship? Probably our passion for the human side of venturing, in our opinion an underexposed subject both in terms of serious research as well as descriptive writing. Much has been contributed to entrepreneurship literature and research. Yet most of it with a primary focus on the processes of opportunity and resource management, the venture team and the uncertainty of the economic environment. Together, we had undertaken a number of interesting research projects where our diverse knowledge and skills (psychologist-economist-researcher and, business executive, three time entrepreneur and latter day academic) combined to provide an in-depth insight into the human aspects of the entrepreneur. In a way, we see this book itself as an entrepreneurial endeavor. Just like entrepreneurs, we took a venturing opportunity and used it to explore the nature, human side and performance of some 60 diverse cases of entrepreneurship and entrepreneurial management. These cases were distributed in a wide geographical area, covering Europe and the United States as well as various life-cycle stages of the firms involved. In this qualitative and exploratory research project we aimed to uncover and document entrepreneurship with a special emphasis on the behavioral aspect. Again, like entrepreneurs, we took a rather risky road in targeting this study and the resultant book at a multiple of market segments such as entrepreneurs, business professionals, students and academics, university managers and communities. We thank our publisher, Martina Bihn at Springer for embracing this vision.

While attending a seminar during the process of writing our last pages of this book the statement by Jerry Engels and David Charron of UC Berkeley: "entrepreneurship is a team sport" appeared as a fitting one. In the seminar they discussed how entrepreneurial success is enhanced by a team endeavor.

We are grateful to people we were able to work with in writing this book and thank all 60 research participants documented in Chapters 8 to 16 for their willingness to share their personal stories and venturing experiences with us. Many entrepreneurs and executives from Nyenrode have evolved to prestigious positions in society which would have made it easy to select participants for our book. We sidestepped that approach to find a balanced group of participants which could be seen as a representative group of the great variety of types of entrepreneurship represented in society.

We thank The Nyenrode Foundation (SNF), especially Jan de Graaff, Herman Bruggink and Eric Wuite, for their confidence, their feedback and material support.

Arie van der Giessen, Frank Tebbe and Job van Harmelen, were all involved from the start in our process of envisioning this study about entrepreneurs. Because of our interaction with them our imagination took concrete forms.

We thank Wim Keizer for sharing his insight and experiences with the Mental Fitness Tracker and Gun Semin also for his insight and experiences with the action and state and promotion-prevention questionnaires. Thanks to Larissa van Woudenberg who helped us to manage the logistic processes of approaching, contacting the participants all with very busy schedules. Thanks to Pipsa Ylänkö for the information she provided on the alumni database. Caroline Knulst and Metty Willemsen for their care and flexibility in letting us use their offices for the research interviews.

We are grateful to the following people who took us back into the history of Nyenrode the business school: Hanna Emmering, Rene Verhulst, Michael Moore, Gert Immerzeel, No Knubben, Thonie Wattel, Arie van der Giessen, Roberto Flören, and Johan de Voogd.

Dr. Albert Heijn honored us by writing the foreword to this book and we want to thank him. Thanks to Bert Twaalfhoven, a serial international entrepreneur and Ben Cohen, a triple bottom line entrepreneur, for their inspiring opinions and experiences on entrepreneurship. Thanks to Cynthia Foster, Job van Harmelen and Frank Tebbe for their tireless advice and proofreading of our drafts. Jacky van Marle gave her valuable input by reading the manuscript in the final stage and her support in our first alumni study. Finally, thanks to the people who have made this book look so good, Eric Fecken for all the photos, John Waller for the cover photo, Mei Li Han for editing and layout, Jason Howard for designing the figures and Onno Frank van Bekkum for the final layout.

Breukelen, July 2006   Sharda S. Nandram
                                                               Karel J. Samsom

Table of Contents

CHAPTER 9:

Venturers 153

CHAPTER 10:

Re-launchers 179

CHAPTER 11:

Trend Entrepreneurs 207

1 The Spirit of Entrepreneurship: Beyond Limitations

"I am enough of an artist to draw freely upon my imagination. Imagination is more important than knowledge."

Albert Einstein

"Strength does not come from physical capacity. It comes from an indomitable will."

Mahatma Gandhi

"In each person's life there comes a time when he or she pursues growth and expansion on the level of form. This is when you strive to overcome limitation such as physical weakness or financial scarcity when you acquire new skills and knowledge or through creative action by bringing something new into this world that is life enhancing for yourself as well as others. This may be a piece of music or a work of art, a book, a service you provide, a function you perform, a business organization that you set up or make a vital contribution to."

Eckart Tolle

"Not everything that can be counted counts, and not everything that counts can be counted."

Albert Einstein

"Your biggest opportunity probably lies under your own feet, in your current job, industry, education, experience or interest."

Brian Tracy

"The ancient wisdom traditions of India identify three components necessary for change. One of them is Simran: to reflect on who we really are. To communicate, to share inspiration. Simran is a profound reflection into the nature of the true self, the essence of you or the spirit of you. When this reflection is done in communication with others, it inspires – infuses with spirit – and unveils or unleashes the collective power of the essential connection we share, serving our inner transformation as well global transformation."

Deepak Chopra

"When you are doing something that is a brand new adventure, breaking new ground, whether it is something like a technological breakthrough or simply a way of living that is not what the community can help you with, there is always the danger of too much enthusism, of neglecting certain mechanical details. Than you fall off. 'A danger path this is.' When you follow the path of your desire and enthusiasm and emotion, keep your mind in control, and don't let it pull you compulsively into disaster."

Joseph Campbell

Reflecting on Entrepreneurship

When we were planning to write the introductory chapter to "The Spirit of Entrepreneurship" we experienced, just like entrepreneurs sometimes do, a need for a moment of deep reflection. Reflection on how our journey started, on the opportunities we envisioned in writing this book, the challenges we saw, and the expectations we held as authors and entrepreneurship researchers. Of course, also the expectations of the Nyenrode community and all others involved were part of our thinking. Our reflections resulted in expressing entrepreneurship through quotes. These quotes are not from scholars of entrepreneurship yet they describe the essence of entrepreneurial activities. Simply put, entrepreneurship is about human behavior and these quotes refer to human behavior. And finally, we reflected on what we would learn from the 60 entrepreneurial stories.

Entrepreneurship is about strong will and the capacity to see and believe, and imagining things others don't see or believe in. It is about the drive to overcome one's limitations. Successful entrepreneurship is also about the inner struggle before taking the first step to become an entrepreneur or to use entrepreneurial techniques in organizations to improve the culture of innovation. It is about the interaction between people, or between teams in a firm or organization. It captures the interaction between the entrepreneur and the business, social, environmental and community relationships. In this spirit, we have dedicated Chapter 3 to the rapidly expanding growth in opportunities for entrepreneurs who address all environments a new venture enters into. Not every entrepreneurial process can be measured but this does not mean immensurable aspects don't count in understanding entrepreneurship. Also entrepreneurship is about reflection, the main driver of inspiration.

Applying the insights we obtained from the 60 entrepreneurial stories to the business context, we are convinced that entrepreneurship is about designing opportunities for which imagination and a strong will are necessary. Entrepreneurship is about visions, dreams, passion, drive, soul, creativity, courage, knowledge, resources, facts and figures. Most importantly, it is about people, teams, leadership and the communities that entrepreneurs serve by creating value in the widest sense of the word. Clients, customers, communities, regions and countries and, of course, the physical environment the venture draws from, impacts and hopefully serves as well.

In the "Spirit of Entrepreneurship" we document what inspires people to leave behind certainty, be it material or immaterial, and to engage in following a vision through venturing, no matter how intangible or ephemeral it may be initially. To anchor these experiences, we will discuss them in the light of what has already been researched and written about the theory and practice of entrepreneurship. We present 60 people who followed their creative vision and drive and engaged in a wide variety of innovative entrepreneurial activities; people from diverse backgrounds, cultures and countries who pursued starting new ventures or leading existing organizations, institutions or corporations, with a refreshing air of entrepreneurial activities and leadership.

The word spirit refers to human activation, passion and enthusiasm and certainly describes the attitudes as expressed by the entrepreneurs and entrepreneurial executives we worked with. Entrepreneurship is about opportunities, ideas that can be realized and value adding creation both in a tangible and intangible sense. These opportunities can have many different sources.

Sixty Cases of "Live" Venturing

Our research illustrates entrepreneurship with the examples of 60 cases of "live" venturing. While much has been written about the creative, innovative and entrepreneurial processes of new venturing, we find that the aspect of human behavior and performance in entrepreneurship is less explored. Yet, in terms of venture performance, the 'people dynamic' appears to be as much a challenge on the road to success as the proper evaluation and exploitation of new opportunities or the parsimonious management of limited resources. In fact, in terms of pre-venture funding due diligence, we have observed in our research over the years, that more is invested in securing business and marketing plans, technological facts, regulatory processes and legal documentation than in in-depth people due-diligence. Thus, in our research of 60 entrepreneurial profiles, we especially zeroed in on this human side of entrepreneurial behavior and performance. As a result, the following types of entrepreneurship will be discussed in this study: (1) entrepreneurial executives, (2) venturers, (3) re-launchers, (4) trend entrepreneurs, (5) family business entrepreneurs, (6) significant business entrepreneurs, (7) small business entrepreneurs, (8) start-ups, (9) enterprising persons.

We have consciously chosen for an individual level of analysis by studying the experiences of entrepreneurs and entrepreneurial executives. We used two primary sources of information. The first source of information was based on a written questionnaire each of the participants completed. The second source consisted of interviews with the participants. All interviews were personally conducted by the authors. The interviews with the entrepreneurs concentrated on the start-up process with questions about their reasons for starting a venture, the factors that hindered or stimulated the start-up process, learning points, and unique experiences within their entrepreneurial career.

The interviews with the entrepreneurial executives concentrated on experiences dealing with innovation, leadership and international aspects. The part of the study which covered entrepreneurial executives was very much explorative in nature with the aim to learn what personal characteristics could be identified within this group. Not one recorded case was similar to another. Reading all the cases provides a good feeling of the many faces of entrepreneurship. Both entrepreneurship and spirit are frequently used as umbrella concepts that are clarified when reading through the cases.

Target Readers

This book is written for practitioners of entrepreneurship, business professionals, academics as well as business students. For practitioners of entrepreneurship, this book seeks to place individual experiences in context. For business professionals, the stories provide a means to discover more about entrepreneurship and entrepreneurial management. For academics, reading our research approach and outcomes presents a new perspective on entrepreneurship. For students, the book offers case materials for entrepreneurship courses. And, this book is also of interest to the Nyenrode University community from which all 60 research participants hailed over the last sixty years.

Structure of the Book

The book is composed of two sections that contain 17 chapters in total. Part 1 of the book presents the central concepts in new venture creation and entrepreneurial management. The latter represents the application of entrepreneurial techniques in larger organizations to reinvigorate the innovative spirit. Part 2 presents case studies covering European and North American entrepreneurs and their companies with a special focus on the personality of the entrepreneur and entrepreneurial behavior. Part 2 ends with the Nyenrode alumni study and entrepreneurial track record of Nyenrode itself in a mini-case format. The book ends with the postscript in which we summarize the main findings and we come with recommendations for stimulating entrepreneurship education at Nyenrode.

Part 1, Concepts and Case Findings, contains Chapters 2 thru 7. In Chapter 2 we summarize *the impact entrepreneurs and their ventures* have on people and society at large. We also highlight attention from European countries to special groups of entrepreneurs in society to stimulate their entrepreneurial activity such as innovative start-ups, women entrepreneurs, immigrant entrepreneurs, and high growth entrepreneurs. In Chapter 3 we focus on the *rapidly emerging opportunities in sustainability and natural capitalism*. It deals with the rapidly growing field of entrepreneurial opportunities and activities in the context of economic, ecological, and social environments. Chapter 4 highlights the *main perspectives on entrepreneurship and the human factor* by integrating the recent line of thinking in academic entrepreneur-ship literature and previous empirical research. Our integration is based on economic models, strategic management models and behavioral models. We conclude that en-trepreneurship is designing an opportunity with the following key processes: (1) recognition or imagination of opportunities, (2) evaluation of opportunities, and (3) exploitation of opportunities. Three types of processes may influence the design process: individual behavioral processes, strategic management processes and eco-nomic processes. In this chapter we also present *a model for understanding entre-preneurship* which forms the conceptual basis of qualitative data collection through interviewing 60 research participants. The six-dimension model of Stevenson (2000) and the three-factor approach of Timmons and Spinelli (2004) have been used to develop the strategic management part of the model. The psychological behavior model of Fishbein and Ajzen (1975) is applied as the basis of the behavioral build-ing block of the study. We enlarged the model by including different psychological concepts not previously studied in the context of understanding entrepreneurial activities. These concepts are promotion and prevention orientation, action and state orientation and moods. We include personality as well, a concept that has been a focus in entrepreneurial research.

In Chapter 5 we describe the research process followed by our findings in *com-paring psychological make up and the company background*. We further contrast our findings of entrepreneurs with those of entrepreneurial executives. Chapter 6

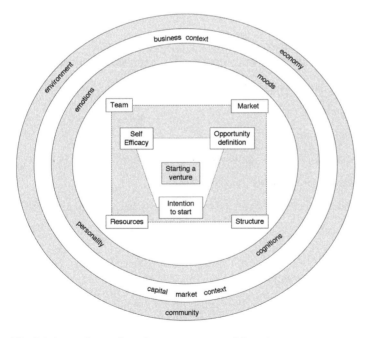

Fig. 1.1 Antecedents of starting an entrepreneurial venture

covers the useful ingredients we explored in our theory building efforts *through the case studies*, based on empirical data presented in Chapters 8 thru 16. Through combining theory and practice in Chapter 6 we develop what entrepreneurship is about, resulting in the following model which incorporates all the relevant concepts discussed in this study (see Figure 1.1).

The model describes the concepts that follow the behavioral processes of undertaking an activity, represented in the middle square of the model. The second part consists of the concepts that cause the interaction and are presented by circles. There is an interaction with the individual background (the psychological make-up), there also is an interaction with the business and industry environment and, finally, an interaction with the bigger picture encompassing society, economics and nature. Within the circle there are two crucial interactive steps.

The first step is between the: (1) opportunity definition, (2) intention to start, and (3) self-efficacy, i.e. the feeling of being capable of taking the necessary tasks successfully. The second step refers to the interaction between: (a) team, (b), structure, (c) resources, and (d) market.

All steps are needed to actually start a venture or implement an opportunity. Starting a venture is the central point in this model yet it can also be applied to other activities such as implementing an opportunity in a not-for-profit organization or in an executive role. This model has been built because of the insights from the case studies. It contains relevant factors for predicting entrepreneurial behavior such as the start-up of a venture. And in Chapter 7, the final chapter of the first part, we pay attention to the conclusions we can draw from our search for the essence of entrepreneurship.

Part 2 – The Case Studies, covers Chapters 8 thru 17. Based on the thinking outlined above, the participants in the study have been categorized as follows:

- Entrepreneurial executives (chapter 8)
- Venturers (chapter 9)
- Re-launchers (chapter 10)
- Trend entrepreneurs (balancing people, profit and planet; chapter 11)
- Family business entrepreneurs (chapter 12)
- Significant business entrepreneurs (above 20 employees; chapter 13)
- Small business entrepreneurs (chapter 14)
- Start-ups (chapter 15)
- Enterprising persons (chapter 16)

The last chapter of this study, Chapter 17, describes the history of *Nyenrode as a business school, the entrepreneurial activity of alumni, and the policy and its impact* related to entrepreneurial opportunities and challenges.

Entrepreneurial Dilemmas

Besides theory building through cases, the data seem to reveal that the various types of entrepreneurs discussed in this book deal with different types of dilemmas. These dilemmas arise because of the entrepreneurial categories we investigated and are detailed in the following discussion. Of course not every entrepreneur always experienced these dilemmas.

- *Dilemma of Transparency.* Entrepreneurial executives described in this book seem to deal with a broader stakeholders framework than entrepreneurs who have more control over their actions because they often build the venture from scratch while the executive has to fit his leadership style, activities and communication within existing frameworks.

- *Dilemma of Previous Network.* Venturers might have to deal with the dilemma of when to decide to lean on their previous networks and when not to.

- *Dilemma of Putting the Past Aside.* Re-launchers and family business entrepreneurs might have to deal with this dilemma. In family businesses a second dilemma of keeping other family members at a good distance from business activities might occur.

- *Dilemma of Scale.* Trend entrepreneurs logically deal with the question of what scale is needed to remain successful in dealing with the bigger picture of entrepreneurship as well as the community, ecology and economics.

- *Dilemma of Delegation.* Often a small business has limited personnel they can build on. The expertise of personnel is not very specialized because often each person is responsible for multidisciplinary tasks. The entrepreneur has to find a balance between what and when to delegate and what and when not to delegate. In busy periods, delegation might be a must. And in less busy times, delegation might not be needed. These situations ask for high flexibility within the team.

- *Dilemma of Growth and Expansion.* Significant businesses frequently have been searching for external finance. They even might need to deal with fast growth as a consequence of their innovative actions.

- *Dilemma of Focus.* The start-up is wide open to creativity, international orientation and growth. The main concern is deciding on a focus.

- *Dilemma of Staying Solo.* The enterprising person works mainly solo and is mainly driven by the need for independence, or doing things their own way. They face situations in which they have to say no to the customer in the fear of not meeting deadlines or delivery of low quality. Some are willing to work with personnel on a temporary basis but others will not because of the specific character of their expertise relying on the capabilities of the person. Another characteristic is that they cannot work in partnership.

Messages

Thus, this study presents entrepreneurship by focusing on spirit; this means the processes that motivate the drive of entrepreneurs and entrepreneurial executives. Most of the chapters therefore offer unusual topics in terms of people related processes as opposed to the familiar issues of finance, marketing, sales, distribution or human resources. Reflecting on our extensive past research as well as listening to the stories of the participants in this study, we are convinced that entrepreneurship, in theory building as well as in practice, will gain a great deal by really understanding the interactive processes between human forces and environmental conditions. This means that entrepreneurship is about interactive processes in defining an opportunity within a dynamic environment.

Another message of this study focuses on the many different types of entrepreneurs which makes the general question 'who is an entrepreneur' not that relevant unless the different types are being recognized. Shane and Venkataram (2000) stated that entrepreneurship has become a broad label under which a hodgepodge of research is housed. To make it a scholarly field it is important to clearly narrow down the topic in addition to just asking general questions about entrepreneurship. We hope that with our contribution, entrepreneurship can escape the label "hodgepodge" (Shane and Venkataraman 2000) or "potpourri" (Low 2001).

In summary, this study aims to rigorously and innovatively explore the basic concepts of applied entrepreneurship in action through insight into 60 venturing cases and related literature.

Part 1:

The Spirit of Entrepreneurship: Concepts and Case Findings

2 Entrepreneurship Today

The impact entrepreneurs and their ventures have on society at large, both in quantitative as well as qualitative terms, is significant. Starting with a look at current economic and social contributions of venturing today, this chapter elaborates on commonly identified personal characteristics of the entrepreneur, the process of entrepreneurship and continues with a brief comparison of entrepreneurial and management styles. The chapter concludes with a look at supporting entrepreneurship through public policy.

2.1   Entrepreneurship and Economy

Richard Cantillon (1680-1734) was the first philosopher who paid attention to the concept of entrepreneurship. In terms of the economic system, Cantillon distinguished between landowners, entrepreneurs and workers within the system. He saw a key role for the entrepreneur in society, i.e. to bring supply and demand in balance, with profit as the motive. Cantillon hypothesized that entrepreneurs differed primarily from landowners and laborers inasmuch as entrepreneurs were prepared to deal with uncertain incomes. In fact, the entrepreneur did not necessarily need to have money or be innovative to start a firm because capital could be borrowed.

Of course today, there are many definitions of entrepreneurship. Due to the great diversity of entrepreneurial activities few if any, fully cover the broad range of venturing activities. From start-up to maturity and from intrapreneurship to the reinvigoration of management styles through to the use of entrepreneurial techniques in large corporations and organizations, the spectrum is broad. Still, we offer two descriptions to demarcate the field. The first recognizes that today entrepreneurship is generally understood to define the risk-taking activity of people who start a new company based on an innovative business opportunity (Samsom 1999). The description by Stevenson (2000) approaches this activity as follows; "In developing a behavioral theory of entrepreneurship it becomes clear that entrepreneurship is defined by more than a set of individual traits and is different from an economic function. It is a cohesive pattern of managerial behavior." Thus, the first description emphasizes the frequently innovative nature of new ventures, the latter brings in the behavioral aspects of entrepreneurship and extends this activity across the life-cycles of companies from start-up to reinvigorating existing companies with entrepreneurial management techniques.

In the annual report for the financial year 2005, the International Monetary Fund (IMF) reported the annual growth of the global economy at 5.1 %, the highest rate in thirty-five years. This supports Wickham (2004), who states that the world is getting richer with North American and Europe producing over 70% of the world's output and China leading the emerging economies. Among the industrialized nations, the USA continued to be the most rapidly growing economy. In the emerging economies, China and India produced the fastest growth (IMF 2005). The Kaufman Index of Entrepreneurial Activity (2006) also reports that between 1996 and 2004, on average, 550,000 new businesses were launched monthly in the USA. That is 6.6 million new companies annually. While this rate of venture creation is not a record for the USA economy, it does express the highly entrepreneurial nature of the American economy.

Generation of material wealth through the commercial provision of goods and services is, in principle, primarily attributed to entrepreneurial and business activities such as self employment, new ventures, and larger and established corporations. Among these, self-employment or solo entrepreneurs, and new and growing ventures fall under the definition of entrepreneurship. Large established corporations are normally not considered as entrepreneurial ventures. However, with the increasing incidence of the application of entrepreneurial techniques to re-energize the innovative capacity of large companies, the field is expanding. Of course, there are also many ways in which entrepreneurship can contribute to non-quantifiable or more difficult to measure well-being and in Chapter 3 we will pay further attention to these trends. Following the above examples of large, highly entrepreneurial and productive economies, governments in other regions, such as Europe, increasingly play a role today in shaping healthy economic environments for entrepreneurship and in stimulating policies in the fields of innovation and new venture creation.

Entrepreneurship Worldwide

The Global Entrepreneurship Monitor (GEM) annually publishes information about the entrepreneurial activity in the Early-Stage Entrepreneurial Activity (TEA Index) by country. TEA expresses the number of people who are in the preparation stage of starting a new venture plus those that are already running a new firm for less than 42 months. The TEA, as previously defined, is thus an indication of entrepreneurial activity as a percentage of the occupational population between the ages of 18 and 64.

Figure 2.1 illustrates that most European nations still score well below the indices for such entrepreneurial juggernauts as the USA and China. Notable exceptions are Norway, Ireland and Iceland, Venezuela, Thailand and New Zealand. These countries show the highest rates of early-stage entrepreneurial activity while very low activity was measured in Belgium, Japan and Hungary. Researchers as well as opinion leaders, the business press and policy makers have written frequently about

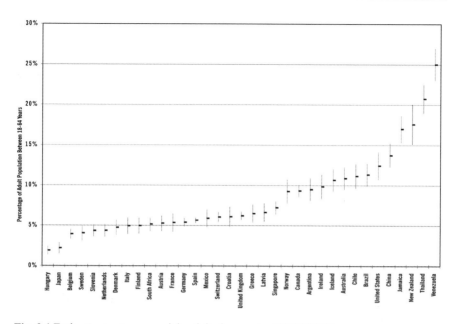

Fig. 2.1 Early-stage entrepreneurial activity by country (GEM 2005)

the need, particularly for some very slow growth European economies, to increase entrepreneurial activity. This reflects the growing recognition worldwide that entrepreneurial ventures produce significant contributions to economic wealth in terms of job creation, innovation and profits. Even without knowing how many employees each of these ventures might have, the TEA index can already tell us that, depending on the country and region of the world, entrepreneurs themselves make up between 2% and 25% (Hungary and Venezuela) of the total occupational population with most countries scoring in the range between 5% and 15%; a sizable contribution to the workforce.

Additionally, GEM 2005 research shows that early-stage entrepreneurs are most prevalent in the 25 to 34 age range. This is confirmed by our own research as well as by our observations of the ages of those business graduates from the universities at which we teach and who start their own ventures. In the established business ownership category, the age range of the entrepreneur is 45 to 54 years.

Entrepreneurship has a positive effect on the economy due to the growth in innovation and stimulation of competition it provides. Innovation refers to such activities as entering new markets, developing new products and services, starting a new venture or rethinking renewed processes and services within a firm. Research by Birch (1989) indicated that 80% of new jobs were being generated in small rather than larger USA firms. This trend was later confirmed for other countries such as The Netherlands (EIM 1997). Therefore new, young firms were considered the engines of growth in the economy. The *High-Expectation-Entrepreneurship*

Summary Report now provides new evidence of the significance of job creation through entrepreneurship (GEM 2005).

The report states that, "The first global study of high expectation entrepreneurship has found that just 9.8% of the world's entrepreneurs expect to create almost 75% of the job generated by new business ventures. The report defines high expectation entrepreneurship as all start-ups and newly formed businesses which expect to employ at least 20 employees within five years. These ventures have far reaching consequences for the economies in which they operate, particularly because of their impact on job creation and innovation."

According to an earlier GEM report (2002), 7% of new entrepreneurs create significant new market niches. The report also shows that 70% of new entrepreneurs provide products and services in existing markets where there is already considerable competition and where the critical technology has been available for more than one year.

Last but not least, entrepreneurship in society can contribute to the quality of life in the community. Besides the self actualization of individuals, creation of wealth, introduction of innovative products and services which increase consumer choices and jobs, entrepreneurial firms can also use strategies to combine resources and opportunities in environmentally and socially friendly ways (environmental and social sustainability). They can also perform voluntary social services for disadvantaged social groups and communities.

To conclude, the primary entrepreneurial contributions to society can be summarized in five main categories:

1. Entrepreneurship as an expression of a person's unique vision, creativity, purpose and fulfillment in life.

2. Creation of material wealth as measured in shareholder value.

3. Innovation through new products and services as well as in stimulating competitiveness in the economy.

4. Job creation through venture employment and additional creation of jobs in supplier and customer companies.

5. Contributions to the quality of life in the local community.

Taking a closer look at the discussion of the contribution of entrepreneurship to society brings to light the following question: in which sectors do early-stage and established entrepreneurs found their business? Figure 2.2 reviews this question. The distinction between early-stage and established entrepreneurs does show significant differences in the areas of transforming or extractive industries. However, higher income countries show an increase in the use of business services and a decrease in consumer-oriented products as compared with middle income nations. Thus, in higher income nations, business services, such as consulting, maintenance and service of office, medical and home equipment, marketing and advertising, and financial services are taking a larger share of sectoral distribution. This shift is facilitated by the greater availability of educated people to undertake these tasks.

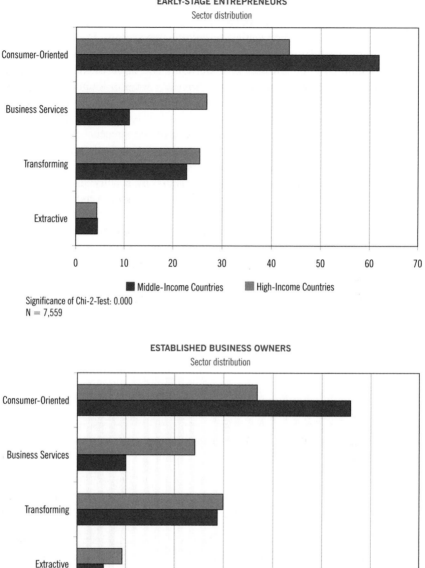

Fig.2.2 Sectoral distribution of entrepreneurial activity by country clusters, GEM 2005

In the transition of the discussion from entrepreneurship as an economic concept to entrepreneurial behavior, the distinction between necessity and opportunity-based venturing offers a fitting vehicle to link the two aspects. The 2005 GEM report provides a useful distinction between people who start a business because they have identified a specific area of opportunity and those who engage in it out of necessity. The latter motivation arises when other ways of finding work are not available or because the work environment is found to be socially or economically unacceptable or just too confining.

Figure 2.3 demonstrates that the great majority of entrepreneurs surveyed across countries pointed to opportunity attraction as the key reason for engaging in venturing. A small group of respondents indicated that they were motivated by the combination of opportunity and necessity. The distribution by country shows interesting differences which could, when further explored, assist policymakers to fine-tune the ways in which they promote and facilitate entrepreneurial activity in their countries. It is not surprising that, given the long entrepreneurial history and "can-do" culture of the USA, opportunity motivation ranks high in that country. In comparison, although The Netherlands is a country with a long history of high entrepreneurial activity, it has during the last four decades not performed as such; possibly because of its growing levels of individual security provided through social welfare, healthcare and the relatively low rate of new venture creation. In recent years, this led to multiple public and private initiatives to stimulate venturing. In the GEM 2005, The Netherlands ranked third in terms of opportunity driven entrepreneurship.

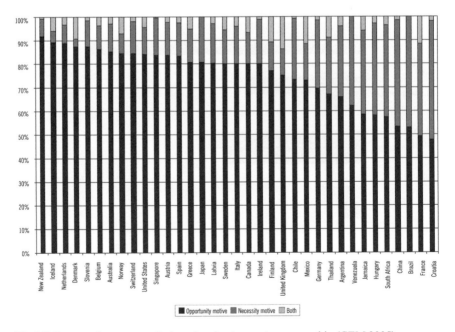

Fig.2.3 Opportunity-to-necessity based early-stage entrepreneurship (GEM 2005)

2.2   Promoting Entrepreneurship in Selected Groups

Many European countries pay special attention to specific groups of entrepreneurs in society to stimulate their entrepreneurial activity. The most important target groups in policy are: (1) innovative start-ups, (2) women entrepreneurs, (3) immigrant entrepreneurs, (4) high growth entrepreneurs.

Start-ups are the drivers of innovation. The expected rise in the aging of the population requires an efficient exploitation of human talent. It is worthwhile to note that much of human talent has not yet been exploited due to the low participation of women and ethnic minorities in the labor market. Entrepreneurship in ethnic minorities can also reduce the high unemployment rate among these groups and it can contribute to increasing living standards of these groups that often belong to the disadvantaged part of the society. A new category might be the potential for entrepreneurship among senior citizens. As an example, Business Week (2005) reports that the population of China over the age of 60 is expected to peak at 400 million by the middle of this century. Activities to target and train this sector of the population for venturing skills is emerging.

Innovative Start-ups

For innovative starters, the following conditions can be seen as critical for success (based on a research of the Ministry of Economic Affairs – The Netherlands 2003): a generally favorable business climate, access to finance, access to skilled labor, and access to knowledge. Indicators of favorable business climate would be: competitiveness, flexibility of the labor market, and the presence of regional clusters of interdependent enterprises.

There is still only limited empirical research on the impact of regional clusters, and it is assumed that these clusters encourage innovation. The same report mentioned above concluded that it is generally difficult to find early-stage funding but that for innovative start-ups it is even more difficult to do so. For this group informal investors seem to be the more suitable financing option. However, though this situation is changing, informal or sometimes called "angel" venture capital is relatively underdeveloped in most EU countries as compared with the USA.

Women in Entrepreneurship

Women in entrepreneurship constitute a venturing group which deserves special attention. Though there are many notable and successful female entrepreneurs demonstrating personal fulfillment through this occupational choice as well as their contributions to the economy and society, female entrepreneurs remain the exception. Possibly because of the dominance of males in this occupation or other cultural constraints, women tend to be less enthusiastic than men about venturing and underestimate their knowledge and skills in this field. Governments as well as private initiatives, such as the EU Commission in Europe and the Grameen Bank in Asia, promote and facilitate women who undertake in entering into entrepreneurship.

The GEM Global Report (2004) concludes that the gender gap continues. Two thirds of entrepreneurial activity is reported to be initiated by men. In middle-income countries men are 75% more likely to be active entrepreneurs than women while in low-income countries and in high-income countries male and female participation rates are statistically identical. There are no countries with more female than male entrepreneurs.

Immigrant Entrepreneurship

The UK is Europe's most entrepreneurial economy according to the GEM (2004). Don de Silva (2006) of ABI Associates summarizes the results regarding the ethnic minorities, stating that ethnic minorities make a large and important contribution to the success of the UK economy (GEM 2004). They tend to have more positive attitudes towards entrepreneurship and better self perceptions of their capacity to establish a business. Ethnic minorities however, are more likely to let fear of a lack of financing prevent them from starting a business and to use family and friends as the key source for start-up finance. Total entrepreneurial activity is highest amongst Bangladeshi people. They most likely face a lack of start-up funding yet are more likely to see opportunities and are less likely to fear failure. Pakistani ventures are most likely expected to start a business over the next three years. They are quick to see opportunities and have a very low fear of failure. Indian (43.6%) and other Asian (48.1%) ventures are most likely to be providing goods or services using new technologies. In contrast, the likelihood of new technology-based venturing among white business people is 14.1%. It seems that women from ethnic minorities are substantially more entrepreneurial than their white female counterparts. Black, Caribbean people are most likely among all ethnic backgrounds to be starting businesses which provide novel goods or services in the UK (36%).

In The Netherlands, the rate of entrepreneurship of Turkish immigrants is comparable to that of the native Dutch population. This is in sharp contrast with the rate of entrepreneurship for immigrants from Morocco, Suriname and the Antilles, which is less than half compared to that of the native Dutch population (EIM 2003). The relatively high entrepreneurial rate among Turkish immigrants is explained by the existence of concentrated groups in specific locations, i.e. clusters. A variety of enterprises serve their own ethnic market and or the general population. Common religion, language and culture all encourage this process, and many Turkish immigrants hail from entrepreneurial families. In addition, this EIM study shows that first generation immigrants are less likely to be entrepreneurs than second generation immigrants.

A study conducted by the Middlesex University (http://europe.eu.int) shows that while in EU countries, the vast majority of organizations do not have any special arrangements for ethnic minority entrepreneurs, Dutch and UK based organizations featured prominently in support for ethnic minority entrepreneurs. Another study conducted by the Middlesex University shows that in EU countries, members of ethnic minorities make up a maximum of 10% of the support organizations. The services provided by the special organizations regard for example training, advice or counseling services, hosting, supporting or developing networks of ethnic minority entrepreneurs, export advice, finance. The Directorate Enterprise and Industry of the European Commission (2006) concludes that businesses owned by ethnic minorities have a significant impact on economic growth in Europe. There are no data available for every EU member yet in at least two member states the percentage of ethnic start-ups is already reported to be proportionally higher than the percentage of native national start-ups. There are many similarities in problems faced by ethnic entrepreneurs and small businesses in general, but the directorate concludes that there are some problems that specifically affect ethnic entrepreneurs. These are identified as access to finance and support services; language barriers; limited business, management and marketing skills; and an over-concentration in low-entry threshold activities where the scope for breakout or diversification into mainstream markets may be limited. Governments have taken some specific initiatives to cope with these barriers for ethnic minorities.

Valdez (2002) concludes that in the USA, since the 1970s, the increase in business ownership has been noteworthy among ethnic groups. Koreans and Cubans exceed rates of business ownership of other groups. Their rates of self employment far surpass that of the general population, 28% compared to 11%. Yet it seems that they remain small business owners. This is comparable with the Indian and Pakistani entrepreneurs in the UK. Ethnic groups may use entrepreneurship as a survival strategy or as a last alternative to unemployment.

High Growth Entrepreneurs

Several definitions of fast growing enterprises are used but usually the term refers to enterprises that have shown growth rates of at least 20% in personnel over three years. *Europe's 500* annually presents the only independent, pan-European listing of high growth, job-creating companies. In the 2005 report, all 25 member countries of the EU are represented plus Iceland, Norway and Switzerland. The fast-growth, high performing mid-sized companies presented in the 2005 edition of *Europe's 500* increased their employment and turnover by 48% over the last three years, maintaining growth at an impressive annual rate of 14%. This offers a positive outlook for Europe in terms of comparison with the USA's 20% or higher growth rate for high performing companies.

2.3   Entrepreneurial People

People frequently choose entrepreneurship because they see an opportunity in the market or they see it as a preferred alternative to employment or unemployment. Some people make the decision based on both motives. To better understand entrepreneurial people that are active in venturing, it is valuable to look at what specific elements stimulate the entrepreneurial spirit in people.

Entrepreneurship begins with individual ambition and intent. From our research at Nyenrode (Nandram and van Dijk 2003), to date we have learned that entrepreneurs choose this profession specifically to be their own boss, to enjoy freedom, to express creative and innovative ideas, to invest in the promise of financial independence and finally, to improve their own financial situation. Women add that they can more easily combine work with care giving tasks in their lives. Some entrepreneurs choose for entrepreneurship out of value driven objectives such as job creation, service to the community or their contribution to a sustainable society.

Every innovation stimulates a reaction in society. When one entrepreneur manages to run his process more efficiently than another, competing entrepreneur, he can serve more customers. This is how competition starts; it stimulates the other players to also pursue improvements in products and services. Competition then stimulates renewal and innovation which, in turn, results in economic growth. Through their level of expended efforts, entrepreneurs confirm their belief that they will be rewarded for their efforts. They have to be able to evaluate the attractive, as well as the unattractive features of their plans and not give up at the first setback. Key to taking decisions is confidence and the ability to believe that they will succeed combined with awareness that they have the right knowledge, skills and vision. Role models are also important for inspirational support but entrepreneurial skills and material resources are equally crucial necessities.

One study by EIM in The Netherlands (1997) showed that 40% of employment creation is accomplished by firms which are less than five years old. Early-stage ventures thus have the potential to become incubators for job creation. Even if people initially start the company out of necessity, rather than opportunity, this will still influence the way society at large values new company start-ups. When failure leads to societal stigma, which in some European countries is still quite prevalent, increased and successful entrepreneurship, whether necessity or opportunity-based, diminishes the fear of failure. Then failure, no matter the pain it inflicts, can become a learning point, as is the perspective in a country such as the USA.

Entrepreneurial Success and Failure

"Success has many parents, failure is an orphan." This saying applies of course to entrepreneurial activity as well. In practice, systematically generated success and failure statistics and additional research based thereon, are hard to come by. This paucity of information applies to most countries and regions of the world. Yet, in order to improve success rates, and understand failure, causes need to be studied

Table 2.1 Overall start-up* and failure rates

Industry	Survival	Failure
All industries	53.6%	46.4%
Agriculture	59.4%	40.6%
Finance	53.7%	46.3%
Manufacturing	58.7%	41.3%
Real estate	63.2%	36.8%
Retail	50.9%	49.1%
Wholesale	51.4%	48.6%
Computer Technology	46.1%	53.9%

BizMiner 2002 Start-up Business Risk Index: Major Industrial Report copyright 2002 Brandow Company Inc.

*Start-ups are defined as firms that are one year old or less

in each country and region. This is one of the more significant opportunities in entrepreneurship research and education. One of the few data sources in this field is the Brandow Company Inc, a USA based market research company, cited in Timmons and Spinelli (2004). The data pertains to the period 1998-2002 and provides survival and failure rates of start-ups after four years by industry group.

Overall start-up survival rates of over 50% after four years, with variations depending on the industry sector, do underscore the need for careful study, planning and monitoring of the quality of the entrepreneurial process in advance as well as during the process of venture building. We do not have comparable data for the European countries but an OECD study (2002) concluded that there is a similar degree of firm churning in Europe as in the US. However the relative size of entrants in the EU is smaller. In the USA there is a greater scope for expansion amongst young ventures than in Europe. We have consistently found in our own entrepreneurial research that this applies not only to detailed, advance opportunity development and resource planning, but especially to human resource management and entrepreneurial team development and dynamics. It is through unattended entrepreneurial team conflicts, potential or acute in nature, that ventures frequently find early setbacks and even failures. Successful entrepreneurs are sensitive to these "soft" issues of entrepreneurial people and team management.

Characteristics of Entrepreneurs

Entrepreneurship represents a sampling of characteristics which facilitate the personal venturing process. Yet the question is how can this be recognized and how can individuals fully deploy these characteristics inside a venture. The spirit of entrepreneurship sees and uses opportunities.

In a new venture, this process leads to a product or service. In existing companies, this process produces renewal of existing processes, yet to succeed, this requires trust and freedom. Studies at Nyenrode (Nandram 2002, 2004) have helped us in identifying seven distinct characteristics which assist in the identification and application of opportunities. Based on the data we obtained, we can present how a group of managers, comprised of Nyenrode alumni, scored on these characteristics, compared with a group of entrepreneur-finalists in the selection of the Entrepreneur of the Year contest in The Netherlands during the period 2002-2004.

It appears that the managers and entrepreneurs did not differ substantially in terms of these characteristics. This could be explained by the observation that both the managers and entrepreneurs pass through the same educational programs and are equipped with similar skills and networks. The finalists of the annual selections for the Entrepreneur of the Year in The Netherlands scored higher than the entrepreneurial managers on the following personal characteristics: (1) achievement drive, (2) leadership ambition, (3) alertness, (4) willpower, (5) trust in others, (6) flexible attitudes, and (7) integrity. With respect to integrity, the finalists of the Entrepreneur of the Year election, showed a lower tendency to project themselves in this area as compared to others. In the competition jury members judge the most outspoken entrepreneurs. They seem to demonstrate higher scores on the entrepreneurial characteristics scale.

Entrepreneurial Employees

Can employees be turned into entrepreneurs? This is a question that remains. The successful entrepreneurial characteristics we identified can also be nurtured in employees in order to promote process innovation. However, the common relationship between employer and employee may hinder this as it is formally based on principles of transactional leadership. That means that in return for compensation, the employee provides work. If the goal is to fully realize the entrepreneurial capacity of the employee, then this formal relationship needs to be changed. One way would be to make the employee a shareholder in the venture, another to provide employees with the freedom to come forward with and develop ideas which might serve the venture or a potential spin-off operation. The interest for the company in supporting such ambitions lies in the creative contributions of employees towards the goals of the venture.

Entrepreneurship and Management

Entrepreneurial and management processes differ in nature. An entrepreneur starts a venture based on his or her personal vision. A manager often steps in later as the company already exists. This implies that a manager is responsible mainly for a policy and its implementation while an entrepreneur remains responsible for the entire vision and mission of the firm, including the required renewal processes at any time. A manager is in charge of defined processes inside or outside the company, while an entrepreneur is in charge of what happens both in and out of the venture. A manager looks at recognizing and solving problems in existing processes while an entrepreneur looks concurrently at new opportunities as well. A manager might first of all aim at cost control of existing processes while an entrepreneur would be more likely to focus on overall profit improvement and strengthening market positions. Unless they are charismatic leaders and/or have previously been trained as managers, entrepreneurs tend to focus on the opportunity they created rather than on imbuing the entire team with the spirit of entrepreneurship. As the venture grows, the entrepreneur will eventually have to consider engaging a manager or managers.

Thus, we now arrive at the transition from the early-stages of entrepreneurship to management phases in the mature company. It would be ideal to retain the entrepreneurial, renewing and creative orientation of the early-stage venture while also incorporating these attitudes into the management phases of the more mature company. Either way, the leadership style will have to be adjusted from transactional to transformational management. The emphasis shifts from management on the basis of transactions to encouraging team members to pursue the continuous renewal of all management processes. This transformational style of management prevents bureaucracy, charismatically keeps employees, managers and executives motivated and increases the likelihood that the venture will continue to grow into a creative, fast growing and renewing market position.

2.4   Entrepreneurial Mentoring and Coaching

The European Union (2003) as well as most European governments focuses on providing services and promotional activities to influence entrepreneurial activity. For instance in The Netherlands, one of the groups targeted is defined as high growth entrepreneurs. Research highlights the existence of 'glass ceilings' for young ventures on the way to achieving growth. Coaching, consulting, networking and supervision are thought to assist in breaking through these glass ceilings towards growth. These services can be summarized as mentoring. The phenomenon of mentoring is well known in the management literature yet less in the entrepreneurial field. In daily life, the word is often associated with a non-professional expertise because everybody can act as a mentor. It is also associated with a voluntary activity.

Clawson (1996) stated that many people tried to define mentoring in the late 1970s and early 1980s. The term became widely used and the meaning of mentoring became diffuse and difficult to recognize. The word mentoring became synonymous with a broad and deep influence from a senior, more experienced and wise individual, to another person. In the venturing situation the entrepreneur or other stakeholders in the new venture might hire a mentor or a coach to guide and stimulate the entrepreneurial process. Mentoring is understood to be a more process-oriented phenomenon while coaching would be more results driven. In mentoring, the individual and his needs are the central starting point, while in coaching the needs of the organization form the starting point.

We also found related definitions specific to entrepreneurship. Sullivan (2000) refers to mentoring as a means of supporting new entrepreneurs through the provision of "expert" help and assistance in overcoming problems. The mentor shares useful insight for running a small business with the new-start entrepreneur, perhaps through learning from the mentor's experience. The role of the mentor is to enable the entrepreneur to reflect on actions and, perhaps, to modify future actions as a result; it is about enabling behavioral and attitudinal change.

Enterprise Ireland states that the mentor assigned to a company has a clear objective to help the entrepreneur grow and develop new skills which will enable him or her to overcome barriers impeding the company's growth. Walton (1998) uses mentoring as an umbrella for different support devices. This could cover career development or psycho-socio orientation. The tools that can be used are dependent on the type of question asked and the culture. Coaching is seen as focusing on the day-to-day work situation and engineered by the line manager. Mentoring on the other hand is thought to be done by a wider range of people and offers possibilities for generating a broader context for the learning process. A mentor can play various roles:

1. Coach – showing how to carry out a task or activity
2. Facilitate – creating opportunities for learners to use new skills
3. Counsel – helping learners explore the consequences of potential decisions
4. Network – referring learners to others when the mentor's experience is insufficient

Yet we can still ask whether we know what impact mentoring might have on entrepreneurial performance. Some results are known concerning the impact on the business, and three examples will be presented:

1. Small and medium sized business
2. Self-employment or unemployed
3. High growth enterprises

In a recent study (Robson and Bennett 2000), respondents from small and medium sized enterprises were asked to identify each area and source of advice they used to pursue their business objectives in the previous three years, and to rate their impact in meeting business objectives. A large sample (2,474) of small firms in manufacturing and business services were surveyed by mail. The results showed statistically significant positive relationships between the fields of advice and employment growth, including capabilities such as business strategy and staff recruitment. There were three areas of advice, which appeared statistically significant in increasing turnover: business strategy, staff recruitment and, fiscal and financial management.

However, in the model of profitability per employee, none of these fields of advice was statistically significant. The researchers found little evidence of statistically significant relationships between government-backed providers of business advice such as Business Link and Venture Performance.

In the White Paper on Enterprise Skills and innovation in the UK (Devins and Johnson 2001) there is a second example. Devins and Johnson explore the paths that long-and short-term unemployed people take prior to enrolling in a venture start-up course. Furthermore, they look at the extent to which such intervention supports the development of business and management skills. The conclusion was that both types of participants were successful in helping themselves transition to self-employment. However, a substantial minority of long-term unemployed participants was not successful in avoiding a return to unemployment.

The third example comes from Enterprise Ireland's Mentor Network. They conducted a survey of companies that participated in the Mentor Network to find out what the impact of mentoring is. The results are based on 60 companies. These researchers found an increase in sales, exports and employment as a result of participation. More than 90% of the respondents described the Mentor Network's input as either very important or important. Yet, not all of the changes can be attributed to the Mentor Network's influence. According to 75% of the respondents the mentor had a significant influence. 78% of the respondents stated that many improvements would not have happened or would have happened differently had a mentor's services not been available. These examples assumed a relationship between support services and business performances existed, and no theoretical framework was explicitly developed. Other research on non-entrepreneurs show benefits on the psychological side, such as understanding other people's situations, personal growth and development, taking a wider perspective on life, and realizing greater self-awareness (Walton 1998).

Given the macro economic importance of entrepreneurship as seen above, government and other public organizations can, particularly in entrepreneurial economies, play an important role in stimulating innovation and reducing barriers for people engaging in self-employment and venturing activities. Governments can also define and implement supportive policies in areas such as taxation, education, mentoring, bankruptcy laws and infrastructure which can contribute to an entrepreneurially friendly culture. In particular, the following policies would be supportive in positively changing the entrepreneurial culture in a region or country:

1. Simplified company establishment, registration and reporting rules.

2. Liberalization of labor regulations and markets providing ventures with greater access to human resources.

3. Suitable adaptations of retirement funding laws for entrepreneurs.

4. Education at all levels of public schooling on the employment, innovation and wealth generation capabilities of new ventures in society.

5. Incentives for the development of scientific and technological inventions at universities and their application in companies.

6. Stimulating spin-off ventures by universities as well as corporations.

7. Attractive fiscal treatment of private research stimulating gifts to universities.

Working on these suggested policies will increase the role of entrepreneurship in society and consequently, the level of economic and social contributions. Especially in a number of European industrial nations, potential as well as practicing entrepreneurs still perceive major distractions from venturing activities because of high levels of rules and regulations, poor economic climates and lack of familiarity with risk taking behaviors. Figure 2.1 offers a clear illustration of those countries which lack a culture which encourages risk tasking, innovation and new venture creation.

Today, distractions from the potential of flourishing entrepreneurial economies are clearly visible in countries such as France and Germany. Even though these nations boost high levels of technological knowledge and innovation as well as large and successful corporations, they struggle with innovation and new venture creation. High levels of labor, bankruptcy and other business regulations, when combined with generous social programs and, finally, the absence of inspiring examples of entrepreneurial venturing, can create cultures which do not support risk taking and entrepreneurship. Education and public policy play a major role in explaining entrepreneurial reality. Steps to facilitate innovation are required to change a traditional economy rooted in established and sizable firms and highly regulated social, business and labor laws. The rewards of opening up to renewal are new venturing opportunities and the promises they hold in terms of individual creative fulfillment, community support, job creation and generation of material wealth.

2.5 Conclusion

This chapter reviewed the qualitative and quantitative impacts of entrepreneurial activity in society, relating specific performance in these areas to a number of individual countries. Typical entrepreneurial characteristics and traits were reviewed as well, including entrepreneurial team and management processes in ventures and established companies. In particular, there was a close review of ways to stimulate effectiveness in entrepreneurs and their teams through coaching and mentoring.

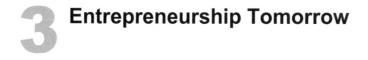

3 Entrepreneurship Tomorrow

As we have seen in the previous chapters, entrepreneurial activity is about discovery of opportunities and creating value. It is also about seeing new possibilities and pursuing them early. This requires an attitude of both focus and detachment; the latter to take occasional distance from the high speeds at which our economies and societies move to be able to observe new trends and possibilities; opportunities that may lie outside the immediate logic of the present moment, the now. Once this bigger, long-term picture, has been carefully surveyed, the entrepreneur needs to focus on possibilities and to verify and select those that offer potentially fitting and new entrepreneurial opportunities. In this chapter we present the bigger picture of the new entrepreneurial opportunities.

3.1 Global Growth in Entrepreneurship and Sustainable Venturing

We observe two trends which offer, as a growing number of entrepreneurs have already found out, a unique new set of venturing opportunities:

1. *Global Growth of Entrepreneurial Activity.* This trend concerns the emergence of increased entrepreneurship and, more recently, the use of entrepreneurial management techniques in established companies to create monetary wealth, innovation and jobs. While the USA has traditionally been the largest and most entrepreneurial economy in the world, in recent decades, other regions, for instance Asia and Europe, have witnessed measurable and continuing growth in entrepreneurship activity and value creation, stimulated by private as well as public parties.

2. *Growing Awareness of Sustainability in Society.* The second trend we note represents a sharp increase, especially during the last decade, of consumer, producer, not-for-profit organizations, and governmental awareness and action in terms of the health and environmental aspects of living in consumer societies. This has led to a modest trend, though as yet insufficient, to turn back long-term depletion and degradation of the physical environment of the Earth. Actions are being undertaken by a variety of public and private parties, nationally and internationally, to reduce the externalization effects of current economic processes such as pollution and resource depletion.

Sustainable venturing or entrepreneurship is on the rise as can be witnessed by the emergence of national and local organizations that subscribe to such business principles. Business for Social Responsibility (BSR), the national organization in the USA, now represents companies with over US $ 2 trillion in turnover and 6 million employees (www.bsr.org). Corporate Social Responsibility Europe (CSR Europe) is a similar organization in Europe (www.csreurope.org). And there are similar organizations in Asia and other parts of the world. At the state or country level too, business alliances for social and environmental responsibility can be found. One example is the Vermont Businesses for Social Responsibility (VBSR) in Vermont, USA. It has 600 company members, mostly entrepreneurial in origin and nature, representing 30,000 employees and $6 billion in turnover (www.vbsr.org). While the traditional Timmons model of entrepreneurship (see Figure 3.1), is depicted as an open system without any limits; the sustainable entrepreneurship model is defined by the physical limits of the economy, the ecological resources and services the Earth can provide and, finally, those limits defined by the community.

Thus, we have placed this model in Figure 3.2 within a circle to indicate the boundaries posed by the Earth's ecological services, the economy and the community (Samsom 2005).

What remains unlimited, and in fact, now becomes an even more important entrepreneurial resource in this new reality, is creativity and innovative ways to: (1) optimize the use and reuse of the available resources, (2) capture the imagination of the customer in building value-based client communities, and (3) build a network

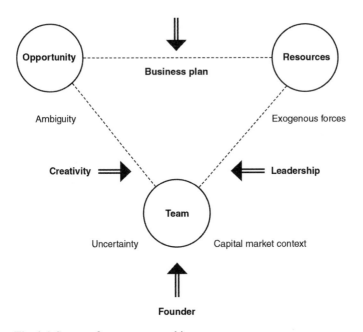

Fig. 3.1 Concept for entrepreneurship

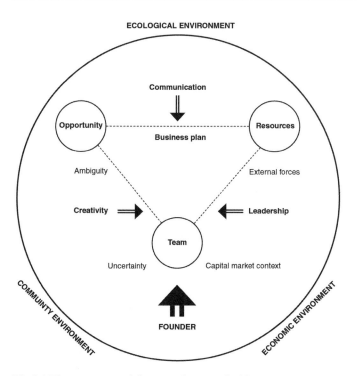

Fig.3.2 The entrepreneurial process in a sustainable context

of strategic partners, including social and environmental stakeholders, and sustainable suppliers of goods and services.

We now review why and how this promising new window of opportunity in sustainable entrepreneurship has come about. This is important as the detailed processes which have led to the separation between ecology and economy are not widely communicated nor commonly understood while today its implications affect all entrepreneurs, be it directly or indirectly.

In his book, *Plan B 2.0 Rescuing a Planet under Stress and a Civilization in Trouble*, Brown (2006) documents in detail how the global rate of natural resource depletion and environmental degradation appears to be accelerating at a rather astounding speed. Today, even some traditionally conservative institutions are no longer insisting on proof of these environmental phenomena, whatever that would consist of, but moving forward in exploring and embracing this likely new reality. Deutsch (2005) reported through an article in The New York Times in November 2005, how Goldman Sachs, the largest investment bank in the world had adopted a policy that details how its 24,000 employees, be they bankers, analysts or purchasing agents, should promote activities that protect forests and guard against climate change. Goldman Sachs, which counts paper companies, refiners and car companies among its clients, stopped short of saying it would reject clients with questionable environmental practices. Instead, it said it would "encourage" clients in "environmentally sensitive" areas to use "appropriate safeguards". It committed itself to investing $1 billion US in projects that generate energy from sources other than oil and gas. And the company strongly endorsed "stringent federal regulations". Scientists from the Intergovernmental Panel on Climate Change (UN IPCC) have reported on global warming as caused by human activities (2001). The New Scientist (2006) reports that the three warmest years on record have all occurred since 1998; and that we have experienced 19 of the 20 warmest years since 1980. Roberts details the history of the present and future of oil and its uses in society in "The End of Oil" (2004). The rate of oil exploration is growing exponentially while the limited reserves of the Earth are becoming more expensive to explore.

Social and environmental sustainability are concepts that are not new. They have been applied to businesses by their owners and managers for centuries based on the personal values they brought to their endeavors. For entrepreneurs the issue of values is usually more personally and directly connected to the pursuit of opportunities than for corporations. For an entrepreneur, a complaint might require reimbursement for returned items or damage done in a community, and the financial impact of that transaction rests directly on the entrepreneur and his venture. It might even threaten reputation and viability of the young firm in the community. The very idea which became the opportunity, on which the new venture is based, is usually rooted in a deeply held personal conviction or belief of the entrepreneur. Many new products and services are built on these personal values.

For instance, at the centre of Ben & Jerry's were the personal values of the two founders. Their vision was to bring premium quality ice cream and fun to the market and, at the same time, connect to the community through their socially and environmentally inspired value chains as well as charities. By keeping local dairy farmers in the USA. State of Vermont in business and on the land, the company worked to contribute not only to individual farming lifestyles, but also to the larger issue of ecologically and economically viable communities which support conservation and tourism; one of the largest sources of economic income in that state. Furthermore, Ben & Jerry's pursued the triple bottom line approach by offering entrepreneurial opportunities for owning ice cream scoop shops in minority sections of the big cities. Their efforts were an example of how sustainable entrepreneurship can take many forms. Application of these values can be systematic through product development, production, marketing and sales as well as in people management, community relations and charity or in any combination of these.

3.2   Economic and Ecological Indicators

To evaluate how entrepreneurial ventures can be based on both economic and ecological values, we also need to understand how these measures have, over time, drifted apart. The terms economy and ecology have the Greek word "eco" in common. Freely translated this refers to "home" or "at home." Economy would be the management of home and, ecology, the physical science of it; that is of the Earth. In economic transactions between people the dominating principle would be utility. Both parties have defined their expected utility from the transaction to which they agree. If in the process, a third party is affected by this transaction, we speak of externalization. Externalization occurs when parties who were not involved with the original transaction are affected by it. Biologist Hardin (1968) labeled such a situation "The Tragedy of the Commons". That is the tragedy of the commonly owned and inhabited community environment in which not everyone treats common property and resources with the same respect and so does damage to "the commons".

Examples of externalization could be pollution or industrially induced global warming and related health issues. These result in negative effects, for instance such as respiratory or carcinogenic in nature, on parties not involved in the original transaction. In an ecologically driven system, the dominating principle would be the precautionary approach or will the proposed transaction also affect parties not involved in it and, if so, how can this externalization be avoided or mitigated. One personal way an entrepreneur can test this is to ask the following question: "Would I expose my children or family to the proposed procedures for manufacturing, marketing, use and eventual disposal of this product?" One critical part of the answer to this question lies in the way economic activity is measured today.

The most commonly used measure of economic activity is Gross Domestic Product (GDP). Unfortunately, it does not comprehensively measure wellbeing. It does not even effectively measure purely economically defined wellbeing in euros or dollars over time. This may be demonstrated by the fact that while three decades ago an average family in many Western economies could manage its financial needs on the income of one single breadwinner, today this is the exception. Equally important, the ultimate costs of environmental degradation and resource depletion are not comprehensively included in GDP. Thus while at the national level economic wealth (as in GDP) has risen, wealth as defined in terms of human and environmental wellbeing, has suffered.

In *Paradigms in Progress*, Hazel Henderson (1995) demonstrates this effect graphically with The Three Layer Cake (Figure 3.3). This illustrates the point as the Non-Monetized, 1/2 half the Cake, Sweat Equity (Social Cooperative-Love Economy) and Mother Nature (Ecological Services of the Earth, resources, climate, nature, etc) are not included in currently used measures of economic wellbeing. While many people perceive this phenomenon at some level through direct experiences with environmental, social degradation or ecological disasters, the detailed economic measurement mechanics involved are often misunderstood. Henderson's point is that national accounting systems do not provide useful indices to manage national economies sustainably because not all elements in the costs of goods or services are properly accounted for. We must further realize that national accounting practices, while representing an indication of annual financial operations, do not provide an annual balance sheet. Imagine a company without a balance sheet as an indication of shareholder or stakeholder value; another serious limitation to consciousness building in the process of management of a country and all its resources, be they economic, social, cultural or ecological because the real, actual costs are not communicated. Finally, the Three Layer Cake illustrates graphically, that without ecology, the Earth, there can be no economy or even social-cooperative economy.

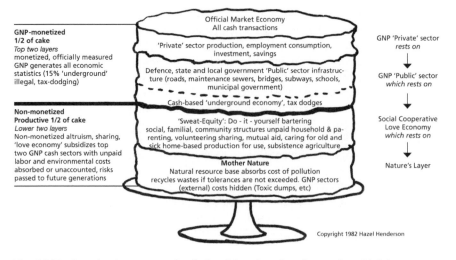

Fig. 3.3 Total productive system of an industrial society three-layer cake with icing

3.3   Externalization, System Feedback and Einstein

Compared to corporate annual statements, GDP, as an indication of wealth is rather limited in what it measures. The situation can be compared to an automobile speedometer indicating a speed of say, 60 miles per hour while, due to the technical reliability of the speedometer, one cannot be sure if the actual speed is in fact, 45 miles or 75 miles per hour. In traffic, this level of speed variance would be considered extremely dangerous and completely unacceptable. In terms of incomplete measures of wellbeing on which much government, social and business policy is based, this state of affairs is of course equally questionable, if not outright dangerous. The implication of this situation is that many ecological resources and services, such as fossil fuels, clean air and clean water on which our daily lives depend are undervalued. This happens primarily because the long-term, future, cost effects of their manufacture, use and disposal are not reflected in their market price. In that sense, these inadequately measured costs are deferred to future generations; a process similar to passing on to future generations the public debts of the current generations but more dangerous as some ecological damage might not be reversible. This imperfect feedback system poses, in itself, yet another source of externalization as it fails to provide the tools to highlight critical situations and provides false security behind incomplete numbers. Externalization occurs due to lack of personally initiated, legislated or otherwise promulgated norms to protect the common good in society. Einstein was not only a leader in science but obviously aware in philosophical matters as well, as the following quote in Eves demonstrates (1977, p. 60):

"A human being is a part of the whole called by us "the universe," a part limited in time and space. He experiences himself, his thoughts and feelings, as something separate from the rest – a kind of optical delusion of consciousness. This delusion is a kind of prison for us, restricting us to our personal desires and affection for a few persons nearest to us. Our task must be to free ourselves from this prison by widening the circle of understanding and compassion to embrace all living creatures and the whole of nature in its beauty."

Consciousness helps to recognize this "optical delusion" of separateness from others; from the communities and countries human beings are a part of. Conscious entrepreneurs and entrepreneurial executives tend to see the opportunity in combining personal interests and the common good. Externalization, as defined above, can only be partially discouraged or eliminated by laws, regulations and rules. For instance a rule to include a "deposit" in the price of a container, as in bottles or aluminum cans, which will be refunded if the empty container is returned to a collection centre to be recycled into new containers. Or, as in some European countries, a "fee" paid with the purchase of an automobile which is reserved to fund the ultimate sustainable recycling and disposal of the vehicle after its useful life. There are also many voluntary ways in which externalization can be reduced. One is by building specific motivations into the value chain which reduce externalization, for instance, by including in the product a service option which allows the user to return all or part of the product after use. Some companies include return envelops for used ink printer cartridges. The consumer keeps the cartridge out of the landfill, and the manufacturer can re-process the item.

Business ethics as well as corporate social responsibility movements contribute to consciousness of values in business and its role in society. Out of these approaches an understanding has arisen that profits, people and planet (Triple Bottom Line) can be served in tandem. Natural Capitalism furthers the path towards a more systemic approach to building the motivation for non-externalizing business behavior as well as new creative and cost reducing strategies directly into the company value chain.

3.4   Natural Capitalism

Natural Capitalism, a term coined by Hawken, Lovins and Lovins (2000) brings an objective, both economic and ecologically based, structure to the concept of business and sustainability. That means, productive and consumptive processes being created and designed in a manner which fundamentally recognizes that the economy is in fact limited by the physical ability of the Earth to absorb its impact. Natural capitalism is grounded in four strategies. As shown below, these can be seen as updates or innovations to traditional business processes.

1. *Radical Resource Productivity.* Here we deal with the supply side of the economy. This activity is based on values which ecology, economy and entrepreneurial activity, already have in common, i.e. doing more with less by creatively re-examining all production processes, resource inputs and their costs. Innovative design, architecture, technology, government stimulated innovation and education as well as fiscal measure to promote sustainability. If fossil fuels were to be charged with their true costs, including externalized resource depletion, pollution and health costs, alternative, ecologically clean sources would not encounter unfair price competition, an example of the tragedy of the commons! A resulting benefit of radical resource productivity would be pollution reduction. Additionally, it might provide for increased employment opportunities. Productivity increases in the range of 4 to 10 multiples are considered feasible. Taken together, these are all good things for economic health. New opportunities for entrepreneurs who, unencumbered by existing business cultures can release their creativity and drive in a market awaiting new opportunities.

2. *Biomimicry.* It is estimated that in the USA only about 6% of all material flows in manufacturing can eventually be found in the final products. Compared with production processes in nature, this appears highly inefficient. Here, Hawken, Lovins and Lovins offer a poignant note: "As long as it is assumed that there are free goods in the world-free water, clean air, hydrocarbon combustion, virgin forests, veins of minerals, large scale energy and material intensive manufacturing methods will dominate, and labor will be increasingly marginalized. In contrast, if the subsidies distorting resources prices were removed, it would be advantageous to employ more people and use fewer virgin materials." (p.15) Think of the gigantic agricultural subsidies of the USA and the European Union which undermine the otherwise praised advantages of free trade. On the positive side, the explosive development of organic agriculture and foods offers a fine example. Biomimicry is thus using nature's examples to redesign agricultural and industrial processes to lower energy input, materials use and promote material reuse. Another example would be the use of biological methods and natural flows to process sewage rather than applying large amounts of energy, building resources and chemicals to run sewage plants.

3. *Service & Flow.* Marketing teaches that customers really only buy the benefits of what products and services deliver. Ownership and possession of the underlying product is not always essential. An example is to buy services for a comfortable office or home climate, thus eliminating the need to own heating and air conditioning equipment. Anderson (1998), founder and CEO of Interface, one of the largest international companies producing floor coverings, introduced the notion of leasing and servicing carpets in tile format, extending the life of the carpet by only needing to replace the high wear areas. Thus leaving the efficient operation and man-

agement of assets, including ultimate breakdown for recycling after the useful live, to the manufacturers of these systems. Manufacturers have strong motivation for the maintenance of the equipment and so lower costs and improve customer service levels.

4. *Investing in Natural Capital*. The most important flow of ecological services which the Earth delivers to its inhabitants' industrial systems can only continue if investments are made to prevent natural disasters caused by man-made events such as global warming, deforestation, pollution, exhaustion of fresh water supplies and poverty to name the most important ones. This might possibly have been demonstrated in 2005 with an all time record of hurricanes in the Gulf of Mexico and the discovery of the radical melting rate of polar ice. Investment would also be required for restoring and enlarging the stocks of natural capital to assist in the functioning of the biosphere which provides ecological services to the inhabitants of the Earth. Water conservation, wetlands restoration and sustainable forestry and reforestation projects are examples. Sustainably grown hardwoods have become a significant new market segment which supports both ecology and economy. So has emissions trading.

Sustainable venturing may especially appeal to the creative inclination of the entrepreneur. Natural Capitalism is thus, about designing new and unexpected value chains that meet customer demands and capture their imagination in terms of image, style, social and ecological value as well as product performance. The value chain, as defined by the traditional marketing mix of product, price, place and promotion is now combined with the product lifecycle from all stages of manufacture or production through to final disposal or disassembly. Not only are the physical benefits of the product or service emphasized but also those of the product life-cycle implications including the implied values of the firm taking this approach. Marketing becomes building value-based communities in the broadest sense of the word.

3.5   The Sustainable Entrepreneur

The personal characteristics and competences of successful entrepreneurs have been frequently studied and enumerated in the literature (Nandram and Samsom 2001, Timmons 1998).

Among these we find a number which not only apply to the traditional entrepreneur but can also be observed in people who are socially and ecologically conscious and engaged. It is in this overlap where the new entrepreneur with a commitment to sustainability can find motivation and empowerment. Characteristics and competencies which successful entrepreneurs, sustainable entrepreneurs and ecologically oriented people might share particularly apply to qualities and orientations as listed (Samsom 2004): consciousness, doing more with less, drive, energy and health, innovative and creative, integrity and fairness, parsimonious, passion, stakeholder orientation, values, willingness to reflect.

When some or all of these characteristics can be found among both successful entrepreneurs and socially and environmentally inspired people, we may conclude that an entrepreneur with a commitment to sustainability may possess a unique focus to share his or her drive, values and competencies and express these through successful sustainable entrepreneurship. Consciousness, which can be found among teams of successful entrepreneurs, deserves special attention (Stockley 2000). Here too we find a similarity with ecologically oriented persons, they are self aware and conscious of all other parts of the ecological world. In his paper *The Making of the Ecoentrepreneur* Isaak (2004), offers a number of remarkable and detailed examples from the practice of sustainable entrepreneurship in which the combination of personal characteristics and competencies as discussed here are demonstrated.

Leadership

The entrepreneurial companies, for instance, such as those represented by members of the Social Venture Network (SVN), which operates in North America as well as Europe, demonstrate a desire to be guided by the triple bottom line of profit, people and planet. The late Dutch business economist Limperg was obviously well ahead of his time when he implied that a company's ultimate purpose is continuity. Companies pursue this continuity by serving all their stakeholders; in today's terminology business relations, customers, community, employees, environment and shareholders. Leadership in creative, entrepreneurial, organizations thus becomes critical. Richard Barrett (1998) in *Liberating the Corporate Soul: Towards a Visionary Organization* as well as Tom Chappell (1999) in *Managing Upside Down* provide insights on how to apply transformational leadership to evolve from a primary focus on individual and corporate egos and goals to one which equally caters to the common good of the company, all its stakeholders and society at large. An organization with a conscious leader and equally inspired work force can, in its pursuit of individual and corporate material wellbeing as well as the common good, minimize externalization while capturing the imagination of its members and customers; a long-term strategy covering multiple perspectives.

In the traditional marketing mix, product, price, promotion and place (which stands for distribution), or the four Ps, are the four elements used to entice customers. While there are many quantifiable variables in communicating each of these "four Ps", the intangible buyer attitudes are harder to read and respond to. The personal values and passions of the entrepreneur and his or her team are a case in point. In the area of sustainable venturing consider the examples from Europe and the USA respectively, of Anita Roddick of The Body Shop and Ben Cohen and Jerry Greenfield of Ben & Jerry's. In their own imaginative ways they succeeded in inspiring both customers and other stakeholders from the beginning of their venturing activities and left an imprint on those who eventually took control of their companies. Successful entrepreneurs create their relationships with their customers and their markets with personal values, involvement and appeals. The vision and messages they communicate appeal to their customers, often at a cost lower than the traditional marketing expenditures. Especially when they start out, these entrepreneurs communicate through the media and through word of mouth with customers intrigued by the products of their venture, which finds itself a welcome place in the community. Add to this the increasing evidence that the buying behavior of the public is influenced not only by the four Ps but also by the perceived set of social and environmental values of companies and their managements. This more recent aspect of consumer behavior too gives nimble and communicative entrepreneurs a potential competitive advantage over larger established companies.

New Breeding Grounds for Creativity

Technology and innovation-based fields such as IT, telecommunications, materials sciences, traditional and alternative energy technologies, biotechnology, organic foods and eco-technology have become breeding grounds for young ventures brimming with creativity and inventiveness. Entrepreneurs and scientists in these areas are driven by a spirit of discovery, speeding often with lower overheads toward new technologies or novel products and services. Large corporations, which for all their market dominance often cannot act as light-footed in inventing and developing new products and services as quickly or as economically, provide a market for such science and technology-based young ventures. Flexibility, agility, speed and well-rooted values are at the core of the competitive advantage of entrepreneurial ventures. Of course, larger companies can, and some do, recover the entrepreneurial spirit. When additionally considering this model in the context of the growing influence of community and ecological considerations, venturing conditions appear to become, at first more complicated but, as some of the entrepreneurs featured in this book will show, at the same time greater numbers of new venture opportunities open up. The physical impact of the relentlessly growing economic activity on the Earth is working its way back into economics as we know it. This places restrictions on business activities as well as on consumption, i.e. through pollution and negative health effects. On the other hand, it offers new opportunities for innovation on the interface between ecology and economics through resource reduction, recovery and restoration as well as entirely new products and services.

The Conscious Consumer

Market sociologist Paul Ray (2004) estimates that in the USA market the conscious consumer makes up as much as 20 to 25% of the population. In practice it appears that the consumer will demand that a green or sustainable product must be as satisfactory in use as a traditional one, and furthermore that a price differential should usually not exceed 5%. Jeffrey Hollender, one of the founders and president of consumer products company Seventh Generation, notes in *What Matters Most* (2004) that honest transparency concerning the social and environmental intentions and claims as well as the actual behavior in those fields are critical elements of the customer relationship. To which extent the trend towards a more conscious consumer will further increase is not really clear. An example of the consumer discontent and even punishment at the cash registers is offered by Albert Heijn supermarkets in The Netherlands after the compensation package of the chain's new CEO had become the subject of a media debate. With shorter lines to its stakeholders and possibly a more personal relationship, an entrepreneurial venture might be less likely to tumble into such an abyss. What is quite clear is that regaining or maintaining customers who perceive dishonest, unfair, asocial or unsustainable behavior is very difficult. Such behavior can provoke unexpected levels of consumer resistance and they can only be regained with substantial marketing efforts, if at all.

Legendary Customer Service

Barlow (2000), the British management consultant, states that customers want to be treated efficiently and maintain a relationship with the company and lays out a very detailed approach to this in-depth service approach. As we have seen in the previous section, the conscious consumer can be expected to require in-depth service levels beyond good products, prices and availability. Barlow appropriately calls this level of deep, loyalty generating service levels, legendary customer service. While Barlow does not particularly aim his approach at companies in the sustainable sector, his approach is quite fitting for products and services which are, in part, bought because of their social and environmental values and those of the supplier! In practice truly legendary service is the exception, rather than the rule. For a young company with a sustainable orientation, truly legendary service, that is faster, more personal, caring and thoughtful client communication offer a valuable and fitting competitive advantage.

New Macro Economic Realities and Opportunities

As demonstrated by the depiction of the sustainable entrepreneurship model in Figure 3.2, in this new ecological reality, the venture operates now in what is a defined ecological system with ultimately limited resources. The only truly unlimited input into the entrepreneurial system is that of the unbounded creativity and innovative abilities of the venture team to overcome the physical limitations imposed by the reality of the ecology of the Earth. The latter would include ecological services such as clean air and water, livable climates, energy and other natural resources and, finally, the ecological recovery and restoration functions of the Earth. This then implies new and increasingly larger macro economic constraints, a reality which applies to all resource consumption, trading and industrial activities. Thus, in terms of the entrepreneurship model of Resources, Opportunities and Team, the latter becomes ever more important in creatively working within environmental limitations and concerns.

3.6   Conclusion

In this chapter we reviewed how non-measured economic externalization under-states the real costs of today's economies and externalizes these deferred expenses to the environment and to future generations. This includes creative and inspired value-based entrepreneurs leading new dynamic ventures which endeavor to con-currently manage customers, financiers, suppliers, customers, community and the environment. Such an ecological orientation can creatively match the values as well as goals of the founders and their new ventures. Natural Capitalism offers ef-fective strategies to go beyond merely adding the values of community and envi-ronment to the traditional economic targets of business. Natural Capitalism offers a model for the systematic and seamless integration of these objectives into the value chain of the company rather than merely adding selected community and environmental values to the mission statement of the venture. Customer expecta-tions regarding the performance of the company in matters of product quality, price, service, the community and the environment offer an opportunity for sys-temic integration of these aspects into the activities of the venture. Experience does show that higher price points in this regard need to be carefully managed.

Two trends were reviewed in second part of this chapter. First, new market op-portunities tend to appear in response to the increasing physical limitations of the ecological system to accommodate traditional economic activity. Second, sustain-able entrepreneurs are uniquely positioned to find and explore new opportunities to build personal and lasting service relationships with conscious customers.

In closing, the connection between consciousness and service, equally applica-ble in private as in business activities, is elegantly summed up in Tagore's poem.

> *I slept and dreamt that life was joy*
> I awoke and saw that life was service
> *I acted and behold, service was joy*

> Rabindranoth Tagore, Poet and Nobel Laureate

4 The Human Factor in Entrepreneurship

Scholars of entrepreneurship dedicated a great deal of research to define entrepreneurship. Highlighting the current thinking about entrepreneurship is valuable to our work. First, we will present our literature research by integrating it into a framework. Second, we will use the inspiration we obtained by doing this literature research, to build a model for approaching the 60 cases which are the main part of this book. Among the positive developments in entrepreneurship is the tendency to define the field by building a theoretical framework, and our case studies are part of this tendency. In the discussion that follows we will elaborate more on the conceptual entrepreneurial framework of our research approach, yet first we begin with a review of existing theory.

4.1 Entrepreneurial Success

One key question in the entrepreneurship literature focuses on the factors which predict entrepreneurial success. The answer to this question could have singled out entrepreneurial winners. Unfortunately there is no easy answer to this question and as such, several theoretical perspectives offer an approach to deal with it (see Low and MacMillan 1988; Gartner 2001; Gartner et al.1992; Ucbasaran et al. 2001). Previously, academic scholars developed economic models, strategic management models and behavioral models. In purely neoclassical economic models there was no place for entrepreneurship because there were too many uncertain processes involved that hindered the realization of equilibrium. The entrepreneur did not have perfect information to take action with the aim of maximizing utility. In this sense, it can even be doubted if maximizing utility in the economic sense is the driving force of the entrepreneur. In the dominant view, entrepreneurship is studied as a disequilibrium phenomenon in which entrepreneurs occasionally disrupt the existing equilibrium by innovations.

Due to empirical results, academics now realize that predictability of entrepreneurial success is very difficult. The entrepreneur can be described as more intuitive than rational and relies much more on expectations than on defined plans based on past results. And, it seems that starting and growing a business involves a more dynamic approach. In the current discussion, cognitive models are offered as tools for understanding entrepreneurship.

The term cognition refers to the collection of mental processes and activities used in perceiving, learning, remembering, thinking and understanding, and the act of using those processes (see for more details about this topic Ashcraft 1998). A widely accepted definition of entrepreneurial cognition refers to the knowledge structure that entrepreneurs use to make assessments, judgments, or decisions involving opportunity evaluation, venture creation, and growth (Mitchell et al. 2002). The study of cognition is a psychological field of research based on fundamental research methods including experimental research designs. Studying entrepreneurs in a laboratory setting and applying experimental designs is not common and that means that entrepreneurship scholars rely a great deal on fundamental psychological insights.

Reviewing the findings of the case studies convinced us that understanding the role of the individual in entrepreneurial processes is at the heart of entrepreneurship. As well, very recent contributions in the literature attempt to develop a distinctive entrepreneurial theory for understanding entrepreneurship. Yet, the big challenge scholars face is defining entrepreneurship.

The current academic discussion is very promising as it encompasses the layman perspective that entrepreneurship consists of very dynamic, subjective and less rational processes. This development implies that entrepreneurship as a phenomenon becomes much more understandable. The new challenge is to make these processes measurable and therefore researchable with empirical data. The models presented here represent a broad view of the main discussions in entrepreneurship literature so far and the expected developments in the field.

4.2   Economic Models

Entrepreneurs who start and develop new businesses are crucial for job creation and productivity growth. They get more recognition when they seem to be successful in terms of realizing profit growth or growth in personnel. The factors that influence the level of entrepreneurial success are questionable, and there is not enough systematic empirical result to review at this point. Looking at economic theory could help in bringing a more systematic review of the research done so far.

A recent book studying new businesses from an economic perspective is that of Bhidé, *The Origin and Evolution of New Businesses* (2000) in which he tries to answer this question. Bhidé states that there is a considerable disjoint between the concrete efforts of entrepreneurs to start and build businesses and the central concerns of economic research. In his study many of the variables lie outside the domain of modern economics. He noticed that there were some incidences of writings by classical economists but these have now virtually disappeared from the theoretical literature. The main reason for the disappearance of the entrepreneur is that the roles classical economists used to attribute to entrepreneurship simply cannot exist within the framework of orthodox economic theory. The critical assumption that makes the theory work, based on perfectly informed and rational decision-making, leaves no room for the classical entrepreneurial functions of coordination, arbitrage, innovation and uncertainty.

Bhidé concludes that in the micro economic theory equilibrium has been defined, yet the micro economic theory does not explain how an equilibrium changes. Equilibrium leads to an optimal allocation of resources within a society. The point at which the demand curve intersects with the supply curve represents the most socially desirable equilibrium. The market reaches this point because of rational and informed buyers and sellers. Yet entrepreneurs face many uncertainties and therefore no perfect information is available and many of them are less rational than the economic theories led us to believe.

The Schumpeterian based innovative activity of entrepreneurs influences the supply and demand curves, even though it lies outside the model. In new elaborations of the economic perspectives represented in agency theory, industrial organization, and behavioral economics, entrepreneurship takes a place; and these theories recognize the consequences of incomplete or asymmetric information and decision-making as a bounded rational process. By using case studies, Bhidé tries to complement the existing framework of economics while pointing out that these type of studies lie outside the normal economic theoretical framework (they contain exogenous factors). He uses business management perspectives to understand activities of entrepreneurs.

Specifically, here we present two research models to demonstrate how empirical studies are conducted with less strict economic perspectives. Eisenhouwer (1995) provides an economic oriented model by combining Austrian and Chicago based perspectives on entrepreneurs. In one Austrian example, represented by Schumpeter, entrepreneurs are claimed to be a rare breed of innovators that create new combinations of resources on a grand scale. In another Austrian view, represented by Kirzner, the entrepreneur is seen as an opportunistic arbitrageur who is alert to potential profits and capitalizes on them. These opportunities are not created by the entrepreneurs, but merely exist because non-entrepreneurs have been inefficient in their allocation of resources.

The Chicago orientation addresses the question of uncertainty. For example, Knight (see Eisenhouwer 1995) was the first to distinguish between risk, a situation in which the outcome of a repeated trial is governed by known probabilities and is therefore insurable, and uncertainty, a situation in which no previous trials have occurred, and which is therefore uninsurable.

In the model created by Eisenhouwer, several of these elements are combined. The entrepreneurial decision is based on a vector of personal or psychological variables such as risk aversion and perceptions of the benefits of venturing, as well as a vector of external or environmental factors including interest rates, accumulated wealth, wages and conditions of work in the wage-sector, the probability of unemployment, the generosity of insurance benefits, and the length of time to retirement. The results suggest that the probability of a worker choosing self-employment responds positively to wealth, the probability of unemployment, and hours of work in the wage-sector. The results further indicate that probability responds negatively to increases in wages and payroll, and insurance taxes provided to laborers. Additionally, increases in interest rates tend to discourage venturing, and younger individuals are somewhat more likely to choose entrepreneurship than older workers, although interest rates and youthfulness do not appear to make a statistically significant difference. As the model contains psychological variables, these variables according to Eisenhower, are rather subjective and difficult to measure while the external factors can be objectively measured.

In developing a model for determinants of successful entrepreneurship based on Dutch entrepreneurs, van Praag (1996) studied the following factors: parental background variables, human capital variables, reason to start a business, macro economic conditions, financial status, social and psychological variables like religion and extraversion. As a result, the following variables occurred as predictors: own capital contribution, father self-employed, father manager, science oriented education, highest education level, number of job changes, low unemployment rate and extraversion. In both models (Eisenhouwer and van Praag) psychological variables were included that all lie outside economic theories. What we can learn is that the human factor can not be ignored not even in economic models.

4.3   Strategic Management Models

In this section we present a few strategic management models that pay attention to the human factor of entrepreneurship. First we will review a model that has been used to explain entrepreneurial performance. Second we will pay attention to two models that describe the start-up of entrepreneurship followed by another descriptive model to describe the development of firms through the life-cycles. Chrisman et al. (1999) discuss the determinants of new venture performance from the perspective of strategic management theory and describe why the concepts of resources, and organizational structure, processes and systems are essential elements of any fully specified model of new venture performance. In their view, entrepreneurship is defined as the creation of new ventures, and entrepreneurs are the creators of new ventures. In addition, new venture performance depends on five factors: the entrepreneur, industry structure, business structure, resources and organizational structure, processes, and systems.

We applied this model for predicting firm growth in terms of personnel growth for a period of three years and turnover growth for a period of three years (Nandram and Boermans 2001). The results indicated that the factor entrepreneur, mainly personality and the factor business structure, mainly the perception of business opportunities, could predict turnover growth and personnel growth. These empirical results will support the conceptual model of entrepreneurship that we build for the research on the 60 cases in this book.

Entrepreneurial scholars such as Stevenson (2000) and Timmons and Spinelli (2004) offer models to describe entrepreneurship. To introduce the subject, Stevenson (2000) defines entrepreneurship as "the pursuit of opportunity without regard to the resources currently controlled". Under this umbrella type definition, wide latitude in interpretation between start-up venturing and any later stages of entrepreneurial behavior is offered. In our view, this would also include the use of established entrepreneurial management techniques in larger firms, not-for-profit organizations and even within the public sector.

In entrepreneurship, it is the ever present opportunity promising the application of new ideas for products or services in society that acts as the driving force in an organization. Stevenson further defines more entrepreneurial behavior, as opposed to less entrepreneurial style, in terms of six dynamic dimensions: (1) strategic orientation: an entrepreneurial attitude is focused on opportunity, (2) commitment to opportunity: knowledge of market, willingness to act, (3) commitment to resources: doing more with less, (4) control of resources: access to as opposed to owning resources, (5) management structure: flexible, (6) coordination oriented, flat, reward philosophy: creation and harvesting of value.

Stevenson offers a dynamic description of entrepreneurship, thereby including corporate venturing and intrapreneurship. "In developing a strategic management theory of entrepreneurship it becomes clear that entrepreneurship is defined more by a set of individual traits and is different from an economic function. It is a cohesive pattern of managerial behavior" (p.13).

Timmons and Spinelli (2004) elegantly illustrate the entrepreneurial process as a continuous interplay between opportunity, resources and the entrepreneurial team in an uncertain environment. Early on the uncertainty can be enormous, if not overwhelming, when contrasting the vision of the market opportunity with the processes of verification, resources acquisition, market forces and regulation, not to speak of the capital market context.

The role of the human factor appears also as an important cause of venture failure. This type of failure often originates in team failure. Thus, a discussion of venturing processes would not be complete without mentioning venture life-cycles. Adizes (1979) breaks down the various task orientations that are required in any stage of the company life-cycle in the PAIE model of task orientations: Productive: producing results, production, marketing, sales, distribution, etc.; Administrative: timing, tracking and controlling productive activities; Integration: team continuously updated on the values, mission and specific goals; Entrepreneurial: creative, innovative, risk taking activities.

This model demands that at each subsequent stage of the venture life-cycle, these four task orientations are pursued and maintained in the appropriate balance. In the creation phase, the idea for the opportunity and its verification in the market place is the dominant orientation. In the infant phase, the emphasis would shift to producing. In the next stage, which Adizes aptly called the "Go-Go stage" when the venture is really taking off, creativity is again called for bringing result-oriented solutions to bear; typical of a fast growing, resources-strapped venture. In new venturing, these first lifecycle stages cover the early life of the company. Thereafter, the innovative and venturing spirit might fade under the pressure of expediency. In extreme situations a company will die or be rescued from the brink by turnaround management, sometimes in combination with being acquired.

Today, there is a greater awareness of the possibility of simultaneously growing companies and retaining an entrepreneurial spirit than thirty or forty years ago. This is where entrepreneurial management comes into play. In the adolescent stage, administration becomes a crucial task orientation to master the business process, for instance, to avoid stock-outs, and manage cash flows and headcounts. The life-cycle demands a different mix of task orientations and skills as the company grows. In the penultimate stage of Adizes model, called bureaucracy (the one preceding death), the dominance of this very administrative orientation leads to the elimination of creativity, flexibility and innovation from the corporate culture. The task orientation common to all life-stages is Integration. In the absence of continuous attention to integration process, common objectives are likely to break down, conflict in the venture team arises as a major threat. Under the stresses and strains of entrepreneurial exploration, expansion and survival, the lack of what often are referred to as "soft skills", "teamship" or "team spirit" can indeed lead to hard failures.

In addition to personal or team failure, common sources of venture failure can be found in insufficient opportunity verification, lack of funding, loss of strategic partners, governmental regulation, competitive innovation, natural or man-made disasters, etc. An indication of new venture failure rates after one year of existence by firm size across industries in the USA is tracked by the Brandow Company Inc. Overall (see Table 4.1); venture failure appears to fall in the range of 45 to 55% (Timmons and Spinelli 2004, p. 53).

Table 4.1 One-year survival rates by firm size

Firm Size (employees)	Survival Percent
1-24	53.6
25-49	68.0
50-99	69.0
100-249	73.2

BizMiner 2002 Start-up Business Index, Majority Industry Report,
Copyright 2002 Brandow Company, Inc.

We conclude that in the strategic management models the human factor seems to play an important role for explaining venture performance or start-up, in describing the development of firms and for explaining venture failures.

4.4 Behavioral Models

Besides economic and strategic management oriented models in which behavior, thus the human factor, takes a place, although often a small one, academics offer behavioral oriented approaches with an exclusive focus on the entrepreneur's personality, backgrounds and traits. In the trait approach, the focus is on personal disposition of individuals. Traits are found by identifying entrepreneurs and non-entrepreneurs (see Aldrich and Zimmer 1986, Begley and Boyd 1987, Chell and

Brearly 1991, Gartner 1988, Low and MacMillan 1988, Bird and Jelinek 1988, Timmons 1978, McClelland 1961, 1965, Miner 1999). For example Brockhaus (1982) who uses demographic data to develop characteristics of the typical entrepreneur. Variables such as birth order, role models, age, education level, and work habits are studied as predictors. However most of these factors have not been found to be unique to entrepreneurs, rather they are common to many successful individuals, including managers.

Low and MacMillan (1988) therefore conclude that the attempts to develop a personality profile of the typical entrepreneur have been largely unsuccessful. It is thus, more useful to distinguish successful and unsuccessful entrepreneurs instead of distinguishing between types of entrepreneurs and managers to find the unique characteristics for each group. In view of the criticism on the trait approach, Robinson et al. (1991) for example, assumed that attitude theory offers a better alternative for predicting entrepreneurial behavior. This shift towards entrepreneurial behavior is also a result of the assumption that traits and demographic variables are of limited use in training and development of entrepreneurs because they cannot be easily modified. Attitudes on the other hand, can be changed more easily.

Another stream of research concerning entrepreneurial variables as predictor for success identifies types of entrepreneurs either by their personality traits (Miner 1999) or their early experiences and entrepreneurial actions (Westhead and Wright 1998). The underlying assumption is that different types of entrepreneurs may use different strategies, capacities and skills in their entrepreneurial activities on the way to successful performance. Differences in performance or goals may exist due to different motives between the various types of entrepreneurs. This elaboration of the literature leads to the conclusion that behavioral entrepreneurial variables are a central focus in research to date. Also, it can be concluded that much is still to be learned about their relationship with entrepreneurial performances as the role of the entrepreneur in this process cannot be denied.

The approaches needed to study the various types of entrepreneurial variables come from different disciplines but most often from psychology. Theories focused on the individual entrepreneur are used to explain personality, behavior and attitudes, cognitive processes of information gathering and decision-making. In view of the criticism of the traits approach it looks as if the individual perspective was getting lost in the entrepreneurship literature.

4.5   Entrepreneurship as a Distinctive Field

Recently however, the focus on the individual seems to be alive again with the new perspectives gained from cognitive and behavioral approaches. The dominant current view has been offered by Venkataraman (1997) and elaborated by Shane and Venkataraman (2000). They define the field of entrepreneurship as the scholarly examination of how, by whom, and with what effect opportunities to create future goods and services are discovered, evaluated, and exploited. The field involves the study of sources of opportunities, the processes of discovery, the evaluation and exploitation of opportunities, and the set of individuals who discover, evaluate, and exploit them. It also concerns three types of questions for research: (1) Why, when, and how opportunities for the creation of goods and services come into existence? (2) Why, when, and how do some people and not others discover and exploit these opportunities? (3) Why, when, and how are different modes of action used to exploit entrepreneurial opportunities?

By defining the field of research, these academics have contributed significantly to the current research paradigm. In the remainder of this section, examples are presented on topics that are related to these three questions.

Opportunity Sources

Sarasvathy (2004) raises the question "whether opportunities exist in the world and need only be recognized or discovered, or whether they are spun into existence from within the minds of the entrepreneurs". In her view, we have to focus on the design of the firm and designing implies an essential role related to the tools 'out there' in the world, as well as, to the purely internal imagination of the designer about what to do with them. According to Sarasvathy what is found in the world is not opportunity but rather possibility. Entrepreneurs use possibility as a tool and fashion it into opportunity through imaginative interaction both with their tools and with the society in which they live.

The Processes of Discovery

Some researchers focus on failures in the cognitive processes to understand entrepreneurial discovery. Baron (1998) for example, developed assumptions for his work. He assumed that entrepreneurial thinking may differ in important ways from that of other persons. Specifically the former may be more susceptible to various kinds of cognitive errors or bias than other persons. He also indicated that differences in cognition do not stem primarily from differences between entrepreneurs and other people with respect to personal traits. Although such differences may well exist, the differences stem from the fact that entrepreneurs operate in situations and under conditions that would be expected to maximize such errors or biases. Baron mentions five biases:

1. The tendency to imagine what might have been in a given situation (counterfactual thinking).
2. Affective states produced by one source influence judgments and decisions about other, unrelated sources (affect infusion).
3. Most individuals tend to attribute positive outcomes to internal causes (such as own talent or effort), but negative outcomes to external causes (attribution style).

4. The tendency of most people to underestimate the time required to complete various projects, or to overestimate how much they can accomplish in a given period of time (planning fallacy).

5. The tendency to continue investing time, effort, or money in losing courses of action because of an initial commitment to this course of action. The desire to justify the initial choice or decision in an escalation of commitment situation (escalation of commitment or self-justification).

According to Baron, the goal of studying the role of cognitive mechanisms in entrepreneurship, therefore, is primarily that of formulating means for holding errors stemming from the cognitive mechanisms in check so that the decisions reached by entrepreneurs, and the strategies adopted, have increased chances of success.

The cognitive entrepreneurship field has very few empirical results, yet Palich and Bagby (1995) found that whereas entrepreneurs and non-entrepreneurs did not differ in overall risk-taking propensity, they did differ in terms of how they thought about business situations. More specifically, entrepreneurs tended to categorize such situations as having more strengths, opportunities, and potential for gain than did non-entrepreneurs.

The Evaluation and Exploitation of Opportunities

Most of the reviewed literature on entrepreneurship presented in earlier sections can be categorized under the heading *exploitation of opportunities*. Research deals with the question of resources needed and the concrete structures to exploit the opportunity; this is the actual design of the opportunity.

After having discovered an opportunity individuals may exploit it by starting a venture or by incorporating it in their corporate career. If there are possibilities to work the opportunity out in an existing firm it depends on the organizational culture and the person's ambition. It can be a part of improving someone's working process and outcome or it can be part of a spin out. For an entrepreneur who discovers new opportunities, there is the possibility to incorporate the new opportunity with current activities by some expansion in the venture structure or processes, or by starting a new venture.

For the evaluation of opportunities, McGrath and MacMillan (2000) suggest that entrepreneurs or potential entrepreneurs keep a dynamic and up-to-date list of new opportunities. This requires a certain entrepreneurial mindset.

Individuals Who Discover, Evaluate, and Exploit Opportunities

In the processes of discovery, evaluation and exploitation of opportunities, the individual entrepreneur or potential entrepreneur, or teams of individuals are the possible actors who make entrepreneurship a phenomenon consisting of actions. This implies that the field can gain not only from cognitive but also from behavioral approaches. One of the current contributions that provides an answer why behavioral approaches did not meet expectations in the past is from Sarasvathy (2004). In the past, entrepreneurial success was studied by referring to firm success, and often the variables used dealt with the behaviors or traits measured at the individual level. Therefore, often weak correlations were found.

In one of our studies we found for example, that from all the 14 behavioral variables we investigated, three of them predicted success (i.e. turnover and personnel growth for three years). As expected, successful entrepreneurs were more market-oriented than less successful entrepreneurs, demonstrated more courage and took more time for reflection (Nandram and Samsom 2000). In another study using the framework of Chrisman et al. (1997), we found that only courage as a behavioral attribute contributed to the explanation of firm success (R-square was only 7%). Variables such as opportunity perception and decisiveness on the other hand explained more variance; 30% of the variance in turnover growth was explained (Nandram 2003). These were also measured at the individual level but the reason for their higher correlations might occur because the variables mentioned refer more to action than traits.

Although weak correlations were found in several studies, it cannot be assumed that individual entrepreneurial variables are not important for venture performance.

Sarasvathy focuses on three faulty assumptions in past research. The first assumption deals with the thinking that the entrepreneur is equal to the firm. The entrepreneur is not the same as the firm, she argued, nor is success of the firm the only or even the most important measure of entrepreneurial success.

In one of our own research efforts we found that entrepreneurial success varies among individuals. To find out how success and failure are defined according to entrepreneurs we used the critical incident technique (CIT) approach, developed by Flanagan (1954) in an explorative study. The CIT is essentially a procedure for gathering certain important facts concerning behavior in defined situations, yet it does not consist of a single rigid set of rules governing such data collection.

From the 205 entrepreneurs that were surveyed by postal questionnaires, 181 answered the questions related to success and 137 gave answers related to failure. In total, 338 incidents related to success were mentioned and 201 incidents related to failure. Incidents mentioned simply and solely were abandoned from further analysis.

Table 4.2 presents the results. The incidents are often related to changes in the ventures rather than personal changes even though the survey was very personally oriented. This implies that an entrepreneur's success is often similar to venture success in the eye of the entrepreneur. Most of the answers can be related to the following changes in the life-cycle of the company: the decision of becoming an entrepreneur, getting and implementing an idea / innovation, growing (personnel, financially), growing by co-operation, growing by take-over, managing changes in the company, managing external changes in opportunities, and coping with resource needs (human capital).

In the early-stage, innovation and the actual start are mentioned most frequently. In the expansion stage, the management of change and growth are the dominant

Table 4.2 Critical incidents referring to success

	Early	Expansion	Maturity	Total
Total	46	136	107	289
1. Termination of wage earning after conflict	5	3	5	13
2. Innovation of product or process	7	8	4	19
3. The actual start of the company	8	11	18	37
4. Was asked to join a company / to take-over	3	13	13	29
5. Privatization	–	4	1	5
6. Internationalization	1	4	5	10
7. Writing a / business plan	2	2	2	6
8. Management of cultural change / re–organization	5	18	12	35
9. Co-operation with other company	5	8	5	18
10. Big orders	1	2	1	4
11. Finish courses	2	1	2	5
12. Occupational change	2	–	1	3
13. Management of growth in sales, personnel	4	21	18	43
14. Management of good team	1	8	5	14
15. Employees commitment	–	3	1	4
16. Big opportunity in the market	–	1	6	7
17. Growth of company to the next phase	–	10	8	18
18. Management of satisfied customers	–	5	–	5
19. Exploration of new market	–	11	–	11
20. Spin-off	–	3	–	3

incidents. And, in the maturity stage, the actual start and the management of growth in sales and personnel, are the most frequently mentioned. Note that all these answers are the result of open ended questions; therefore every incident mentioned more than once can be seen as relevant. We conclude therefore, that in practice entrepreneurs often tend to attribute entrepreneurial success to firm success.

Table 4.3 summarizes the incidents related to failures. These incidents described many types of problems due to the lack of experience, the lack of good co-operation and different external factors such as permission and reasons related to market opportunity. It appears that attribution bias occurs, as mentioned by Baron earlier in this chapter. The entrepreneurs had the tendency to attribute failures much more to external causes while the successes were attributed much more to the entrepreneurs themselves. In each phase, the category 'wrong decisions' is frequently mentioned as critical. In the early phase, liquidation, bankruptcy and rejected plans are mentioned as failures frequently. And in the expansion and maturity stage a crucial factor is having the wrong business partners.

Table 4.3. Critical incidents referring to failure

	Early	Expansion	Maturity	Total
Total	39	77	58	174
1. Conflict with superior	3	8	4	15
2. I act too impulsively to foster problems	2	2	4	8
3. Business Partner dropped out	2	1	3	3
4. Wrong decision (investment, purchase, personnel)	6	11	14	31
5. Financial problems	1	6	2	9
6. Wrong business partner / co-operation	4	10	5	19
7. Liquidation / bankruptcy / cancelling of big order	5	6	1	12
8. Did not had the expertise of running a business	3	7	5	15
9. Plan rejected by advisory board / bank / government	5	3	3	11
10. Take-over of a company	2	1	–	3
11. Too many people were involved at the beginning	2	1	1	4
12. Conflict with suppliers / customers did not pay	1	2	1	4
13. Good employees quit / distrust	–	4	3	7
14. No sufficient orders / lost of contract	1	1	3	5
15. No sufficient experience / preparation	–	–	3	3
16. Too many changes in company	–	2	2	4
17. My aspirations / motivation decreased	–	2	2	4
18. Delay in getting permission	–	3	1	4
19. Personal problems / I got sick	–	6	1	7
20. Did not manage the target	2	1	–	3

Referring to the problematic assumption pointed about by Sarasvathy, namely the thinking that the entrepreneur is equal to the firm, this assumption could not be confirmed by the results presented so far. And the second problematic assumption according to Sarasvathy is the homogeneous goals on the part of the firm's founders and management team. The entrepreneurs' goals are assumed to be either homogenous in the sense of some optimization problem (usually profit maximization) or are assumed to be collapsible into some well-specified ordering that can be smoothly mapped to firm goals. Therefore, she argued that firms are products of individual abilities and expectations that are heterogeneous to begin with. According to Sarasvathy, the heterogeneity at the root continues to diverge unchecked, leading only to more variety and novelty, rather than otherwise.

The third faulty theory Sarasvathy points out refers to the strong assumption of opportunity on individual behavior. Studies have shown that the intelligent altruist beats both the unintelligent altruist and the selfish individual in survival along certain key measures of fitness (p.522).

Sarasvathy summarizes her thinking by saying that one simply cannot get away from the fact that firms are created by entrepreneurs, and entrepreneurs are human beings; evolved socio-biological beings whose psychology, history, and culture matter. "By refocusing our attention on the person(s) who is making it happen, we are able to unhook ourselves from preconceptions of "it" and allow it to float and transmogrify into a variety of possibilities, many of them yet to be imagined", says Sarasvathy (2004, p.522).

The literature review leads to the conclusion that focusing on key activities of entrepreneurship, such as designing the firm may open new ways of thinking about the role of entrepreneurs and the human factor within entrepreneurial processes; the role of the entrepreneur is part of this thinking. Entrepreneurship is then, designing a firm with the key entrepreneurial processes defined on the basis of earlier studies.

Yet because of our wider view on entrepreneurship, we narrowed the design process to the opportunity, as detailed below. It starts with an opportunity that can be a real, existing opportunity or a belief that is based on imagination. This opportunity could be designed by creating a new firm or organization, by adjusting an existing firm or organization, or by adding to an existing firm or organization.

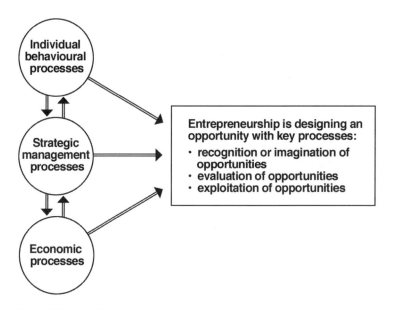

Fig. 4.1 Concept for entrepreneurship

In Figure 4.1 we summarize the main perspectives of entrepreneurship based on the literature review. On the left side of the figure we include three clusters of concepts namely individual behavioral processes, strategic management and economic processes. These are presented as predictors of entrepreneurship. *Entrepreneurship is defined as an umbrella concept consisting of different processes such as the recognition or imagination of opportunities, the evaluation and implementation of opportunities.*

Here we can conclude that different processes influence the design of key entrepreneurial processes. Behavioral expectations and strategies, strategic management practices and strategies and striving towards various types of economic goals can all effect entrepreneurship. This framework can be applied to entrepreneurial management as well because we focus on a process oriented view. To investigate the 60 cases we need a more detailed conceptual framework to approach the human factor more on a micro level. In the following sections we will develop such a conceptual model by elaborating on individual and cognitive concepts. These seem to play an important role in the recent academic discussion about entrepreneurship. However there is very little research with empirical results to give meaning to these types of concepts.

4.6 The New Research Model for Entrepreneurship

We have presented different academic views of entrepreneurship and aim next to build a model in which the human factor is more dominant in comparison with any other model presented in the previous sections. The main reason is that the human factor is our focus. We believe, based on our research results so far, that the human factor can not be ignored. In fact, we believe that we have to explore it further. Understanding entrepreneurship asks for understanding processes of individual entrepreneurs and executives experience. Further insight into the entrepreneurial processes from an individual perspective with a focus on management of emotions and behavior is of value because these factors influence decisions that entrepreneurs or executives take. Furthermore because these factors influence the perception of opportunities and in some cases indirectly, the performance of firms. Specifically, we will look closely at strategic orientation, decision orientation, emotional stability and behavioral attributes.

Based on our review of the literature in the previous sections, the discussion that follows takes a business management research approach, with a strong emphasis on the individual entrepreneur and a review of psychological variables. The question of how opportunities are created and designed from the perspective of the individual entrepreneur as the source of information is central, encompassing their perceptions of the design of opportunities. A part of this research approach also contains psychological concepts and strategic management concepts adapted from Stevenson.

The Strategic Management Approach

In the previous sections we already discussed some strategic management models and therefore we will spend only a few words on this approach. The six-dimension model of Stevenson (2000) and the three-factor model of Timmons and Spinelli (2004) have been used to develop a strategic management model for the case studies presented. Both models are considered in the context of the growing influence of community and ecological considerations, when venturing conditions appear to become at first, more complicated. However, as some of the entrepreneurs featured in this book show, at the same time greater numbers of new (venture) opportunities open up. The physical impact of the relentlessly growing economic activity on the Earth is working its way back into economics as we know it. This places restrictions on business and consumption (in one sense) i.e. through pollution and health concerns. On the other hand, social and ecological challenges also offer new opportunities for innovations, resource conservation and reduction. Often referred to as sustainable venturing or natural capitalism, this has been discussed in Chapter 3. The big challenges lie in finding a balance between the available resources, and the strategic decisions that are targeted.

The Role of Attitudes

The field of entrepreneurship, according to current academic discussion, deals with the design of opportunities by discovering, evaluation and exploitation. The key actor within these processes is the individual person. Therefore, our case studies in this book concentrate on this key actor, the entrepreneur. The following sections focus on psychological concepts such as attitudes for understanding (some) entrepreneurial processes in this regard.

We approach the psychological side from three perspectives. First, we focus on the two self-regulation basics related to decision-making processes, namely prevention and promotion orientation. Next we focus on the regulation of emotions in the individual to explain the concepts of action and state orientation. The mental aspects are examined, especially when dealing with a setback. And third, certain behavioral attributes are discussed. By approaching the psychological side of the entrepreneur, insights into the key entrepreneurial processes can be gained.

We also consider the design of an opportunity as a process which contains several behavioral actions. One of the most frequently confirmed behavioral models in social sciences stems from Fishbein and Ajzen (1975). In their model behaviors can be predicted by intentions. This model, which has been based on the work of cognitive psychologists, has been elaborated with empirical results (Ajzen 1989, Ajzen and Madden 1986). The model is based on the assumption that individuals act on good reasoning. It has been primarily applied to behaviors that are under complete volitional control. Volitional control means that the individual does feel he has complete control over his intended behavior. Intentions have been conceptualized as being a function of beliefs that provide a link between beliefs and subsequent behavior. People form attitudes toward performing a given behavior based on beliefs that performing the behavior will result in certain consequences. The attitudes are also based on normative beliefs about the behavior. A person's attitude is the positive or negative evaluation of performing a specific behavior.

We approach attitude as a multidimensional construct, the tripartite model (Chaiken and Stangor 1987). According to this approach, an entrepreneur will have three types of reaction to everything such as a place, a thing, an event, an activity or even an opportunity. Psychologist call these reactions affect, cognition and behavior. This means that regarding an opportunity, an entrepreneur will have positive or negative feelings towards it (affect). He will have beliefs and thoughts about the opportunity (cognition), and he will develop a certain behavioral intention, a certain way to behave towards the opportunity seeking process.

In Ajzen's model, intentions come from attitudes and become the immediate determinant of behavior. According to Fishbein and Ajzen (1975) asking for the individual's intention to perform a specific behavior is the most efficient way of knowing if the person is going to express that behavior. An intention is based on one's attitude, and the attitude can be predicted by one's own beliefs and the perception of the beliefs of significant others (social norms), and refers to the perception of pressure towards performing the behavior. This model has been revised by Ajzen and Madden (1986) and is called the theory of planned behavior. This narrows the application of the model to behaviors that are less volitionally controlled. The model of Ajzen and Madden (1986) assumes that both intention to a specific behavioral act and the perceived self-efficacy of conducting that act are the best predictors of the behavioral act.

The assumption that behavior is reasoned does not hold for every entrepreneurial behavior. We therefore expanded the model with the introduction of the concepts of prevention and promotion orientation, action and state orientation, and mood orientations.

Applied to the design of an opportunity (which is behavior) implies that the intention to design and the perceived self-efficacy of designing the opportunity are the best predictors together with the orientations. The intention and the self-efficacy can be influenced by the three aspects of attitudes. Using attitude in entrepreneurship literature has advantages because attitudes are seen as being relatively less stable than personality traits, as they change across time and across situations through interactive processes with the environment. It can be considered therefore, as a dynamic and interactive way by which an entrepreneur relates to the opportunity or any other entrepreneurial activity. Figure 4.2 shows the concepts that we believe are important in understanding entrepreneurship from a human interactive approach.

In our example we use the orientations that have a direct influence on the intention of the person and on the attitudes. The three types of orientations and their behavioral attributes are discussed further in the following sections.

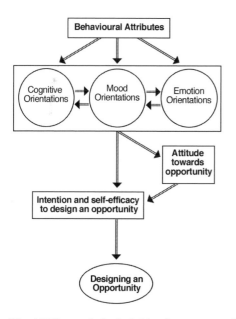

Fig. 4.2 The psychological side of entrepreneurship

Promotion and Prevention Orientation

People have two basic self-regulation systems (Higgins 1998). One system regulates the achievement of rewards and focuses people on a promotion goal. In contrast, the other system regulates the avoidance of punishment and focuses people on a prevention goal. Specifically, Higgins (1998) proposes the term promotion for pursuing positive outcomes and prevention for avoiding negative outcomes. Higgins (2000) also developed the concept of promotion and prevention in relation with decision-making.

The decision-making process is explained in the next section. It is not only the economic costs that counts but also the psychological costs and the question does it fit one's values (the subjective fit).

Higgins' theoretical views lead to the conclusion that a good decision is not simply a matter of rational cost and benefit analysis or a social and rational cost and benefit analysis. There are individual differences in orientations that influence whether an entrepreneur strives for a promotion goal or if he strives for a prevention goal. This orientation is not a stable characteristic; it can vary for example, due to the stage of the design of the firm. A decision is good when there is a fit between the situation and the entrepreneur's orientation. An entrepreneur who has a promotion goal, such as a profit growth, will be motivated highly when there are opportunities to realize this goal. A lack of opportunities will only serve to frustrate, as a decision to expand is a good one and a decision not to expand is a bad one (see Table 4.4).

Promotion and Prevention in Entrepreneurship

An entrepreneur who has a prevention goal such as not hiring permanent personnel and consciously staying small, will feel better when he does not need to hire fixed personnel and instead can make use of flexible personnel or do things on his own. Yet when he does not manage to do the tasks he is responsible for on his own or he cannot find flexible personnel, the situation will frustrate him.

In this scenario, a decision to hire fixed personnel is a bad one because this does not fit with the entrepreneur's orientation. As such, a decision not to hire fixed personnel is a good one. By introducing the concept of promotion and prevention orientation it is assumed that an entrepreneur's actions can vary and therefore their decisions can vary due to their subjective orientation. In the case studies it will become clear that entrepreneurial types that we distinguish might have different promotion and prevention orientations which predict their purposes and dilemmas they experience. From the information we received regarding the motivation of the enterprising person we may conclude that they are more prevention oriented which means that they will strive less for high achievements, in comparison with the significant growth entrepreneurs for whom promotion orientation is an important drive. A prevention oriented person will therefore gain more from an enterprising route to entrepreneurship.

Table 4.4 Promotion and prevention

Promotion and prevention	Description
• Promotion focus	• Tendency to achieve rewards
• Prevention focus	• Tendency to avoid punishment

The Process of Decision-Making

From a psychological and economic perspective, we all want to make good decisions. Each individual evaluates the beneficial outcomes with the cost of attaining the outcomes. The costs include not only the goods or services one must give in exchange (the economic costs) for receiving the benefits but also the costs of the decision-making process itself. From an economic theoretical perspective one will strive for optimizing outcomes. A psychological perspective would say that an approach to optimize outcomes might not be used by an individual because the costs in cognitive effort or time are too high. In explaining the concept of promotion and prevention orientation, Higgins (2000) introduced three concepts to understand decision-making:

1. *Value of outcomes.* He equates value with worth and not with utility and questions 'is the final decision worthwhile'. Higgins states that the final decision is worthwhile because the benefits of the decision are relatively high compared with alternative decisions (the opportunity costs in economic models). With respect to outcome costs, the decision was 'worth it' because the costs of the

decision are relatively low compared with the benefits. So there are two steps; first comparisons of the benefit of the decision with alternative decisions; and second, a comparison of the costs of the decision with the benefits.

2. *The means by which the outcomes are attained.* There must be a fit with a purpose. Utility of a good decision is, according to Higgins, more than value from worth. Another factor that makes a decision good is value from fit. The fit is the relation between a person's orientation to an activity and the means used to pursue that activity. From our view, some entrepreneurs discover and exploit opportunities that others don't. Their behavior might be influenced by their orientation, so more entrepreneurs can pursue the same goals (i.e. starting or surviving a business, or higher profit or sales) from the available or imaginative opportunities but their orientations and means might differ. For example, all surviving start-ups will have benefits regardless of their orientation and means.

3. *Subjective fit.* Independent of this value from worth, Higgins stressed an additional value from fit. When the goal someone pursues fits with his regulatory or management system, the value he experiences will increase; so there is a sort of subjective fit occurring when activities fit with the system. The development of this individual management system is based on situational factors (loss – non loss situation versus gain – non gain situations) and individual factors (security needs versus self-actualization needs; ought self versus ideal self).

The Regulation of Emotion and Moods

Manstead and Fischer (2001) defined emotion regulation by making a distinction between mood regulation (negative or positive) and the regulation of specific emotions. They see moods as broad, affective states that are primarily characterized by hedonic qualities and not the appraisal of a specific object. So someone can have a happy or sad mood due to cheerful or depressive music, whereas emotions are more specifically based on appraisals that are relevant to an individual. Emotions have a sequence of processes that are cognitive, affective, and behavioral. Emotions can be regulated by reappraising or avoiding the emotional stimulus whereas moods cannot. Individuals vary in their abilities and inclinations to engage in emotion regulation and in mood regulation. One concept referring to emotion regulation stems from Kuhl and Beckmann (1994). And, according to Gross, emotions have the following functions (1999).

1. They tailor cognitive style to situational demands.
2. They facilitate decision-making.
3. They prepare the individual for rapid motor responses.
4. They promote learning.
5. They provide information about behavioral intentions to give clues as to whether something is good or bad and to flexibly script complex social behavior.

We will focus on the cognitive regulation of emotions from a perspective of the control theory (Kuhl and Beckmann 1994), as it is a concept that could be applied to the entrepreneur. Entrepreneurs deal with several situations where emotions can run very high such as bankruptcy.

Action and State Orientation

Kuhl and Beckmann (1994) developed the concept of action versus state control from the action control theory, a frequently applied approach to predict human behavior. The control theory assumes that behavior is never caused by a response to an outside stimulus. Instead, behavior is inspired by what a person wants most at any given time based on his basis or luxurious human needs. This means that an individual will actively formulate intentions towards behaviors (Ajzen 1989). This control theory is applicable to entrepreneurial behavior such as actively seeking opportunities. Action control is the self-regulatory mechanism that mediates the enactment of action-related mental structures. According to Kuhl and Beckmann people differ in their disposition toward, or capacity for, action control. Those with a low self-regulatory capacity are called *state oriented* persons. Those with a high self-regulatory capacity are called *action oriented* persons; both lie on a continuum (see Table 4.5). A state oriented person has a tendency that reflects inertia to act. An action oriented person shows readiness to act. Action and state orientation was developed as a variable influencing goal-striving and it has to do with the ability to initiate and maintain intentions, the ability to make timely decisions, commit to a course of action, initiate action, aid procrastination, handle multiple competing demands, maintain challenging goals, and persist despite failures or setback (Kuhl and Beckmann 1994). State orientation refers to a low capacity for the enactment of action-related mental structures, whereas action orientation refers to a high capacity for this type of enactment. Action oriented persons can decrease their negative affect, whereas state oriented cannot easily decrease their negative affect. State oriented persons have therefore, a high level of negative mood.

Individuals with a strong action orientation are able to devote their cognitive resources to the tasks at hand, thus enabling them to expediently move from a present goal state to some desired future goal state. They flexibly allocate their attention for the purpose of task execution and goal attainment. They have the ability to complete tasks after minor failures or setbacks, especially when dealing with high stress situations, uncertainties and setbacks; entrepreneurs will behave different because of the interpersonal differences in the action or state orientation.

Table 4.5 Action and state orientation

Action and state orientation	Description
Action orientation	a high capacity for the enactment of action related mental structures
State orientation	a low capacity for the enactment of action related mental structures

Mood Regulation

As stated above there is a difference between emotions and moods. A mood is continuously present and it is not easy to figure out its source. Moods have obviously less intensive appearances and moods influence behavior only in an indirect way by having influence on the cognitive processes.

A positive mood state is one in which a person feels good and therefore will act more socially, cooperatively, creatively and deal more easily with setbacks (Reeve 2001). People with positive moods tend to have more enjoyable thoughts and recalls and they act towards positive thoughts and recalls. Mental fitness is a concept consisting of five facets on a continuum of negative and positive moods.

We will focus on the concept of mental fitness developed by Keizer and Vooren (2006) on the basis of the flow theory of Csikszentmihalyi (2003). The flow theory tries to explain motivation based on elements such as the feeling of enjoyment, capability of control, clearness of goals, concentration level and experiencing the moment itself. Mental fitness is a concept consisting of five facets on a continuum of negative and positive (see Table 4.6). The five facets are: self-confidence, energy, alert, tension and satisfaction. Self confidence stems from Bandura's self-efficacy (1991), the confidence that one can execute specific tasks to obtain a certain goal. Energy tells us if someone is capable of carrying a load. A person with low energy will not be able to put effort in tasks and feels exhausted. Alert refers to the concentration level to fulfill a task. Tension refers to the level of arousal when dealing with a task. A satisfied person will have a positive evaluation of the situation. These five concepts can be divided into three groups. The first deals with self-confidence and energy as antecedents of behaving in a certain way in situations. Self confidence represents the cognitive aspect and energy represents the physical aspect of having control towards the situation. The second deals with the experienced moment itself facing tension and alertness. The third category deals with the evaluation of situations based on the concept of satisfaction.

Table 4.6 Mental fitness

Mental fitness	Description
Self-confidence	The subjective feeling that one is capable of executing a specific task to obtain a certain goal
Energy	If someone feels psychically capable of carrying a load
Tension	Refers to the a level of arousal when dealing with a task
Alertness	A sharp concentration level to fulfill a task
Satisfaction	Positive evaluation of a task

Behavioral Attributes

Personality variables may have an important role to play in developing theories of the entrepreneurial processes. One of the first studies dealing with personality stems from McClelland (1961) who developed the concept of achievement motivation for comparing entrepreneurs with non-entrepreneurs. From qualitative studies he concludes that achievement motivation is a good predictor for entrepreneurs' perceived success. From that time, several studies have been conducted mainly using non-psychological measures of personality variables. Therefore, many inconsistent results have been obtained leading to the conclusion that the trait approach does not offer anything towards understanding entrepreneurship. A recent article of Zhao and Seibert (2006) presents a meta-analytic review of the role of personality variables and entrepreneurial status. This review method tries to conclude what role can be prescribed to personality by comparing results of studies and taking into account the criteria of reliability and validity of measures used for personality variables. They state that most studies included a confusing variety of personality variables, sometimes with unknown reliability and validity and often with little theoretical justification. In the vocational psychology, overwhelming evidence exists for differences in mean personality scores across jobs, occupations, and work environments. Results indicate significant differences between entrepreneurs and managers related to personality dimensions.

In the psychological literature the five factor model of personality has been widely accepted (McCrae et al. 2004). Within this model personality consists of the five big factors: conscientiousness, openness to experience, neuroticism, agreeableness and extraversion. Each factor consists of several variables that consist of more specific traits. Zhao and Seibert (2006) conclude that this personality model brings together over 40 years of research on the emotional, interpersonal, experiential, attitudinal, and motivational style of an individual.

Therefore we are convinced that it is worth using this model for understanding the entrepreneurial processes in our case studies. In addition, during our past research efforts, we attempted to start from a dynamic perspective by not simply using the same personality factor model for entrepreneurs. We therefore approached entrepreneurs by using the critical incident technique (Flanagan 1954) for assessing the personality variables that are linked to entrepreneurial success and failures. In that study we asked entrepreneurs to think of successes and failures and then to describe their actions. From their descriptions we made a list of personality variables which we refer to as behavioral attributes, as they are derived from specific actions (Nandram and Samsom 2000, Nandram 2002).

To frame this list we used the big five personality factors, yet not every facet seems to occur in our list. We carried out a project with the Dutch Association of Venture Capitalists and the Ministry of Economic Affairs to develop a systematic tool for assessing entrepreneurial personalities. They were critical of the existing personality questionnaires because of many clinical terms which might not motivate entrepreneurs to fill in those questionnaires. Therefore we developed items for each facet in our list. These items have been validated by use in several studies including the selection of the Ernst & Young Entrepreneur of the Year competition. An adjusted list of items based on previous findings was analyzed in an advanced statistical method, the structural equation model in AMOS. This analysis has resulted in a definite scale for using entrepreneurial attributes that we call the EBAI (Entrepreneurial Behavioral Attributes Inventory, see Table 4.7). It consists of seven variables that have been exclusively developed for entrepreneurs and tested.

5 Case Study Design and Participant Background

While many theoretical foundations have been presented in the early chapters of this book, we have consciously chosen for an individual level of analysis by studying the experiences of entrepreneurs and entrepreneurial executives. This is the basis of our case study design. We concentrated on individual backgrounds by looking closely at their personal experiences, delving into what makes these people who they are. The questionnaire was specifically designed to probe their histories, and to inspire a diversity of stories to surface during the interviews. Our questions ranged from asking about their motivations, experiences, setbacks, behaviors to strategies concerning their involvement with entrepreneurship. The case studies seek to represent the spirit of various aspects of entrepreneurship. In the first section of this chapter we present information about the research sample and sources of information we used. We continue with the research model which formed the basis of our research, and detailed information concerning concepts in the model is also presented.

5.1 Entrepreneur and Executive Selection

In 2003 we conducted a study to ascertain the level of entrepreneurship among Nyenrode alumni. We defined entrepreneurs as founders who also had the role of top executives of their ventures or owners with the role of top executives. A questionnaire was sent to a group of alumni of which a total of 725 returned responded; this represented a response rate of 10%. 275 of those responses qualified as entrepreneurs. In the questionnaire we included a question about the willingness to participate in future research; nearly half of this group (150) was willing to participate in this research project.

For the 2005/2006 study we aimed to include a diversity of entrepreneurs and entrepreneurial executives in a case study approach. An additional selection criterion was that every venture had to have at least two employees. Our aim was to form a group of 50 entrepreneurs and 10 executives. Therefore, we selected at random a group of 40 entrepreneurs from the pool of 150 responders of the 2003 study. These 40 entrepreneurs received an invitation letter, a letter of agreement and a description of the objectives of the study. At this point, we did not yet reach the required number of 50 entrepreneurs. We wanted to reserve the option to subjectively select about 10 participants to include various different types of entrepreneurs we aimed to describe in the book, such as female participants, members of the not-for-profit sector, entrepreneurial executives from large companies, recent start-ups, and enterprising persons.

Because not everybody was willing to participate in the study, a second round of random selection (with invitations) was conducted. The same procedure was examined for the entrepreneurial executives. To reach a total of 50 participants we randomly approached nearly 70 alumni. People who refused to participate mentioned the fact that they did not want publicity, did not see themselves as role models, and were involved in a bankruptcy while some did not provide any reason. Appendix 1 provides additional detail of the participants and the number of participants per category.

To further describe and analyze the results, we divided the group of entrepreneurial executives into two types; profit and not-for-profit organizations. We distinct special case entrepreneurs and general entrepreneurs. The categories within the two types of entrepreneurs are not totally distinctive, for example a start-up could also be categorized in a group of special entrepreneurs such as venturers. Our aim was to use broad categories with specific focuses to address in the profiles of the entrepreneurs.

The Entrepreneurial Executive

The entrepreneurial executives are (potential) leaders who initiate an innovation, introduce a new way of working, realize an international business impact, or act as a charismatic leader resulting in the incorporation of their views at various levels of the organization. They can be found in the for-profit as well in the not-for-profit sector using entrepreneurial skills and techniques. A list of participants is included in Appendix 1.

The Special Entrepreneur

The category special entrepreneurs can include venturers who spin off businesses from existing firms. They leave a business to start a new one based on their personal learning and experiences. The re-launchers have bought a company which they give new direction and which they therefore developed further by applying their own efforts and abilities.

Trend entrepreneurs are owners of new businesses who are dedicated to the implementation of a triple bottom line stakeholder orientation (people, planet, profit). The family business owners have taken over a business or a part of a business from their family.

Table 5.1 Type of executives and entrepreneurs / numbers

Entrepreneurial executives	Special case entrepreneurs	General entrepreneurs
• Profit sector (7) • Not-for-profit sector (3)	• Venturers (8) • Re-launchers (8) • Trend entrepreneurs 6) • Family businesses (4)	• Significant business and growth founders(10) • Small business founders (6) • Start-ups (2) • Enterprising persons (6)

The General Entrepreneur

The general entrepreneur category included the significant and fast growing venturers. This group is composed of business founders who have been able to create a business that is significant in the sense of personnel, turnover and innovativeness. Some of these ventures have experienced a fast growth rate, for example 30% per year over a period over three years.

The second category is the small business founder. This can be compared with the enterprising person with the difference that they have personnel and are much more sensitive to market needs.

The third category is the start-up venture with the entrepreneur's intention to grow into a significant or high growth business. The products or services of this venture have the potential to enter a large market.

And the fourth category covers the enterprising person who started a firm with the primary aim of self employment, individual independence, and creativity development. This entrepreneur was also conscious of not working with personnel on a long-term contract. For this type of entrepreneur, their own needs are dominant in their way of doing business. Due to past experiences with personnel some were not open to hiring personnel on a long-term basis. And for some, their products or services relied much more on their own expertise which made hiring a person with the same expertise somewhat difficult.

5.2   Source and Type of Information

We used two primary sources of information. The first source of information was based on a written questionnaire regarding: (1) current position, (2) background data of the firm, if applicable, (3) short personal history, (4) headcount and turnover and firm development, if applicable, (5) strategic approaches to opportunities pursued, (6) psychological items dealing with the regulation of emotions and behavioral attributes. The second source consisted of interviews with the participants.

They were asked to complete the questionnaire before the personal interviews were held. This offered the possibility to learn something about the interviewee in advance and to clarify any unclear answers given. Four of the interviews were held by telephone or video conferencing as some participants were not able to travel due to the location involved. All interviews were personally conducted by the authors.

The interviews with the entrepreneurs focus on the start-up process with questions about their reasons for starting a venture, the factors that hinder or stimulate the start-up process, learning points, and unique experiences within their entrepreneurial career (one positive and one negative experience each).

The interviews with the entrepreneurial executives concentrated on their experiences dealing with an innovation, and their leadership and international experiences. The section of the study concerning the entrepreneurial executives was very much explorative with the aim to learn what personal characteristics could be identified within this group. The section of the study referring to entrepreneurs was much more framed within the current insights about entrepreneurial processes. In both parts the person is a central theme of the research.

Several types of variables could directly or indirectly influence the design of opportunities into firms. We wanted to take a more explorative approach in this view and therefore included open-ended questions in our questionnaire (see Appendix 2). In analyzing the case studies we aimed for a more specific definition of the behavioral and strategic processes that describe the start-up and evolution of a firm or the management behavior of executives in an organization.

For the analyzes we used the case study descriptions and the data we collected through the questionnaire. Quantitative data has been analyzed in the statistical program Statistical Package for Social Sciences (SPSS). Information about the measurements is included in Appendix 3. We did not have enough cases for every variable to test for significant differences. Although significant differences can provide more reliable outcomes we illustrate average scores when dealing with small numbers of cases to see what type of trends could be traced.

In popular terms we would say that a difference is significant statistically if there is an indication that the difference is large enough to represent an actual difference or trend in the population rather than occurring only by chance in the sample of study. For example as a result of factors we were not aware of or that we did not control (Jankowicz 2000). When differences are not tested statistically we would only say that the difference pattern is found in this study without claiming that it will occur in every other sample. For assessing statistical differences we used the 95% chance of being true, which means that a p score of $\leq .05$ is considered as significant, implying that the finding has a 5% (.05) chance of not being true.

5.3   Psychological Background of the Entrepreneur

Behavioral Attributes

The scores of entrepreneurs that took part in the case studies are compared with each other and with a benchmark score of entrepreneurs (5-point scale). This benchmark score stems from other previous research data (Nandram and Samsom 2005). The entrepreneurs were divided into the general category and the special form.

Only for one attribute, hardiness, do these groups differ significantly. This shows that special types of entrepreneurs score higher on hardiness in comparison with the general entrepreneurs. The special entrepreneurs reach almost every benchmark score (Figure 5.1).

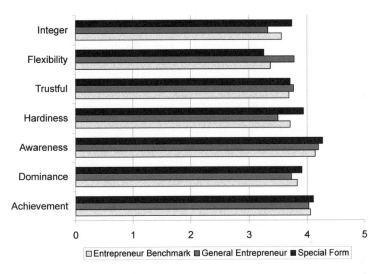

Fig. 5.1 Behavioral attributes of entrepreneurs

We compared every case study group presented in Chapters 8 through 16 (see Table 5.2). Due to the small numbers of cases per group we could not test differences; instead we focused on the average scores for each group.

- *Achievement Drive, Assertiveness.* All groups score high on achievement drive and awareness which are seen as the key entrepreneurial characteristics.

- *Dominance, Integrity and Trustful.* The scores on dominance, integrity and trustful behavior are more or less the same for every group.

- *Hardiness.* Start-ups show low scores for hardiness. They face less challenges and setbacks in comparison with the others and therefore have fewer experiences in dealing with them which is expressed in their scores on hardiness. High scores for hardiness were found for trend entrepreneurs, enterprising persons, re-launchers and family business entrepreneurs.

- *Flexibility.* Enterprising persons and start-ups have the highest scores on flexibility whereas family business entrepreneurs and re-launchers show the lowest score. This is explainable. They do have to act more than others within an existing framework that has been defined by others before they became the person with influence in the business. The enterprising person works solo which in part is also true for the start-ups and for whom flexibility can be higher.

Table 5.2 Behavioral attributes of entrepreneurial case groups (average scores)

	Venturer	Re-launcher	Trend	Family Business	Signifi-cant	Small Business	Start-up	Enter-prising
Achievement	4.15	4.06	4.03	4.42	4.06	3.94	4.25	4.08
Dominance	3.79	4.10	3.83	4.00	3.93	3.47	4.47	3.80
Awareness	4.29	4.33	4.17	4.33	4.29	4.17	4.33	4.17
Hardiness	3.75	4.00	4.11	4.00	3.60	3.36	3.25	4.00
Trustful	3.79	4.11	3.39	3.17	3.54	3.72	3.83	3.83
Flexibility	3.50	3.00	3.58	2.25	3.19	3.67	4.25	4.00
Integer	3.64	4.25	3.33	3.75	3.44	3.25	4.00	3.25

Mental Fitness

As part of our study we looked at the mental fitness of entrepreneurs (see definition in Appendix 3). We used a 10 point scale. Our results did not find significant differences between general and special case entrepreneurs, yet between the different case study groups we did see differences in patterns (see Table 5.3.).

- The small business entrepreneurs have almost the lowest score on each concept which means that they more often have mental problems and have less positive moods, low levels of energy, and low satisfaction, as well as low self confidence and low level of alertness.

- The concepts of satisfaction and moods show the widest range of variety between the groups. Enterprising persons are the most satisfied. Family business entrepreneurs and small business entrepreneurs are less satisfied. Differences between the other groups regarding satisfaction are small.

- Start-ups and significant business entrepreneurs show the highest scores on self confidence which means that they are relatively more self confident in comparison with other groups.

- Significant entrepreneurs, enterprising persons, start-ups, venturers, re-launchers and trend entrepreneurs have the least problems in maintaining a positive energy level followed by enterprising persons and venturers.

- Family entrepreneurs face high levels of negative moods followed by small business entrepreneurs.

- Family business entrepreneurs, start-ups, venturers and re-launchers show a high score on alertness which means that they feel more often alert in comparison with the others. These entrepreneurs might face more competition and therefore feel more alert.

- Enterprising persons, trend entrepreneurs and small business entrepreneurs have lower levels of alertness. This might have to do with the less competitive surroundings they operate in.

Comparing all the scores we can conclude that the mental fitness of small business and family business entrepreneurs are the lowest.

Table 5.3 Mental fitness of case groups (average scores)

	Venturer	Re-launcher	Trend	Family business	Signifi-cant	Small business	Start-up	Enter-prising
Energy	8.10	6.95	7.25	6.80	7.80	5.57	7.13	6.73
Moods	6.30	6.53	7.68	5.83	6.50	5.95	7.77	7.13
Self-confidence	7.90	7.60	7.40	7.73	8.24	6.37	8.53	6.93
Satisfaction	6.67	6.33	6.70	5.87	6.78	5.57	6.93	7.67
Alertness	7.97	7.83	7.85	8.13	7.93	6.87	8.00	7.27

Promotion and Prevention Focus

It has been proposed that people have two basic self-regulation systems. One system regulates the achievement of rewards and focuses people on a promotion goal. In contrast, the other system regulates the avoidance of punishment and focuses people on a prevention goal. The results (see Figure 5.2) show that all types of the entrepreneurs studied score higher on promotion than on prevention orientation. Family business entrepreneurs tend to have a promotion orientation more often then other entrepreneurs. Entrepreneurs tend to achieve rewards and avoid negative outcomes. The Y-axis represents the average score on the seven point scale.

Action and State Focus

People differ in their disposition toward, or capacity for, action control. Those with a low self-regulatory capacity are called state oriented persons. Those with a high self-regulatory capacity are called action oriented persons. A state oriented person has a tendency that reflects inertia to act. An action oriented person shows readiness to act. The state orientation characteristic was measured by counting the

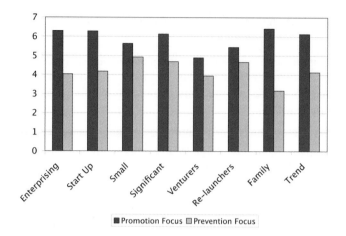

Fig.5.2 Prevention and promotion focus

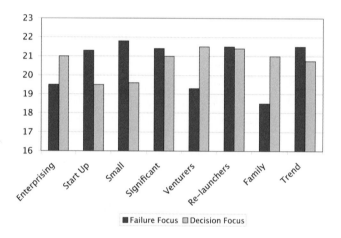

Fig.5.3 Failure and decision related focus

frequency of failure related actions and the action orientation characteristic was measured by counting the frequency of decision related actions on hypothetical situations. Figure 5.3 presents the results.

Enterprising persons, venturers and family business entrepreneurs often show more readiness to act. Significant and trend entrepreneurs take a middle position. Start-ups and small business entrepreneurs show a low readiness to act. Comparing the different groups of entrepreneurs shows that the decision related scores are more or less equal for the groups with the exception of start-ups and small business entrepreneurs. These groups might have a lower capacity for the implementation of action-related mental structures. Re-launchers score high on decision focus and failure focus.

5.4   Personal and Company Details of the Entrepreneur

The personal and company details of the entrepreneurs included in the sample may be characterized as follows:

- The number of employees varies; yet most of the participants have less than 50 employees. Three entrepreneurs have more than 500 employees; 5 between 100 and 500, and 4 between 51and 100.

- The majority of the participants have turnover levels less than 5 million annually.

- Only six entrepreneurs did not found any business as they either bought it or took over a family business. Few of the re-launchers have founded businesses themselves.

- The entrepreneur's international orientation was also assessed. We drew a distinction between three categories. The categories are as follows: *European* (17 persons): Ventures / companies are based in the EU and are commercially active in more than one EU country (i.e. manufacture and / or market and / or distribute in more than one EU nation). *Other continents* (17): Ventures / companies are based outside Europe and are commercially active in manufacturing and / or marketing and / or distribution outside their home country. *The Netherlands* (16): Ventures / companies are Dutch if their services, distribution and marketing processes are primarily based in and aimed at The Netherlands market.

Company Results

Entrepreneurs were asked to mention if they had achieved positive financial results or not. Those who achieved positive financial results were compared on several variables with those who did not. The differences were tested using ANOVA in SPSS. We only mention the statistical significant differences.

Entrepreneurs who mention positive results score relatively higher on achievement drive (mean score is 4.1 and 3.8 respectively). This means that those who have a high drive towards achieving results seem to have realized positive results. Those who have a low drive towards achieving results realized less positive results. Entrepreneurs who mention positive results score relatively lower on flexibility (mean score is 3.3 vs. 3.9). They might have a well structured framework and are therefore less flexible.

Entrepreneurs who mention positive results score relatively higher on self-confidence indicating that they are more self-confident (mean score is 7.0 compared to 6.3). Entrepreneurs who mention positive results score relatively higher on alertness) indicating that they have a more alert focus toward their surroundings (mean is 7.9 vs. 6.9). The results indicate the entrepreneurs with certain mental fitness (self confidence and alertness) scores have realized positive results. Whether the moods influence the result or the other way around is not clear.

Entrepreneurs who mention positive results score relatively lower on failure focus. They feel less difficulty in dealing with failure related situations (mean is 20.4 vs. 22.3).

Entrepreneurs who mention positive results for the last three years of their involvement in the venture use techniques for stimulation of their own creativity process more often in comparison with those that did not achieve positive results). For the other variables we did not find significant differences.

Entrepreneurial Family

About half of the entrepreneurs hail from entrepreneurial families. Those who come from an entrepreneurial family are more promotion oriented in comparison with those who do not come from an entrepreneurial family background (mean score is 6.1 vs. 5.4). This means that entrepreneurs who hail from an entrepreneurial family background focus more on achieving rewards and therefore they may have more winning strategies.

5.5   Designing an Opportunity

It is assumed that entrepreneurs who manage opportunities by using criteria systematically and by stimulating their own creativity will increase their chances of maintaining the entrepreneurial spirit and even the chance to innovate. We asked entrepreneurs to tell us if they stimulate their own creativity, and about half of them responded that they did. We also asked them if they formulate criteria in advance, during or after the process. The results found that two-thirds formulate criteria in advance. And these two criteria were tested on differences using a selection of variables.

Entrepreneurs who formulate criteria in advance score statistically, significantly higher on hardiness compared with those who do this during the process or afterwards (mean is 33.8 vs. 3.5). For the other variables we did not find statistically significant differences.

The results also show that entrepreneurs who stimulate their own creativity score higher on hardiness which means that they believe in themselves, they believe that accomplishments and setbacks are within their own control and influence (mean is 3.9 vs. 3.1). We did not find any other significant differences. Results were measured with a dichotomy variable indicating no positive results for the last three years versus positive results in the three years.

Entrepreneurs who stimulate their own creativity score higher on variable results (mean score is 0.9 vs. 0.7). This indicates that they have more often realized positive financial results for the company.

5.6   Entrepreneurs and Entrepreneurial Executives Compared

In this section we present the results of our analysis regarding the comparison between executives and entrepreneurs. These results are presented here as a comparison between behavioral attributes, mental fitness, promotion and prevention focus, action and state orientation, and opportunity management. The group of executives was too small to test reliable differences in SPSS; therefore we can only illustrate differences according to the average scores. The findings indicate that there are no big differences between the groups. Yet some differences occur for the variables dominance and trustful indicating that executives are more dominant and trustful in comparison with entrepreneurs in our case studies.

The executives in our sample deal with many types and a wider range of stakeholders. Therefore they might deal with more issues concerning trust and showing a dominant attitude. Yet because the sample is too small we have to be very cautious with any general conclusions. The Y-axis represents the average scores on a 5 point scale (see Figure 5.4).

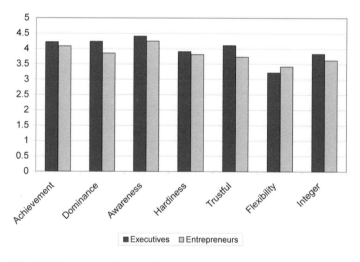

Fig.5.4 Behavioral attributes of executives and entrepreneurs

For each mental fitness variable the executives show higher levels indicating that they have a higher mental fitness. The Y-axis represents the average scores on a 10-point scale (see Figure 5.5).

The comparison on promotion focus shows that entrepreneurs are more focused towards achieving rewards in comparison with executives (mean is 5.8 vs. 5.5). In addition, they seem to focus more on preventing negative situations or setbacks (mean score is 4.4 vs. 3.8). Regarding action and state orientation the groups score more or less similar.

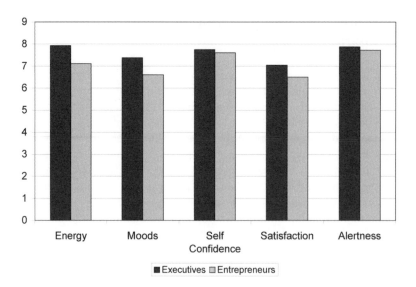

Fig.5.5 Emotions of entrepreneurs and executives

5.7   Conclusion

In the preceding sections we presented a selection of the differences between groups of participants in our case studies. Note that not all findings are tested statistically due to the small number of participants per group. Still, we were able to test meaningful differences among the larger sample groups, specifically in cases where there were 20-30 people per group which applies to company results, entrepreneurial family background, opportunity criteria and encouraging creativity. In all other instances the differences can be seen only as tendencies that might become clearer in larger, quantitative research designs.

Our research model, as presented in Chapter 4, appears to have the best fit with testing of larger datasets. In smaller sample groups it was not possible to test the model statistically.

Furthermore, the results tend to indicate that behavioral attributes, as measured within these case studies, are linked with company results. Good mental fitness tends to relate to positive business results. Failure focus tends to relate with less positive company results. In the process of seeking opportunities within the context of designing a firm, behavioral attributes such as hardiness also play a role. The overall conclusion is that demographic and psychological background variables do play a role in leading to greater understanding of the entrepreneurial process, such as seeking out opportunities or achieving positive financial results. We can summarize more specific trends regarding the characteristics of different types of entrepreneurs and executives.

- *Entrepreneurial Executives.* Entrepreneurial executives showed high levels of dominance and trust as well as mental fitness. In comparison with all entrepreneurs in the study they tend to be less promotion oriented, less achievement oriented. However they showed higher mental fitness levels. We may assume that their professional settings demanded a more stable profile. Entrepreneurs however showed more extreme scores indicating that they are more promotion oriented but also more prevention oriented. They act more in extreme terms while the executives try to find more balance.

- *Venturers.* Entrepreneurs who started a venture based on their previous experience in a corporate career show a good level of mental fitness. They score high on decision focus which indicates their readiness to act when dealing with negative experiences.

- *Re-Launchers.* Entrepreneurs who bought a part of, or a whole firm, show a good level of mental fitness. They often implemented reorganizations which do not make them popular among personnel. These situations might influence their flexibility, and they score low on flexibility.

- *Trend Entrepreneurs.* The trend entrepreneurs showed relative high levels of hardiness meaning that they are experienced in dealing with setbacks.

- *Family Business Entrepreneurs.* Family business entrepreneurs are less flexible, and show a lower level of mental fitness. Yet, they do demonstrate a high level of hardiness, maybe because of setbacks that they experienced in the past. They show a high level of alertness and they tend to be more action oriented. It can be assumed that they showed a need to prove themselves to the former owners and employees.

- *Significant Business Entrepreneurs.* Entrepreneurs who founded a significant business showed high levels of self-confidence and a good state of mental fitness. However, they are relatively less flexible, meaning that they established an organizational structure which provides less room for flexibility.

- *Small Business Entrepreneurs.* Entrepreneurs running a small business showed relatively low scores on mental fitness variables meaning that they faced mental problems more often. They often lack sufficient personnel which might give rise to lower levels of mental fitness. They are too small to grow because of the type of products or services they deliver. They might face a high fluctuation in projects / demands from the market to support a stable level of personnel. Their scores showed a tendency to be state oriented which means that they have a low self regulatory capacity to act.

- *Start-Ups.* Start-ups are also very flexible; they have a good mental fitness in terms of high self confidence. They are alert which is necessary for exploring and implementing opportunities they perceive. They show relatively lower scores on hardiness meaning that they are not that experienced in dealing with setbacks. This might be understandable because due to the fact they tend to be young, the chance that they have already experienced many setbacks is low. They are at the beginning of an entrepreneurial career which can take many forms.

- *Enterprising Persons.* Solo entrepreneurs seem to be very flexible, very satisfied, and they have positive energy. Generally speaking they have shown good mental fitness. They are also more action oriented persons which means that they will take initiatives easily. These characteristics can be described in terms of their motivation to be an entrepreneur but, based on their personal drives, to remain a solo entrepreneur without much worries from the environment. Some support for this assumption can be found by the fact that they seem to show a low level of alertness. Their span of control in terms of complex relationships with others is relatively small because they function as solo persons. Being an entrepreneur is a way of life for them and a way of earning money.

Entrepreneurial Attitudes

In general, we assume that for an optimal entrepreneurial attitude the following characteristics are needed: high achievement drive, high awareness, and a high promotion focus. Among entrepreneurs we found no differences regarding these concepts.

Entrepreneurs who had achieved positive results during the past three years showed the following characteristics: (1) higher achievement drive, (2) lower flexibility, (3) higher self-confidence, (4) higher alertness, (5) low failure focus, (6) stimulate their creativity. Additionally, entrepreneurs who come from an entrepreneurial family are more promotion oriented meaning that they focus more on achievement.

Finally, entrepreneurs who stimulate their own creativity are more capable of dealing with setbacks; they have greater sense of control. Those who are better prepared for setbacks (high score on hardiness) seem to be better as well at seeking opportunities and define their criteria in advance.

6 Theory Building Through Case Study

6.1 Understanding the Entrepreneurial Venture

The conceptual framework in Chapter 4 provides a basic introduction of the relevant concepts explaining the field of entrepreneurial processes. In our case studies we applied this framework, specifically to investigate the dynamics of starting a venture. By using the case study approach we aimed to learn more about these dynamics. Entrepreneurs and executives were indeed very open about their experiences which resulted in the rich data that we present in Chapters 8 through 16. The results regarding the executives will be presented in 6.4. All results regarding the entrepreneurs will be presented in 6.1-6.3.

The stories of the entrepreneurs and executives have taught us that there are three different driving forces for starting a venture. Of course all three may play a role but usually one of the drivers dominates at start-up.

1. A person starts by facing an opportunity. It can be an opportunity he or she faces by chance. He or she then deals with the serious questions "do I have the capabilities to design this opportunity" (self-efficacy) and "do I really want to do this (intention to start)." An opportunity can be developed by perceiving or imagining a certain customer need, mostly by experiencing it, and knowing the solution for it. Sometimes entrepreneurs told us that they saw opportunities that others did not, which makes the source of opportunity rather imaginary instead of a tangible facet. Examples of dealing with opportunities as the first driving point in their entrepreneurial activities can be found in the profile of Zieleman (Ch. 14), Verstraaten (Ch. 11), Ypes (Ch. 11), and Spoorenberg (Ch. 11). Zieleman started a wholesale vending machine business when he was already working in this industry. Verstraaten's cousin died of lung problems caused by asbestos. This inspired him to create an asbestos removal business. The trading company for which Spoorenberg was working for went bankrupt. He noticed that many products were damaged during transportation and this inspired him to start a firm in damaged goods and products. Ypes developed the idea of a shredding business. An opportunity can also occur by facing the need for an entrepreneurial spirit in an existing firm. Examples are given in the profiles of Schipper and van den Hondel (Ch. 15), van Schaik (Ch. 14) and Kindler (Ch. 13). After a while van Schaik stopped with his firm when the market collapsed. An op-

portunity can simply appear through the question "do you want to succeed in the family business?" (Dekker and Hodes in Ch. 12) or "do you want to join by starting a firm?". Examples of being asked by family members are given in the profiles of Govers (sister) and Bellingwout (father-in-law). Some people see opportunities by buying a firm or part off the firm such as in the case of Blomsma, Brink, Houtman, Moore, de Knoop, Ruigrok, Velthuis, and Versluis (Ch. 10).

2. A person starts with the intention to become an entrepreneur and therefore begins searching for opportunities that fit his or her capabilities. From these experiences, we have noticed the importance of a good match between capabilities (self-efficacy), serious willingness (intention) and the type of opportunity he or she is going to define and implement. A good fit between capabilities, opportunity and intention will increase the chances of success. Some have dreamed of becoming an entrepreneur since youth. Examples could be found in the profiles of van Wezel (Ch. 13), Wolbrink (Ch. 14), van Rozendaal (Ch. 13), Westendorp (Ch. 13), de Wolf (Ch. 13), Brink (Ch. 10), and Inden (Ch. 11). Others have just developed a strong intention because of less positive experiences in a corporate career. Examples can be found in the profiles of Gunning Ho (Ch. 16) and Klok (Ch. 14).

3. A third starting point comes from discovery of one's talents in designing and implementing activities suitable for earning an income and / or serving some need in society. This talent or capability can be discovered in activities stemming from a corporate career or in a firm founded by someone else. Examples are Boskma, Sterken, van Rooijen, Reeders, Pullens, Maassen, and de Jong (Ch. 9). By noticing his or her own capabilities in successfully executing activities an idea can be formed to implement these or similar activities by starting a new venture. Other examples are found in the profiles of Vuursteen (Ch. 16) and Te Gussinklo Ohmann (Ch. 14). Sometimes people discover they do not fit a salaried job by not being able to work for a boss. Examples of this situation are found in Aardewerk and Van Straten (Ch. 16).

Each of the three situations could act as the main driver, thus they all can lead to the start of an entrepreneurial career. Not one case is similar to another. Reading all the cases shows that entrepreneurship has many perspectives as does the start-up process.

In this chapter we endeavor to structure these perspectives into bigger patterns by using concepts from our conceptual model. During their adventures, entrepreneurs had to deal with challenges and setbacks. Many of these were unknown or could not be imagined in advance but decisions had to be taken along the journey. Decisions were based on previous experiences; or on intuition, and still others were based on emotions, moods and behavioral characteristics. We also learned from the case studies that there is always an interaction within the individual (intra-personal interaction) and between the individual entrepreneurial characteristics and the business environment with its financial resources and possibilities. And there is a bigger picture defining limitations through economics, community and environmental needs.

The combination of insights from theory and practice leads to the following model in Figure 6.1 which presents the elements of starting a venture, proposing that there are two fundamental steps in starting a venture:

- *Step 1* consists of finding a match between: (1) an opportunity, (2) a serious intention to become an entrepreneur, (3) the evaluation of one's capabilities (self-efficacy) to really create an opportunity by defining and implementing it.

- *Step 2* consists of combining four activities: (1) Obtaining relevant market knowledge and finding a market for the products or services; (2) Creating a structure for designing the opportunity. This refers to structure by writing plans about the products or services the venture wants to deliver and structuring venture processes including finding customers in the very initial stage; (3) Finding resources and making them accessible or by seriously exploring them and / or discovering what can be done with less resources; (4) Formulating a team of people needed in starting the venture. This refers to partners, employees, mentors, sounding boards and / or suppliers.

The sequence in which these four activities are developed varies yet both Step 1 and 2 are necessary. Step 1 is not enough. Only implementing Step 2 is also not enough; although it can be imagined that some people start without having a serious intention to become an entrepreneur, without a real opportunity or without asking if they possess the capabilities. It is this first step that makes the process of starting an entrepreneurial step. The starting process contains these ingredients but the endpoints can be different as are the starting points. The model consists of two parts:

- *Part 1* refers to the two processes as described in Step 1 and 2.

- *Part 2* refers to the conditions that influence the start-up processes which includes three categories: (a) The individual, psychological characteristics consisting of personality (behavioral attributes), moods (mental fitness), cognitions (promotion or prevention orientations) and emotions (reflected in action or state orientation); (b) The traditional economic business environment such as the industry sector and capital market context; (c) The macro environment consisting of social, community and environmental conditions for producing products and services.

The experiences of the 50 entrepreneurs are presented using this model in the next paragraphs. In the following section, we will pay special attention to their fears, difficulties and abilities for dealing with setbacks.

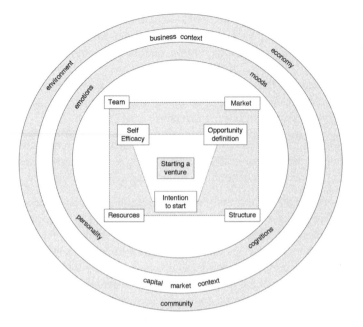

Fig.6.1 Antecedents of starting an entrepreneurial venture

6.2   The First Step in Starting a Venture

6.2.1   Defining an Opportunity

Entrepreneurs identify opportunities by experiencing certain needs or by perceiving that others have certain needs for which a market might exist. Examples are Entrop (Ch. 9) who noticed by living in Suriname that there was a need for retreaded tires for cars and trucks. This idea might not have been born if he was living in The Netherlands.

Entrepreneurs can also arrive at an idea for an opportunity by working somewhere, as is the case with Kindler (Ch. 13) who noticed that the company where he worked did not do anything with the product line of work gloves which led him to launch a glove distribution and marketing company. Van Well (Ch. 13), another example, was familiar with the wholesale food sector because he worked for his parents' business and developed his own opportunity. Boskma (Ch. 9) came with a new idea of setting up a unit in an existing consultancy regarding interim management which did not exist in those days. The idea came into existence because of the downward economic trend at the time which required working towards more efficiency. Ypes (Ch. 11) designed an opportunity because one day he saw a piece of shredding machinery at an equipment dealer lot and wanted to try that out. It appeared to be a very useful tool in the waste recycling industry. His imagination to formulate an opportunity helped him as well.

People can start a venture just by being asked to start a business s was the case with Entrop (Ch. 9) with his second firm. He was asked to start Intal (International Aluminum Corporation). He himself did not notice there was an opportunity yet others did, however they thought he should start the company and further develop the opportunity. Additionally, Entrop (Ch. 9) also started two companies based on his own ideas.

Opportunity Design – Buying a Business

Blomsma (Ch 10) applied a word-of-mouth marketing technique to promote the activities of the part of the firm she bought with her business partner within the shipbuilding industry. Her systematic marketing approach had a significant impact on the business.

In another instance, Brink (Ch. 10) took over a company with a number of people. Currently he works with a small team of 12 employees which asks for a rather different approach. Brink, together with his business partner, re-built the company. A third example is Moore (Ch. 10), who bought a company and realized a very fast growth of 40% in turnover within the first year. His approach contains radical changes for the company at all levels of the value chain. For other examples, see Chapter 10.

Opportunity Design – Family Business

Some of the participants were asked to take-over a family business as was the case with Dekker or Damen (see Chapter 12). Damen was asked to manage a part of the family business related to real estate, and she noticed a need for custom de-signed houses in the region of Barcelona where she lived. She recently created a niche with her new venture in real estate to capture this opportunity. Another ex-ample is Zieleman (Ch. 14) who helps manage a family business with his sister and parents although he has founded and currently runs his own business. Van Kraaikamp (Ch. 12) took over his father's venture which provides consultancy in the public sector. While involved in this business he designed his own opportuni-ties. Van Kraaikamp noticed that there were many fields for consultancy devel-opment in the public sector and therefore put his ideas, passion and effort in build-ing and further developing an existing venture.

Hodes (Ch. 12) is another example who took over her parents' company with her brother and gave it a new life inspired by her and her brother's effort, vision and passion. Her restructuring resulted in founding new ventures related to the family business. Dekker also brought new spirit to her father's company. In her case she had to prove herself to her father, even though her father asked her to join the company. She convinced the employees as well that she was capable of doing the job. Her entrepreneurial spirit did not stop in the family business and she started another firm and bought another firm as well.

Criteria Used for Opportunity Evaluation

Every participant was asked which criteria they used for opportunity evaluation. The 50 entrepreneurs mentioned a total of 129 criteria that were later quantified into the following categories: customer, personal, structure, team (all referring to the broad label of people), quality (referring to the broad label of planet), market, power, resources, and results (all referring to the broad label of profit).

- *People Related Criteria.* Several entrepreneurs mentioned very *personal* criteria such as creativity stimulation, fun, excitement, intuition, interest, challenge, willingness to change, prior experience, and distance between home and work. Another type of people related criteria concerned the *team*. Criteria are support from existing contracts, developments with subcontractors, fit with competencies in the company, with the company network, and with the quality of staff. People related criteria such as client relationships, convincing customers, implications for customers, and match with current customers, all were labeled under the heading people-*customer*. Another people related criterion identified is the *structure* which can include the relationship with distributors, the way to reach the market, and the order level of existing clients. These forms the structure in which the entrepreneurs functions.

- *Planet Related Criteria.* Only a few entrepreneurs mentioned criteria related to planet in terms of company image, product image, and values fit with clients. Other criteria are a match between personal and business values, and are labeled as *quality*.

- *Profit Related Criteria.* Figure 6.2 shows that the profit related criteria were mentioned most frequently. The profit related criteria of *results* refer to, for example, added value, company benefits, effects on margins, growth, feasibility of results, financially good deals, financial parameters, gross margin, revenue, profit, returns on investment, and turnover. Profit related criteria of *power* refer for example to, market size, ownership, competitor strengths, market growth, and competitor players. The profit related criteria of *resources* refer to variables such as risks, time needed, efforts expended and required costs. The profit related criteria of *market* refer to the fit with the market, fit with the product, and fit with life-cycle.

Techniques Used for Opportunity Evaluation

Entrepreneurs use a variety of techniques for the on-going evaluation of existing or possible opportunities. The 50 entrepreneurs mentioned a total of 163 techniques which are quantified in broader categories. These are presented in the next table. The strategy related techniques such as re-definition, re-differentiation, re-designing and re-segmentation of the products, services and markets are the most frequently mentioned followed by competence related techniques and techniques to stimulate creativity.

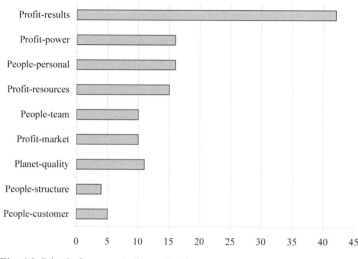

Fig. 6.2 Criteria for opportunity evaluation

6.2.2   Intention to Start

For some entrepreneurs it was a dream to start a venture. Van Wezel (Ch. 13) first had a salaried job but decided to follow his dream when the time was there. Now his company is the 13th largest in the global sneaker market. In the golf market he is 2nd in the UK and in the outdoor market his company is 4th in the world. Wolbrink (Ch. 14) always knew he wanted to be his own boss because he is an impatient person. Van Rozendaal (Ch. 13) worked for a few years for a television producer and decided to follow his dream. Westendorp (Ch. 13) also worked for a company before he decided to become an entrepreneur. De Wolf (Ch. 13) could not bear criticism and he thought becoming an entrepreneur suited him the best. Brink (Ch. 10) followed his drive to achieve when he decided to buy a company to realize his dream. Inden had high goals and a drive to be creative which made her follow her dream (Ch. 11).

There are entrepreneurs who were primarily driven to start because they did not enjoy their job. Gunning Ho (Ch. 16) is an example of someone who started a business to enjoy what she is doing. She also wanted to raise her children in combination with having a career. Van Straten (Ch. 16) was encouraged to start his venture through a conflict with his boss and people around him encouraged him to start a venture of his own. Tuinenburg (Ch. 13) started in the same sector he worked after losing his job.

Mutsaerts (Ch. 13) came back to the Netherlands after working abroad but a position in The Netherlands was not challenging enough. Therefore he decided to start a business. The time was right, he did not have responsibilities and he was young and felt he could afford a financial risk. The path to start-up was based on trial and error. Vitzthum (Ch. 13) was also looking for a new challenge when she decided to start a business after selling her first venture.

Table 6.1 Techniques for on-going evaluation of opportunities

Techniques	
Competencies	
Adjust leadership	1
Developing specific competencies	24
Strategic business techniques	
Re-defining products / service / markets	37
Re-differentiation of products / service / markets	24
Re-designing products	2
Re-segmentation of products / service / markets	21
Creativity	
Bonus for creative ideas in venture	1
Creativity team / office day / discussion groups for creativity	6
Associative methods	3
Mediation / yoga	2
Building time for reflection on ideas	4
Learning by talking about cases	1
Brainstorming	6
People / communication	
Talking with customers	7
Meetings with employees	3
Talking with business partners / entrepreneurs	4
Adjust communication styles	1
Updating information	
Fairs / workshops / courses / reading material	12
Studying markets / registering trends	5
Writing plans	2

6.2.3   Self-Efficacy Regarding Starting a Venture

Examples of discovering talent by working in an existing firm could be found in the case of Aardewerk (Ch. 16), who found he was drawn to silver while working accidentally for his parents who had a jewellery and antiques business. Ter Heege (Ch. 16) discovered her competencies in dealing with recruitment. She built her expertise further, in executive management search. "Why don't I start for myself", was one of the questions she asked herself.

Van Rozendaal (Ch. 13) noticed that people around him said it was time for him to stop with the business and to get a job. He was convinced of his capacity to implement the opportunity he created and that enabled him to proceed with his ideas.

Van Wezel (Ch. 13) and van Wijk (Ch. 13) were very ambitious while starting their firms and both took financial risks based on their confidence that the risk taking was worth it. Other examples can be found in the profiles of the re-launchers in Chapter 10 who were convinced that they could perform better because in most cases the companies they bought were leaning towards bankruptcy. They bought them in order to develop the business based on their own vision. Another example is Spoorenberg (Ch. 11) who says that his self-confidence helped him especially in the beginning years.

6.3   The Second Step in Starting a Venture

6.3.1   Positive Factors Influencing the Start-Up Process

We asked every entrepreneur to mention factors that stimulated their start-up as a follow up question after talking about their real motives to start an entrepreneurial career. As discussed in the previous section, we concluded that they all had a high drive to start but their goals varied. They were inspired by either seeing or imagining an opportunity (opportunity) or a strong intention to be their own boss or noticing having relevant competencies to become an entrepreneur (self-efficacy). In Chapters 9 through 16, all factors are mentioned in the profiles. We produced a list of these factors and started to quantify the qualitative data. The 50 entrepreneurs mentioned about 70 positive factors. In order to categorize the factors mentioned, we focused on the concepts of team, market, structure and resources (see Figure 6.1). To make this tangible these concepts are specified in Figure 6.3.

- *A Good Team.* Entrepreneurs mention having a good team available most frequently. This refers to starting with a partner and having congruent competencies, meeting people who can help realize the start-up. For example, people acting as a sounding board, people who support ideas, and people who share knowledge from the beginning. For the re-launchers, employees of the former firm were sometimes very supportive. In many cases however, the personnel in businesses that were re-launched had a defensive attitude.

- *Relevant Competencies.* Entrepreneurs were convinced that they had the relevant competencies to start an entrepreneurial career by actually initiating a venture. These convictions were based on the perception of having control over the required competencies, which refers to the concept of self-efficacy. Some were more specific about their perceived competencies and mentioned financial expertise, capacity to organize, and chemical expertise.

- *Entrepreneurial Drive.* Although in the previous question during the interview we talked about their motivation, some entrepreneurs felt they had to stress their drive in relation to their entrepreneurial behavioral attributes. They mentioned their creativity, persistence, achievement drive, self-confidence, action related drive, optimistic approach, enthusiasm as factors that stimulated the start-up process.

- *Relevant Experience.* Some entrepreneurs founded more than one firm and they believe that their previous experience helped them substantially in the start-up process. Other referred to the experience of setting up a previous firm with someone else.

- *Knowledge of the Market.* Entrepreneurs mention also that they could easily obtain market knowledge which led to a good state of preparation. Some knew the market already when they developed the opportunity in their minds.

- *Market Responses.* Entrepreneurs mention how responses from the market stimulated their start-up. Suppliers reacted very positively and they began to think in terms of delivering good products. Examples of this include potential customers reacting positively, opening communication with customers in order to obtain feedback and, finally directly approaching the customers for relevant input.

- *Immediate Existence of Market.* A few entrepreneurs were in the position to have customers or a project at the very beginning that stimulated their start-up because they had to design a concrete structure to implement the opportunity. They needed a building, an organization or venture with a name to actually conduct the project or deliver the service they promised to the customer.

- *Availability of finance, Lack of financial pressure.* For a few entrepreneurs the fact that they did not have any financial responsibility freed them to experiment with an entrepreneurial career. Few of them were able to launch their entrepreneurial career with a salary and they did not earn an income for a couple of months. A few of the entrepreneurs interviewed had saved money earned in their corporate careers and a temporary lack of income did not have big consequences so they could afford a trial period of six months. Some noticed that because they started young, they were in a better position to afford trying an entrepreneurial career. In the case of failure, they expected to easily return to a corporate career. A few also mentioned that since they did not have a family they did not feel a financial burden which made it easy to start. Entrepreneurs mentioned that finding bank loans facilitated the start-up.

- *Low Cost Entry.* Some entrepreneurs, especially the enterprising persons and the start-ups stressed the fact that they did not need a large amount of money to start. Therefore the cost to enter an entrepreneurial career was low.

- *Good Network.* Many entrepreneurs mentioned the important role their network played during the start-up period. Many of them referred to the network they built for example during their corporate career or previous job. This applied especially to the venturers, re-launchers or those with a family business.

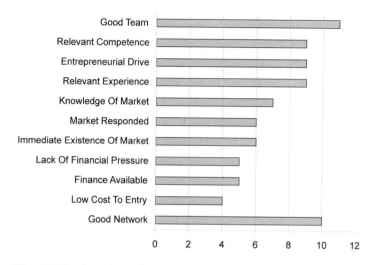

Fig. 6.3 Stimulators in starting a venture

These results are presented in Figure 6.3 indicating the frequency of every positive factor that had an impact on the start-up.

The 11 factors mentioned in Figure 6.3 can be summarized in the four broader categories of Team, Market, Structure and Resources. We found the following pattern of positive factors influencing the start-up (see Table 6.2). It seems that Team (having a good team available and a team with competencies, drive and experience) is the most important positive factor. The other important factors relate to resources (lack of finance pressure, finance available, low entry cost and good network). Having market knowledge comes in third place followed by structure, which is logical because structure follows the other ingredients.

Table 6.2 Positive factors encouraging starting a venture

Factor	
Team	29
Resources	19
Market	13
Structure	6

6.3.2   Negative Factors Influencing the Start-Up Process

The 50 entrepreneurs mentioned a total of 65 negative factors that hindered their venturing efforts. These are categorized in Figure 6.4.

- *Team – history with the firm.* Firms that had been taken over faced the problem of unmotivated or de-motivated employees with too much resistance to change.

- *Team – own capacity and expertise.* Team capacity and expertise refer, for example, to not being prepared for the skills needed to start-up, not having the accounting expertise, not being able to master the art of persuasion, not being a good networker, and not being familiar with technology.

- *Team – personnel.* Quality of the team refers to the employees that were hired and did not match the expectations of the entrepreneur, or difficulty assembling a good team of employees.

- *Market – knowledge.* Entrepreneurs related their negative experience during the start-up to a lack of specific market knowledge.

- *Market – impact.* Negative factors mentioned refer to, for example, changing markets because things needed more time, difficulty in finding a first project, conflict with former owners, and negative image of the product (i.e. cigarettes).

- *Structure.* Entrepreneurs mention that more time was needed to build a structure, that there was a need to identify a structure while at the same time there was no project, the difficulty to find good supply partner, and the departure of business partners because of accidents.

- *Resources.* The lack of money and banks reluctance to loan money for the start-up were the main items mentioned in relation to resources.

- *Other.* There were other personal and specific factors that could not be placed under one of the four concepts. These included problems with obtaining visas, the combination of work and child care, financial reporting rules and requirements while the time needed for reporting could have been spent on more beneficial things, loneliness of working alone, no support from the government, problems with family, mentality issues related to dealings in foreign countries, and spouses that did not support the start-up.

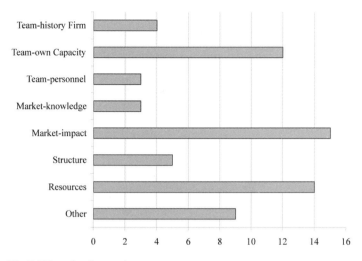

Fig.6.4 Negative factors in start-up process

Table 6.3 Negative factors discouraging starting a venture

Factor	
Team	19
Resources	14
Market	18
Structure	5
Other	9

The results are presented in Figure 6.4 and in Table 6.3, which summarize the findings within the four broader categories of Team, Market, Structure and Resources. Most challenging were team related factors, followed by market related factors while resources could be ranked third.

6.3.3   Dealing with Fears, Difficulties and Setbacks

Eleven of the 50 entrepreneurs mentioned they experienced fears in the start-up process. Three others stressed that fear is a big word and they would rather speak about concerns or special events. The other entrepreneurs stated that they did not have fears; this might itself be a characteristic of an entrepreneur.

Entrepreneurs were honest about the difficult decisions they had to take. They mention 65 difficult types of decisions that include dealing with uncertainty, dismissing personnel, availability of money, leaving a salaried job, acquisition of projects, fear of bankruptcy and more time needed for achieving results (Table 6.4).

Table 6.4 Difficult decisions taken by entrepreneurs

Types of difficult decisions	Number
Dealing with uncertainty	9
Dismissing personnel	8
Availability of money	5
Leaving a salaried position	5
Acquisition of projects	4
Fear of bankruptcy	4
More time needed than expected to realize results	4
Approaching banks / others for finance	3
Partnership with other consultancy	3
Employees don't like you as the new owner	3
Pressure to have enough projects for his employees	2
Significant others not convinced of his capabilities	2
Spending money	2
Dependency on suppliers	1
Having one big client	1
Hiring personnel	1
Inviting a third party to solve problems	1
Maintaining focus in doing business	1
Maintaining strong reputation	1
Not being able to sell	1
Practical aspects of running a business	1
Predicting if your intuition is right	1
Pressure because of specific expertise	1
Pressure to grow while not wanting employees	1
Replacing absence of employees in small firm	1

Examples of Setbacks

In the interviews we asked participants to tell us about serious setbacks they experienced in their entrepreneurial careers. This type of information was often confidential and personal and therefore we present it in an anonymous way. The box below offers examples of some of these setbacks.

Supplier Produced Stress

> *"I had franchise plans that were not successful. From my experience, I learned that you should have really good communication with the supplier in order to set high standards for quality. In our business, we were too dependent on them. Another difficulty was the computerization process that was contracted out. The problem was that we did not have any influence on the speed and quality of the process. We had to accept that we could not manage every process. Today, this dependency on one single supplier is not the case anymore."*

> *"Suppliers came with terms of delivery and one of the conditions was to pay in advance. For (business) starters money is always a problem and in our case this was not a good condition. Still, we found that when you face problems, you become motivated and therefore you get energy to cope with every negative and stressful situation."*

> *"With the first contract, the supplier delayed finalizing the contract due to their lack of knowledge and experience. This was a very stressful financing phase of the start-up. Putting pressure on suppliers did not work and we found that they adopted a lazy, laissez faire attitude towards us. Now they are more realistic in providing services on time given the culture in the supplying countries."*

Doing business in foreign countries. Doing business in foreign countries can bring problems because of a lack of local presence of the entrepreneur or because of cultural misunderstandings.

> *"I cooperated with someone in an Asian country and the delivery took a long time. While everything looked good on paper, I was supposed to present my collection at a fair, and at the last moment the Asian supplier informed me that they could not deliver for the price that we had agreed on. So, I had to make a new agreement. For me, this was a signal. The timing was not good and I was forced to negotiate a lot. At one point I had to go to an important meeting and the supplier came there to tell me he did not agree with the price. It was at that moment that I decided to quit doing business with him."*

> *"The good thing was that I was forced to make my own product collection. My private life at that time was difficult as well. My mother was very sick, she died in that year. Also, my wife was pregnant. Mentally speaking it was a very hard period for half a year. "Loosing my mother, at the same time having to deal with problems in my venture was a challenge. The positive thing during this time was the birth of my twins."*

> *"The production of clothes in other countries and working with business partners from China and Turkey eventually led to a big clash with the agent in Turkey. It was not profitable to produce the clothes in Turkey anymore and therefore I went to China. Emotionally it was a big decision to switch production strategies and suppliers."*

> *"I hired a Dutchman to run the business in a foreign country and this turned out to be a big problem. It was not easy to run a business from a long-distance approach. For example, when there were technical problems it takes resourceful thinking and immediate solutions and this necessitates a strong and able local person to solve problems immediately. I tried this long-distance approach for one year and finally I sold the asset for half the price I bought it. Yet it felt like a good decision to me and that was the most important thing."*

"Clients that went bankrupt and choosing the wrong agents in foreign countries are big risks in working overseas. You have to look carefully at risk factors, and getting insurance for debtors and confirmed letters of credit is a very good idea."

Critical personal events. There might be critical events in the personal life that lead to stress.

"My divorce! It left a lasting scar! Going through the divorce really weighed heavily, both mentally and emotionally, on my ability to work. I was still employed at that time, and my boss supported me in dealing with the situation and understanding how to come to terms with it! I took the time I needed to consider things, and thought about the divorce a lot. It still remains a scar though!"

"My physical health was okay, yet with the increased workload I am now flying far too often and I find that it is bad for the body!"

"I had to choose between my business and my marriage. It was a difficult situation. Working with the business made it impossible to take time for holidays, for example. Ultimately, I had to continue with the company to sort out the financial problems."

Financial situation. Financial pressure can give a lot of stress.

"The venture had problems with liquidity, the bank refused to pay the salary and I had debts. Eventually, I was able to find a smaller bank that was willing to work with me."

"A new factory was built as part of an expansion plan and the project went over budget. As the work continued on the factory, the costs kept increasing and I simply intervened too late. From all of the stress, I got a stomach ulcer."

"Dealing with stressful events raises the question for me of "How to go on and solve the problem" versus "I give up." One extreme situation was a time when we had far too much inventory on hand. As a result, there was bank pressure too to reduce the inventory! After searching, I found suitable channels to reduce inventory and products sold, even if we had to move the inventory at very low prices. It was a very intense process for us because a negative outcome of quickly moving the inventory could have potentially ended the business. "

Ethical issues. Ethical issues and the feeling that one has been cheated can release many negative moods and emotions.

"In general dealing with ethical issues is very hard. I am sensitive to this, and these issues are always an energy drain for me."

"Something happened in my business dealings which was both really unfair and inappropriate! I eventually sold my company to a Dutch individual who indicated he would continue the business as a venture. But it soon emerged that he bought the business to use it as a front for another company. I found this situation very unethical. His plan was to merge with a company which was going public on the stock exchange. When the Nina Brink affairs hit the press, the stock market collapsed. Thus, the venture came under immense pressure. Given the opportunity to do this all over, I would find a better, more reliable and experienced investor. Yet, it is important to realize that you have to accept your losses somehow. That's the way it is in the real world."

"A client really left me in a bad situation and I lost a lot of money and no matter what I tried to resolve the problem, nothing worked. For me, this experience has been a huge emotional trauma, and I fear that in future business dealings I might be faced with the same situation! I simply feel very, badly cheated."

Rebuilding is hard. Rebuilding a company makes it necessary that one is able to cope with employee emotions.

"It was very painful to have to remove people with whom I initiated the business and built it. The decision to let people go was taken by the non-executive board of this publicly traded, hot, company. I realized that some of the team was no longer functioning well, so I discussed the issue with the founders, and the decision was to let a number of people go."

"Personnel issues are always difficult. When things are good you don't hear much but when things go wrong they come and complain".

Partnership failure. Sometimes partnerships end in failure when expectations do not seem to meet reality.

"The business partnership that was in place at the start-up stage ended after we had been in business for a short time. I was then in a situation that I had to fire people when we decided to separate. Still, after we decided to end the partnership we found it best to continue working together for six months. In fact, we had to because agreements with customers were made five months prior to our decision. Working with someone and knowing that your business relationship is over was difficult, and our last joint project was awful."

"I started a company with someone I knew and we each had 50% ownership of the business. When we went our separate ways it cost me a lot of money and in many ways I felt as if I was taken for a ride."

Company accidents. An accident such as fire can give rise to a lot of stress.

"There was a fire in the factory and it completely burned down. When people asked if we planned to continue with the company, I realized that many people were dependent on the firm for their livelihood. At that time I was also pregnant. And I was faced with such a high level of commitment from the employees and dealing with the decision of how to continue with the business. It was a challenging time for me, running a company, re-building a factory of 10,000 square meters and being pregnant."

"The headquarters of the company burned down to the ground, and the entire administration office also burned. We were left with no administrative information, and didn't have any sort of back-up archive."

Leaving a company. Leaving a company knowing that you don't have faith in good performance is painful.

"The moment of selling the company was painful. I was disappointed with the fact that the good plans we had in place would never be realized by the new owners. And leaving employees in a situation where you don't have faith in the new owners of the company is painful."

6.4   Entrepreneurial Executive Specificities

In 6.4 we present the main findings regarding the entrepreneurial executives. We could apply the insights of the previous sections by stating that the main opportunity and willingness to manage exists already. The key is confidence in having the capabilities needed to effectively manage the existing opportunities and developing new ones within the existing framework. This refers to the self-efficacy of being able to meet the needs and the ability to work within the existing framework.

Before we describe our findings regarding the 10 executives in our sample, we define the characteristics of an entrepreneurial executive. In the questionnaire we asked the 10 participants to indicate what characteristics applied to them and what characteristics were missing.

Activities of Entrepreneurial Executives

The actions of executives are usually based on a team process which means that actions do not immediately follow their own creativity or ideas. Usually the actions are born through communication with different stakeholders involved. The activities could be summarized in four groups as follows: (1) The initiation and implementation of new products or services; (2) The initiation and implementation of new working methods (market strategy, re-organising internal business processes); (3) Breaking taboos usually as a by product in the first two processes; (4) Activities that have a large impact crossing national bounders.

Self-Efficacy of Entrepreneurial Executives

The qualitative data reveals the following competencies: (1) Showing leadership and people management and the ability to inspire others and mobilise change; (2) Ability to convince stakeholders and therefore make situations transparent and if possible also include accountability; (3) Flexibility and the ability to cope with competing interests and communicate about these; (4) Coping with highly complex and demanding situations from the outside world; (5) Fundamentally positive attitudes towards their own vision; (6) The ability and drive to achieve high performance.

Values of Entrepreneurial Executives

The stories of the entrepreneurial executives highlight some of the values in dealing with problems and meeting goals: (1) Fundamentally positive attitude towards the organisational goals or the common good; (2) The ability to show respect to others involved; and (3) Building a reputation of integrity.

Dealing with Fears

The entrepreneurial executives identified dealing with the following fears presented in the table below. The table presents how many times each fear has been mentioned. The people part appears to be the hardest one for executives.

Table 6.5 Fears of entrepreneurial executives

Fears mentioned	Number
Adjusting to new working methods, and expected successes	1
Ability to convince personnel of growth goals	1
Processes that can go wrong / not able to meet deadlines	3
Firing personnel	3
Taking decisions without full information	1
Coping with uncertainty	1
Political conflicts	2
Uncontrollable activities	1
Management of people	3

Table 6.6 Criteria for opportunity evaluation

	Criteria for opportunity evaluation	Number
People	Creating trust between people	1
People	Commitment of people	1
People	Learn from own experience in the past	2
People	Who is responsible / experience of employees	2
Planet-development	Process development	1
Planet-group	Decrease obstacles to bring people together	1
Planet-group	Cohesion of people	1
Planet-process	Process of implementation	2
Planet-quality	Quality	1
Profit	Performance goals	2
Profit	Returns	1
Profit	Costs	1
Profit	Financial risks	1
Profit	Possibility of earning money	1
Profit	Likelihood of success	1
Profit	Number of clients	1
Other	Speed of development	1
Other	Feasibility	1
Other	Time span needed	1

The criteria they use for evaluation of opportunities in their work setting are presented in the following table. The table offers insight into a variety of tangible and less tangible goals; some easy to relate to such as profit (8 times), planet (6 times) or people (6 times) and others (3 times) more difficult to relate to these concepts. The group of participants is too small to generalize the findings, however for executives the focus appears to be more on finding balance between people, planet and profit in comparison with the entrepreneurs who mainly seem to focus on profit related criteria. The executives' framework of stakeholders is a complex and demanding one since usually many interests are involved. The framework for operations is usually already defined for an executive while an entrepreneur is often building the framework from scratch with the possibility to influence it substantially.

Entrepreneurial executives use a variety of techniques for the on-going evaluation of opportunities. The 10 executives mentioned a total list of 51 techniques which are quantified in broader categories.

It appears that these executives apply entrepreneurially stimulating techniques in their activities to continuously encourage their opportunity registers.

Table 6.7 Techniques for on-going evaluation of opportunities

Concrete techniques	
• Translation of goals into actions	6
Competencies	
• Leadership	5
• Developing breakthrough competencies	4
Strategic business techniques	
• Re-segmentation of the market	2
• Re-differentiation of goals	4
• Re-design of products or services	8
• Creating new competitive advantage	3
Creativity	
• Thinking out of the box / reflection	4
• Creativity approach to designing winning strategies	2
People / communication	
• Finding sounding boards	2
• Interactive sessions	4
• Dialogues / creating consensus on goals	3
• Adjusting communication styles	4

6.5   Conclusion

These 50 case stories of entrepreneurs reveal that though we have been searching for similar ingredients for theory building, the entrepreneurs offer their unique experiences. The first step in starting a venture deals with an intention to do so, based on an identified opportunity, and the feeling of having control over the needed capabilities (self-efficacy). Once this decision has been taken, several other processes have an impact, such as team availability, resource availability, knowledge of the market and the structure needed to really design and implement a venture. Factors commonly having an indirect effect stem from personal psychological characteristics, developments and constraints in the business sector, and the economy at large (see Figure 6.1).

These findings leads to the conclusion that various factors influence starting an entrepreneurial career. From all positive factors illustrated in this chapter, those related to the team were the most frequently mentioned. Considering the negative factors listed which influence the start-up process, it turned out that team related factors were also the most frequently mentioned as having an impact. Just as other professionals, entrepreneurs have to cope with difficult situations. These types of setbacks caused the participants in our study a lot of stress. Many of these are very hard to control. Thus, entrepreneurs deal with several types of setbacks in their career, and most of them are very hard to control.

The entrepreneurial executive career requires activities that refer to innovation of products or services, innovation of processes, breaking taboos, and possibly initiating activities with international impact. The frameworks in which to operate for executives are much more defined in comparison with those of the entrepreneur. It requires a set of abilities to work within the boundaries defined. These include leadership, coping with demanding tasks, striving for high achievements, interest in the organisation and the common good, flexible focus and the ability to convince stakeholders. A majority of entrepreneurial executives have stressed certain values in their way of dealing with people. It seems that for the participants of the study, the people factor is the most challenging issue to address. Possibly in part due to the defined frameworks of the organisation they perceived these executives had to search for more balance between people, planet and profit issues on their way to evaluating opportunities.

Application of creative entrepreneurial techniques in existing companies or organisational frameworks seems to relate to the entrepreneurial attitude of the executive. In transforming these attitudes into the company or organisation, fitting leadership and communication styles is critical to creating an entrepreneurial climate for innovation.

7 The Human Side of Venturing: Lessons

In the course of this study we identified three distinct trends in entrepreneurship:

- Today the field of entrepreneurship as a distinct subject receives much more academic attention than 20 years ago. Especially in the European context, entrepreneurship has become a main topic for education and policy in recent times.

- Entrepreneurial skills, tools and knowledge are increasingly being applied in large corporations to encourage creativity and innovation as part of the growing positive attitude towards entrepreneurship.

- New, real market opportunities are appearing in response to the increasing signs of the physical limitations of the ecological system to accommodate traditional economic activity. And, sustainably inspired entrepreneurs are uniquely positioned to find and explore new opportunities to build personal and lasting service relationships with conscious customers.

In this final chapter of the first part of this book we pay attention to the conclusions we can draw from our search for the essence of entrepreneurship as related to these trends. How can we fit our insights into existing frameworks and theories and contribute to the field of entrepreneurship? What did we learn that can be applied in practice to entrepreneurship in the future? Is entrepreneurship predictable and how? What can be done to encourage entrepreneurship?

7.1 Summary and Conclusions

In this study, we reviewed the qualitative and quantitative impact of entrepreneurial activity in society today; relating the case studies to specific performance of ventures in a number of individual countries. Typical entrepreneurial characteristics and traits were reviewed as well, including entrepreneurial management processes in established companies and organizations. We also observed two trends which we believe offer a unique set of venturing opportunities for the near future.

1. *Growth of Entrepreneurial Activity:* This trend concerns the emergence of increased entrepreneurship rates and, more recently, the use of entrepreneurial management techniques in established companies to increase monetary wealth, innovation and job creation.

2. *Growing Awareness of Sustainability in Society:* The second trend represents a sharp increase in awareness, especially during the last decade, among consumers, producers, not-for-profit organizations and governments, in terms of the health and environmental aspects of living in consumer societies.

We have presented different academic views of entrepreneurship. Here we conclude that different processes influence the design of key entrepreneurial activities. Behavioral expectations and strategies, management practices and strategies, and striving towards various types of economic goals can all effect entrepreneurship. This framework can be applied to entrepreneurial management as well because we focus on a process oriented view. Thus, in order to investigate the 60 cases we needed a more detailed conceptual framework to approach the human factor at a micro level.

In approaching these case studies, the human factor was a dominant focus. Specifically, we looked at strategic orientation, decision orientation, emotional stability and behavioral attributes. Therefore, this study is unique in the different perspectives it offers: (1) Case studies normally focus on venture performance and less on the entrepreneurial processes involved in designing a firm. In our study the person behind the entrepreneur was the central focus; (2) In contrast to other studies we describe a wide variety of entrepreneurial types; (3) From the perspective of qualitative research we covered a rather high number of profiles; (4) We investigated positive experiences as well as negative experiences to gain a broader perspective, as often only positive cases enjoy attention; (5) The case studies can be used as learning material for students who study entrepreneurial activities.

It should of course be recognized that as a qualitative study with, in some cases, limited numbers of participants, our comments should be interpreted as exploratory in nature. We will not pay attention to achievement drive and awareness in the summary of the findings because all the entrepreneurs had high scores on these variables. Our findings per entrepreneurial type are summarized as follows.

- *Entrepreneurial executives.* Entrepreneurial executives showed high levels of dominance and trust, and high levels of mental fitness meaning they can manage their emotions and moods very well. In comparison with all entrepreneurs in the study they tend to be less promotion oriented, and less achievement oriented. We can also assume that their professional settings demanded a more stable profile. The entrepreneurial executive career track requires a focus on innovation of products or services, innovation of processes, breaking taboos, and possibly, initiating activities with international impact. For executives, the framework in which they operate is much more defined in comparison with those of the entrepreneur. These frameworks require a set of abilities to work within defined boundaries, and leadership, coping with demanding tasks, striving for high achievements, interest in the organization and the common good, flexible focus and the ability to convince stakeholders. A majority of entrepreneurial executives stressed certain values in their approach to dealing with people. It seems that for the participants in the study, addressing the human factor is the most challenging.

- *Venturers.* Venturers spin-off businesses from existing firms. Entrepreneurs in this group had the highest score on energy, they have positive moods, and they are self-confident, satisfied and alert. They have often left a business to start a new one based on their personal learning and experiences. They score high on decision focus which indicate their readiness to act when dealing with negative experiences. Venturers might have to deal with the dilemma of when to decide to lean on their previous networks and when not to.

- *Re-launchers.* Entrepreneurs who bought a part of a firm or a whole firm show a good level of mental fitness as well. As buyers they must convince previous employees or suppliers of the firm that they will be more successful in running the business. They often implement reorganizations which do not make them popular with the previous personnel. These situations might influence their flexibility as they scored low on flexibility. Re-launchers might also have to deal with the dilemma of putting the past aside. Former employees sometimes resist change that seems necessary to the re-launcher.

- *Trend entrepreneurs.* The trend entrepreneurs showed relatively high levels of hardiness meaning that they are experienced in dealing with setbacks. Trend entrepreneurs are founders of new businesses who are dedicated to the implementation of a triple-bottom line stakeholder orientation as a logical part of their business strategy. Trend entrepreneurs deal with the question of what scale is needed to remain successful in dealing with the bigger picture of entrepreneurship as well as how to address the community, ecology and economics in relation to their business.

- *Family business entrepreneurs.* Family business entrepreneurs are less flexible, and show a lower level of mental fitness. Yet, they do demonstrate a high level of hardiness, maybe because of setbacks they experienced in the past. They show a high level of alertness and they tend to be more action oriented. It is also assumed that they showed a need to prove themselves to former owners and employees. In family businesses, a dilemma of keeping other family members at a good distance from business activities might occur. It is also the case that putting aside the past can present real challenges. Working within a family business and facing expectations from family members might raise tensions.

- *Significant business entrepreneurs.* Entrepreneurs who founded a significant business have shown high levels of self-confidence, and a good state of mental fitness. However they are relatively less flexible. This means that they have established an organizational structure which provides less room for flexibility. Significant business founders are also entrepreneurs who have been able to create a business which is relatively important in terms of personnel, turnover and innovation, as significant businesses frequently search for external finance. As well, significant business founders might need to deal with fast growth as a consequence of their innovative actions.

- *Small business entrepreneurs.* Entrepreneurs who run a small business demonstrated relatively low scores on mental fitness variables, including a low level of energy, less positive moods, an average level of self-confidence, relatively less satisfaction and an average level of alertness. This means that they face mental problems more frequently, they often lack sufficient personnel which might cause lower levels of mental fitness and they are too small to grow because of the type of products or services they deliver. In addition, they might face high fluctuations in projects and market demands which make it difficult to maintain a fixed team of staff. Their scores indicate a tendency to be state oriented which means that they have a low self-regulatory capacity to act. Often a small business has limited personnel to rely on. And, the expertise of personnel is not very specialized due to the fact that each person is responsible for a number of multidisciplinary tasks. The entrepreneur has to find a balance between what and when to delegate and what and when not to delegate. In busy periods, delegation might be a must and in less busy times delegation might not be needed. These situations ask for high flexibility within the team.

- *Start-ups.* Start-ups also appear very flexible, show high levels of hardiness, they show high levels of energy, positive moods, high self-confidence, they are satisfied and they are alert. These characteristics are necessary for exploring and implementing new opportunities. They score relatively lower on hardiness, implying that they are not quite experienced in dealing with setbacks. That would be understandable as many start-ups are initiated by young entrepreneurs and the chance that they have already experienced setbacks is low. The start-up entrepreneur is therefore wide open to creativity, international orientation and growth. The main concern is deciding on which direction to focus.

- *Enterprising persons.* The solo entrepreneurs in the study were very flexible, very satisfied, and demonstrated positive energy. Generally speaking, they also demonstrated good mental fitness, meaning they have high energy levels, positive moods, a high level of self-confidence, they are highly satisfied and they are highly alert. They can also be characterized as action oriented persons, meaning that they are more likely to take the initiative to start something new. These characteristics can be ascribed to the fact that they are motivated to be entrepreneurs. Additionally, based on their personal drive to remain a solo entrepreneur, they are more relaxed in dealing with external factors. Some support for this assumption can be found in the fact that they appear to show low levels of alertness. Their span of control in terms of complex relationships with others is relatively small because they function as a solo person. Being an entrepreneur is a way of life and a way of earning money. It appeared that staying solo is a rational choice even though this might give rise to tension. It can therefore be assumed that a characteristic of the enterprising person is the dilemma of staying solo in comparison with the alternative of seeking partnerships or hiring employees.

7.2   Miscellaneous Findings and Recommendations

- *Factors leading to success in entrepreneurial activities.* From the findings in theory and practice we conclude that the following factors improve success: (1) achievement drive, (2) awareness of opportunities, (3) alertness focus, (4) focus on winning, (5) good mental fitness, (6) self-confidence regarding required capabilities, (7) creativity stimulation, (8) ability to cope with setbacks, and (9) preparation in dealing with opportunities. These factors can be learned or trained to be prepared for successful entrepreneurial activities. Of course having all these capabilities does not guarantee success but they encourage success.

- *Characteristics of successful entrepreneurs.* We have found that entrepreneurs who achieved positive results during the past three years showed characteristics such as: higher achievement drive, lower flexibility, higher self-confidence, higher alertness, and low failure focus and creativity stimulation.

- *Achievement orientation of family business entrepreneurs.* Entrepreneurs who hail from entrepreneurial families are more promotion oriented meaning that they focus more on achievements. Family members who act as role models for them might stimulate winning strategies.

- *Creativity enhancing entrepreneurs.* Entrepreneurs who stimulate their own creativity are more capable of dealing with setbacks as they have a greater feeling of control. Those who are better prepared for setbacks (high score on hardiness) seem to be better prepared as well in seeking opportunities, and these entrepreneurs define their criteria in advance. This confirms the idea that good preparation brings benefits.

- *Factors influencing the start of an entrepreneurial career.* From all positive factors identified, those related to the team were the most frequently mentioned. Considering the negative factors that influence the start-up process, it turned out that team related factors were also the most frequently mentioned as having an impact on the start-up.

- *Entrepreneurial tools for the business community:* (1) An evaluation register assessing new business possibilities based on criteria can give a higher level of focus on the most relevant type of opportunities; (2) The on-going evaluation of opportunities using techniques such as brainstorming or creativity stimulation by working with a multidisciplinary team; (3) Reinforcing risk-taking and creative employee behavior with a reward system; (4) Developing entrepreneur training to provide time for reflection; (5) Developing training for assessing entrepreneurial characteristics and supporting career development.

- *Entrepreneurial tools for education.* Universities and business schools can use the following tools to encourage entrepreneurial attitudes[1]: (1) Entrepreneurship as a core course requirement in the curriculum can create the possibility for everyone to become familiar with the basics of entrepreneurship; (2) Developing training to assess entrepreneurial personalities and assist students with career development focused on entrepreneurial opportunities; (3) Let alumni participate in mentoring programs for new entrepreneurs; (4) Create facilities such as incubators and multidisciplinary working groups to stimulate entrepreneurial teams to become innovative; (5) Business planning and developing sources of funding and other resources; (6) Participation of entrepreneurial role models in education; (7) Research on business school alumni-entrepreneurs that provides insight into entrepreneurship and builds ties with important stakeholders; (8) Assessing business ideas for business plans from the perspective of different disciplines or multiple mentors; (9) Create a variety of electives for students to get familiar with a range of entrepreneurial activities.

---

[1]   See: Technology Entrepreneurship Education, 2006 of Jerome S. Engel and David Charron for additional recommendations for educators.

Part 2:

The Spirit of Entrepreneurship: Case Studies

8 Entrepreneurial Executives

8.1 Introduction

In this chapter we present seven profiles of entrepreneurial executives from corporations and three from not–for–profit organizations and public sector. (see Appendix 1). Each of the participants from these corporations has initiated and implemented new innovative processes. The entrepreneurial executives in the profit organizations include Anthony Burgmans, Tanja Dik, Edwin van Houten, Arnold Koomen, John Schollink, Thomas Versterre, and Lodewijk de Vink. The entrepreneurial executives in the not-for-profit organizations include Rudolf Deutekom, Wim Kok and Harjan van Dam. Their activities logically included breaking taboos and initiating new processes in creative ways.

Mr. Burgmans designed and implemented the creative idea to build on the corporate multinational strategy with a team of top executives by spending time in the forests of Costa Rica. Amongst his several activities he implemented the idea of a path for growth which included the introduction of new working methods, breaking with old ones and taboos. He implemented the idea of innovation centres to encourage creativity. Mr. Burgmans further managed the realignment and reduction of the number of the brands at Unilever. Ms. Dik developed a performance model which is being been used as a benchmark for all venues of Stage Entertainments. Mr. Van Houten creatively reorganized the sales force through the introduction of business units at Organon Mexico. His new working method contains a plan for profit sharing which will increase the personnel commitment and the efficiency of Organon. Mexico. Mr. Koomen also dealt with increasing employee motivation through management processes such as employee communication and team building at Koninklijke Jongeneel. Mr. Schollink led the process of new building construction at Etam Retail Services paying special attention to managing employee expectations and risk aversion. Mr. Versterre is director at Smits Vuren B.V., a production company of Sovion. In his experiences as an entrepreneurial executive, he managed several changes to improve company results by introducing a new control system for processes and outcomes. Mr. De Vink created an atmosphere that encourages innovation in Warner-Lambert, a pharmaceutical company. Most important was the radical change in new product development procedures so that at every point in the operations of the company the process was less about the pharmaceutical product and more about what it will bring in benefits to the user.

The participants from the not-for-profit and public sectors also dealt with managing change processes and implementation of new working methods often resulting in breaking taboos. One of the main required characteristics here is the competence to deal with multiple interests while maintaining the focus on organizational or societal goals.

Mr. Deutekom introduced business management principles within UNICEF. He stressed that even in an institutional not-for-profit organization, there are opportunities. However, patience to find them through creativity is required. Mr. Van Dam has applied business principles while trying to shake off the municipality culture in BV Sport, a local sport facilitator in the municipality of Leeuwarden, in the Netherlands. In politics, Mr. Kok in his role as Dutch Prime Minister, encouraged multiple initiatives with his capacity to mediate, to empower people and groups of people by building teams and initiating discussions between them. One of his main contributions concerns the initiation of the so called "polder model." This refers to the on-going process of consultation, communication and contacts between people from widely varying institutions in society while trying to find common grounds in opinions and goals which creates a winning strategy for all parties involved.

All participating entrepreneurial executives in this research demonstrated the capacity to act as entrepreneurial leaders with personal characteristics in terms of dominance, high achievement drives, and perseverance. They all have had to deal with demanding environments that called for a flexible attitude and the ability to cope with multiple, often widely diverging, interests. Trust and integrity were also mentioned as main facets of their behaviour. These stories reveal that entrepreneurial processes such as opportunity evaluation and setting up a strategy with clear goals are also part of entrepreneurial management. The entrepreneurial executives and leaders in the not-for profit and profit sectors also deal with fears and difficulties in managing goals, budgets, teams, the social environment and the market and, finally, the structural framework in which they function.

It seems that for the participants of the study, the people factor is the most challenging issue to address. Possibly in part due to the defined frameworks of the organization they perceived these executives had to search for more balance between people, planet and profit issues on their way to evaluating opportunities.

Application of creative entrepreneurial techniques in existing companies or organizational frameworks seems to relate to the entrepreneurial attitude of the executive. In transforming these attitudes into the company or organization, fitting leadership and communication styles is critical to creating an entrepreneurial climate for innovation.

8.2   Anthony Burgmans, Unilever

I have been working at Unilever for almost 35 years. I am a non-executive chairman of Unilever. Unilever is one of the largest manufacturers of food and home and personal care products in the world. In the 1990s it had already been decided to concentrate on "Fast moving consumer goods" (FMCG). A major strategy change came with Unilever's "Path to Growth" in 2000. This was a five-year program for more focus throughout the business, especially to concentrate on fewer but more profitable brands to stimulate faster growth. In 1999, Unilever had 1,600 brands and I have been able to reduce the total number of brands to 400, for example to strong ones like Knorr, Hellmann's, Dove and Omo. There was 5 billion Euro available for restructuring and decreasing the number of brands. Through "Path to Growth" I achieved a major transformation in Unilever. As a result, Unilever itself has changed dramatically, the structure is much simpler now and the activities are clearer.

Company Profile

Company dynamics. During the last few years Unilever accomplished an overhaul of its brands and product offerings, reviewed its dual ownership structure and implemented changes to its corporate governance arrangements. Profits, dividends and turnover for 2005 increased over the previous year and market shares remained stable.

Strengths, weaknesses and success. Strong points include the deep roots of the company which operates worldwide in more than 100 countries. The company is also diverse and multicultural. Looking at weaknesses there is the point of speed of decision making; because of the multicultural composition of the company there is a high tendency to negotiate in order to get the same starting point and to connect with each other and this process takes a lot of time. Yet the strengths dominate the weaknesses.

Defining Opportunities

Evaluation criteria. "It takes patience to build a new market proposition. The margarine market for example was not built in one day; it took many years of effort and investment. It required patience, consistent marketing investment and research and development. Financial markets work with a short-term framework but the development of new markets and brands need a long-term vision and sometimes you face major dilemmas".

Experiences with innovation. Unilever is very decentralized meaning that each country organization has a significant degree of responsibility. When he was working for Unilever in Indonesia, Mr. Burgmans noticed that it was better to concentrate on the local needs and structure. Later, as a Unilever board member, he worked hard to achieve a step change in marketing and research and development (R&D). He set-up innovation centers in a number of countries, of which four were in Europe. The aim was to concentrate the specific expertise in order to make the organization more effective and as a consequence to perform better. It was an enormous cultural change. The danger was that the centers were too much focused on the local needs.

   While Mr. Burgmans had restructured the process of innovation, he noticed that there were different stages in the innovation process, including: (1) A creative part with not much structure and reasonable tolerance; (2) A process of evaluation of ideas; (3) The structure and discipline that was needed for a framework of judgment; (4) An implementation phase of working out the plans in a disciplined way; (5) Launching the product in the market. During these processes and stages he used an instrument of goals with gatekeepers who monitored the whole process. A second tool was a team of professionals who were allowed to assess the processes. The success per innovation phase differs and so does the acceptance.

Experiences

Remarkable initial experiences. Mr. Burgmans took 100 top managers of Unilever to Costa Rica as part of a project to build leadership and entrepreneurship. The focus was on the role of the entrepreneur, personal responsibility, willingness to take responsibility and developing a clear strategy. There were people from all over the world with different cultural backgrounds. The aim was to formulate a shared approach towards strategy and management style. The style concerned empowerment and entrepreneurial inspiration. It needed an atmosphere of trust and transparency. It was therefore important to provide clarity in order then to have an acceptable system of empowerment and accountability. The experience in Costa Rica offered the group an environment without the comfort that the people were used to. It created a climate where they were able to break taboos, and to think differently.

Fears and difficult decisions. "If the position asks you to stick your neck out, there are always things that do not work out as you had wished or had planned. That is part of it. It is important to communicate about things that are difficult or about setbacks but it is critical that you move on," says Mr. Burgmans. He goes on to say that, "It is difficult to determine when to intervene after you notice that someone does not perform well. You can influence sometimes by coaching but often you tend to wait for it too long. Only afterwards you may conclude that you should have intervened earlier but this remains a problem because you do not want to create an organization based on fears and one of not making mistakes. By making mistakes you learn a lot, so you need to find a good balance in this".

Initial learning points. Mr. Burgmans stresses that it is very important to weigh the different interests in a conscious way. A decision should be supported legally, be taken with integrity, and "feel good".

Message to new entrepreneurs. "Be enthusiastic and put in 100% effort, keep things simple, enjoy your work and be yourself. Do not do too many different things but try to improve your expertise in a particular area," Mr. Burgmans also says. "Nowadays students find it very difficult to choose; therefore I would suggest to go for things that you really enjoy. When, after two or three years, it does not feel good, then try something else. You can switch your career once or twice, and if you then are 27 or 28 years old, you can still start a different career. But do not use all that time just thinking about what career you would like to pursue. It does not matter if it is a corporate career or one by starting an own firm, always try to work in a professional way".

Entrepreneurship and Spirituality

Societal contribution. As a multinational Unilever provides many jobs and through its activities it contributes to the range of foods and other products for daily use that people can choose from in order to improve their personal well-being. According to

Mr. Burgmans, "integrity is the basis for every action; it is the boss of everything. You can have a lot of rules but earning money with integrity is the most important one. Then you are, of course, dependent on how employees behave regarding these rules". Mr. Burgmans is known for advocating the social and ecological responsibility of big business. His work at the World Water Forum and the World Wildlife Fund underscores that environmental issues have his interests. He frequently speaks out for the development of cross-cultural awareness and diversity in society and organizations.

Summary Profile Anthony Burgmans

Entrepreneurial executive roles	He started his career with Unilever in 1972 in marketing and sales in The Netherlands and Germany. He then moved to Indonesia as company chairman. In 1991 he was appointed as a member of the board of Unilever, by heading up the Personal products group. In 1994 he moved to Ice cream & Frozen foods Europe. In 1999, he went on to become the chairman of Unilever N.V. and the vice-chairman of Unilever PLC. And, since 2005 he is non-executive chairman of Unilever.
Place of organizations / roles	Head office in Rotterdam, The Netherlands
Involvement	1972 to present
Business sector	Fast moving consumer goods
Venture activity	Manufacturers of food and home and personal care products around the world.
Customers	Consumers world-wide
International activities	Operations in more than 100 countries
Characteristics of an entrepreneurial executive	Initiation of an innovation which logically leads to the introduction of new working methods, breaking taboos, charismatic leadership and designing and implementing creative ideas Inspiring employees Awareness of the international impact of your actions

8.3   Tanja Dik, Theaters Nederland

I am director of Theaters Nederland, a part of Stage Entertainment. The organization has passionate and highly driven personnel and it offers an inspiring environment where people can be happy and creative. The organization has grown fast by expanding the amount of theatres and products. Stage Entertainment currently has about 5,000 employees, Theater Nederland has 1,800 employees. When I started in 1999, there were about 250 employees. In the past, the positions I held consisted of a fixed set of tasks. In the current situation, each venue and business unit acts as an entrepreneurial firm with a high level of responsibility. In the Netherlands, I have developed a benchmark with my team which can be applied to all the other venues. The Netherlands was the first country in the group to become commercially oriented.

Company Profile

Company dynamics. The company has become more professional, and now hires more highly educated people. Growth remains the key of the strategic approach. Within the Netherlands the organization is a market leader and customers are found mainly in the Netherlands at the top of the Dutch corporate businesses.

Strengths, weaknesses and success. Strengths of the company include a high degree of flexibility, passionate people, and high achieving personnel. Among the weaknesses, Ms. Dik points out that the degree of professionalism within the organization needs to proceed at the same speed as growth. Yet, in order to achieve this, it is clear that multiple processes must be running at the same time. Still, Ms. Dik thinks the organization is very successful, and it has been profitable and still growing.

Defining Opportunities

Evaluation criteria. When Ms. Dik pursues market opportunities she defines her criteria for success in advance as well as during the process. For her the most important criteria to evaluate market opportunity are the speed of development, the returns, and the way the process develops.

Opportunity evaluation techniques. Ms. Dik practices different techniques as part of her business strategy. She took part in brain storming sessions with colleagues, sessions to think out of the box and creating moments of detachment. Some of these techniques include the re-design of goals, the adjustment of leadership style and communication.

Experiences

Remarkable initial experiences. Ms. Dik worked on creating more structure by writing about the process in detail. This required thinking about goals, and the change process took her three to four years. First she started with a pilot study. The model she developed became a handbook containing processes about how, what and when to act. This resulted in developing a one page performance report which is now handled by every venue director.

The model is primarily financially oriented with attention for qualitative processes as well. It encourages personal responsibility and efficiency, freedom, and autonomy. It is based on a series of small steps that aims to identify what is needed for the business unit to perform well; to be profitable. The model also contains a sample of a balance sheet that looks closely at the consequences of a decision and the costs and benefits.

Fears and difficult decisions. The most difficult issue was adjusting to this new working method as it contained more tasks, and more responsibility for each person involved, implying that earnings would increase as well. Personnel had to make choices between growing the business or not. Not growing meant staying at the same level while growing meant developing yourself as a person. These changes were necessary and it did not result in higher salaries but did lead to other qualitative outputs, such as more autonomy and personnel development.

Initial learning points. The new environment proved to be addictive, yet about 15-20% of the personnel left within three years. One important point that Ms. Dik learned is that changes need to be implemented slowly.

Message to new entrepreneurs. Ms. Dik says, "Make sure you are happy and that you are open to new experiences. Structure your plans in terms of concrete actions to be taken. This will enable you to make the best choices for yourself and to follow your own intuition. When you grow personally, your organization will grow as well."

Entrepreneurship and Spirituality

Role of intuition. Intuition plays an important role in Ms. Dik's life and financial analysis forms the basis. "Intuition plays a role when you ask yourself how others would react, and what people to connect with. You should know what people like, and show openness for feedback."

Societal contribution. Through her position Ms. Dik makes people happy and contributes to the culture.

Summary Profile Tanja Dik

Entrepreneurial executive roles	Director Fortis Circustheater Director Theatres Nederland (the holding is Stage Entertainment)
Place of organizations / roles	The Netherlands
Involvement	2001-2003 Fortis Circustheater 2003 to present Theaters Nederland
Business sector	Live Entertainment
Venture activity	Exploitation of theatres Production of musicals Productions, ticketing
Customers	Theatres visitors, corporations for business events
International activities	International musical producer Stage Entertainment has venues in The Netherlands, Germany, Italy, France, Spain, Russia, USA and UK
Characteristics of an entrepreneurial executive	Introduction of new working methods Breaking taboos Designing and implementing a creative idea

8.4   Edwin van Houten, Organon

I am general manager at Organon Mexico. During my tenure, the organization further developed from a hierarchical and traditional form into a modern organization. The company experienced quantitative growth through increased turnover and profit and faced qualitative growth through increased professionalism. I changed the traditional profit sharing system in Organon Mexico, which was based on the number of years in the company of an employee and overall fiscal profits, to a bonus system based on real company and personal performance. As such initiatives are often met with a great deal of mistrust and resistance, I personally explained the new system to all levels of the organization. I believe that personal involvement of the CEO with all organizational levels is the only way to achieve everybody's commitment to real change.

Company Profile

Company dynamics. The company achieved positive financial results during the last three years, and both turnover and employment increased significantly. The turnover for Organon Mexico was 25-50 million euro per year. Organon Mexico directly and indirectly employs 330 people on a full-time basis. It worked through many changes under my management such as reorganization, a merger process, and a major change in the compensation systems.

Organon Mexico now invests in the education of its employees; and strives to hire more highly educated employees. Mr. Van Houten dealt with reorganization of the sales force and with the sales and marketing structure by introducing business units. Furthermore, the training department was expanded and placed under the responsibility of Human Resources. The Business Development unit was added. PR and Design departments are now in-sourced because of efficiency reasons and there was a merger with Diosynth. In order to change the compensation and benefit systems, the legal entity of Organon Mexico had to be taken through some changes. As a strategic approach, the sales force was restructured within a bigger project, called Sales Xlence, for improving sales force efficiency and effectiveness. The market position as a whole has grown little but in specific segments significant growth occurred. Besides the customers in the private market, the government became an important client as well.

Strengths, weaknesses and success. The organizational strengths that Mr. Van Houten points to were drive, commitment and flexibility. The weaknesses were a decline in basic educational level, and dealing with a traditional heritage. According to Mr. Van Houten the company is very successful. The company achieved growth in the quality of personnel, and growth in turnover and profit. From a personal perspective, Mr. Van Houten feels it was quite successful too.

Defining Opportunities

Evaluation criteria. When Mr. Van Houten pursues market opportunities he defines his criteria for success during the process. For Mr. Van Houten, the most important criteria to evaluate market opportunity are: what was done well or poorly, what can we learn from it for the next time, and were the goals reached.

Opportunity evaluation techniques. Mr. Van Houten practices different techniques as part of his business strategy. He tries to find similarities in goals. Then he translates the goals into clear actions (i.e. why are we going to do this?). Some of these techniques also include a structured business planning process, where everyone involved has the opportunity to give feedback.

Experiences

Remarkable initial experiences. Next to involvement from the top, hierarchical structures also should be respected in change processes. Through combined presentations, subsequent management levels demonstrate their commitment to their reports. Each level in the organization had to convince the next level. Meetings with trade unions contributed positively to this process. Less positive were the time pressures, the administrative work and distrust that remained with some individuals.

Fears and difficult decisions. The fear that the entire process could go wrong and the chance that things would go wrong were real for Mr. Van Houten. From his perspective, it was a difficult decision to move forward as the downside risk was that the whole project could turn out as a personal mistake. He prepared by pre-defining a threshold level that determined the go-no go decision.

Initial learning points. If he would have the chance to carry this process out again, he would do it the same way. Mr. Van Houten says, "…it is easy to decide on change but it is difficult to implement it. Actually this is the most difficult part of the process".

Other experiences. "I introduced business principles and values in every unit in Mexico. The project was initiated by head office as part of their global strategy, and fitted very well with our needs to further improve the local company. Rather than just presenting the business principles we decided to talk extensively about their application in our environment, involving all company levels, and define a realistic implementation path and goals. Looking back, I am very satisfied with the results, not only because we really improved, but also because we had a real discussion on the application of business principles in our company. I have gained experience in how a business culture could be changed. Of course you do not know beforehand how it will work out. But through these processes you get to know the employees and they learn how to grow and develop," says Mr. Van Houten.

Message to new entrepreneurs. Perhaps the most important factors to be aware of as a new entrepreneur for Mr. Van Houten are drive, ethics, being a good role model, and sound implementation after launching a change.

Entrepreneurship and Spirituality

Role of intuition. Intuition plays only a partial role for Mr. Van Houten, yet it always does play a role.

Societal contribution. To survive in the long-term, community engagement is a must. The company, wherever it is, contributes to job creation, environmental issues, charity and partly to culture. "Ethics is an issue, which especially in less sophisticated countries, should be attended to," says Mr. Van Houten.

Summary Profile Edwin van Houten

Entrepreneurial executive roles	July 2005 to present: Manager Global Learning Department Organon 2000-2005: General Manager Organon Mexico 1995-2000: General Manager Organon Russia
Place of organizations / roles	The Netherlands, Russia and Mexico
Involvement	From December1989 to present
Business sector	Previously: Marketing, Sales, General Management Currently: Human Relations
Venture activity	Pharmaceutical Industry
Customers	Patients, health care providers
International activities	Organon is a global company, with products sold in more than 100 countries worldwide and subsidiaries in more than half of these. Organon strives to become or remain one of the leading pharmaceutical companies in each of its core therapeutic fields through a combination of independent growth and business partnerships in research & development, production, packaging, marketing and sales. Personal international activities were: the double degree program Nyenrode – EM Lyon, France 1985-1988 Organon, Russia, 1991-1993 and 1995-2000 Organon Mexico 2000-2005
Characteristics of an entrepreneurial executive	Introduction of new working methods Breaking taboos Charismatic leadership Designing and implementing creative ideas

8.5   Arnold Koomen, Koninklijke Jongeneel

I am general manager at Koninklijke Jongeneel since 2003. I characterise this organization in terms of passion, performance orientation, achievement orientation, improvements, openness and ambitiousness. I have experienced changes such as a take-over, mergers of business units, and the sale of a business unit. The organization also develops initiatives to grow, to improve efficiency, and partnering. I have reviewed the back-office process and I conclude that this works better. This concerned 100,000 orders per year, and 3,000 invoices per day. I introduced the redefinition of the whole process with the aim to reduce costs and to secure more continuity in the long-term.

Company Profile

Company dynamics. The company achieved positive financial results during the last three years, and turnover increased but employment decreased. The turnover was more than 50 million euro per year and the company employs 700 people on full-time basis. Mr. Koomen tries to give education and development a more prominent place by providing more structure and hiring a new coordinator for education. For each part of the organization he has introduced the goals of growth and operational excellence to increase employee motivation.

Strengths, weaknesses and successes. Strengths include customer orientation, high quality employees, and a bottom line focus, while weaknesses are short-term orientation, and consistency in strategy. For Mr. Koomen, the organization is a success. It has been able to be profitable and realize positive growth even in times of recession in the building industry and it has a qualified group of dedicated people.

Defining Opportunities

Evaluation criteria. When Mr. Koomen pursues market opportunities he defines his criteria for success in advance. For Mr. Koomen the most important criteria to evaluate market opportunity is achieving performance goals compared to the plan and the question of why and how this was achieved. This results in knowing what was learned and how this new learning can be applied to other situations.

Opportunity evaluation techniques. Mr. Koomen practices different techniques as part of his business strategy. He strives to find consensus about goals. Then he translates the goals by connecting them to budget and the formulation of concrete activities. (What are we suppose to do). Some techniques include the redesign of products or services; he also adjusts his leadership and communication styles.

Experiences

Remarkable initial experiences. A positive factor for Mr. Koomen was the passion of the employees, the reward system, and the return on investment recognized at each level in the organization. Negative factors included a high degree of delegation due to the 35 establishments and it was difficult to find qualified IT analysts.

Fears and difficult decisions. Mr. Koomen did not experience fears; he started the process with a positive attitude. So far he has not been in a position to fire anybody, and views this as a potentially difficult decision. Otherwise, Mr. Koomen has not taken difficult decisions as part of the management process.

Initial learning points. He had a total project plan but not enough detail was considered in advance. He learned that it is good to plan things in advance and, upon implementation, to have a full-time analyst responsible for the process.

Other specific experiences. Arnold Koomen noticed that his predecessor often blamed the shareholders for not having success. He therefore started to mobilize employees to change this attitude. Now they focus on thinking what influence and control they can have over things that happen. Thus the team gained self-confidence. This process was very time consuming as it was equivalent to changing the working culture of the organization. His perseverance and passion worked positively, and people in the organization appreciated that he took time for them. Changes and especially closing business units caused fears. He stayed rational. "Communication is so important. The people part is the most difficult one. Things are not clear immediately. It takes more time. But honest communication works".

Message to new entrepreneurs. Execution is much more important than strategy, says Mr. Koomen.

Entrepreneurship and Spirituality

Role of intuition. Nowadays intuition plays more of a role than in the past for Mr. Koomen. He feels that is experiences allow him more room for intuition.

Societal contribution. His organization gives jobs to nearly 650 people and it contributes to addressing environmental issues.

Summary Profile Arnold Koomen

Entrepreneurial executives roles	Before his executive roles Mr. Koomen held different positions such as Management Trainee Rabobank the Netherlands, Product Manager Euro Relais, Consultant, OC&C Strategy Consultants. His executive roles started: In 1997-2000: Chief Financial Officer, Axxicon Group 2001: Chief Operating Officer, Axxicon Mould Technology 2001-2003: Financial Manager, Koninklijke Jongeneel 2003-present: General Manager, Koninklijke Jongeneel
Place of organizations / roles	Axxicon Group NV, Eindhoven, The Netherlands Koninklijke Jongeneel B.V., Utrecht, The Netherlands
Involvement	1997 to present
Business sectors	Metals and Plastics Wholesale building materials
Venture activity	Manufacturing of injection moulds and plastic parts National network of construction material wholesalers
Customers	Automotive, medical, electronics Contractors and wood product manufacturers
International activities	Customer services International purchasing activities International consulting assignments, worked among others in Russia, Germany, Austria and Switzerland
Characteristics of an entrepreneurial executive	Initiation of innovations Introduction of new working methods Designing and implementing creative ideas Fundamental positive attitude "Can do" mentality Standing still implies decline

8.6   John Schollink, Etam Retail Services

I am general manager at Etam Retail Services. The organization has experienced many changes since my involvement. Its characteristics are: open, young, informal, professional and willing to face challenges. I was in charge of the construction of the new central building for the Etam group. This included overseeing the whole logistics, infrastructure, and construction of the building. It was a big project that concerned implementing a vision for the long-term and required the involvement of every level of the organization. The processes were very dynamic. I noticed that people were risk averse and change averse.

Company Profile

Company dynamics. Etam Retail Services employs 170 employees on a fulltime employment basis. The company has been profitable since its beginning. The demand for educated and experienced people continues to increase, while the demand for people with lower levels of experience is decreasing. To a large degree, work processes have been automated. Turnover remains stable, and the company works for market leaders.

Strengths, weaknesses and successes. Strengths that Mr. Schollink points out include the ability to act quickly, flexibility, and the continuous drive for improvement. Weaknesses include primarily the ability to finish activities. According to Mr. Schollink, the organization is successful financially and operationally.

Defining Opportunities

Evaluation criteria. When Mr. Schollink pursues market opportunities he defines his criteria for success in advance. Criteria he uses for assessment are costs, quality, time span and sometimes the financial risks.

Opportunity evaluation techniques. Mr. Schollink practices different techniques as part of his business strategy. Most of the time he starts with describing his approach towards opportunities as he expects the situation will unfold, then he uses brainstorming sessions to make the approach more concrete. Some of these techniques include re-design of goals, developing competencies in order to gain winning strategies, and adjusting the style of leadership to the situation. Mr. Schollink stresses that there is a big difference between being absolutely right and getting to the right outcome.

Experiences

Remarkable initial experiences. "It was remarkable that some people were defensive at all levels, it was not related to someone's position," and Mr. Schollink says he had to manage their expectations. He found that everyone he interacted with had their own questions and expectations, therefore it was very important to communicate and frequently inform those concerned: And sometimes he found that he had to be very willful. Positive factors detailed by Mr. Schollink include that the organization was growing, there was a positive climate in the organization that made it easier to get people enthusiastic, and people were familiar with change from past experiences. Negative factors were related to the fact that turnover was too high to produce the winter collection in the old building which meant that there was a formal deadline. The positive thing related to this challenge was that this was accepted by everyone, so the need to let the project become successful was shared.

Fears and difficult decisions. The main fear for Mr. Schollink was that he would not be able to meet the deadline due to issues that could cause problems like the software not working, etc. For the construction work itself he hired a supervisor with whom he was in constant communication. And, in the end there were some delays in the construction due to several problems. During the process Mr. Schollink experienced difficult decisions as well. When employees did not function as expected or agreed upon, he was left with the decision to fire them which always felt difficult. Mr. Schollink says, "It is painful to dismiss personnel yet it is better than not taking action for a long time."

Another difficulty was going on with work while at the same time knowing that the project was not finished. In Mr. Schollink's view this was a risky approach yet is was necessary to meet the deadline. The other difficulty was realizing that decisions regarding the infrastructure had to be taken without being completely informed, some things were not clear. "Taking decisions without full information and coping with uncertainty were very important for the continuation of the process", says Mr. Schollink.

Initial learning points. Looking back, Mr. Schollink noticed that the results could have been less satisfactory, and although things could have been done better, in general he was satisfied with the results of the project. Still, according to Mr. Schollink, "Satisfaction is the death of innovation". Among the learning points that he lists, Mr. Schollink learned what processes are important for the management of changes. For example, he gave training sessions to the personnel at the lowest level in the organization. During these sessions he noticed that for most of them it was the first time they went to a training course, and many of them were very nervous. He learned a great deal from these experiences, including how to tailor processes to people and understanding the emotions of people involved in the training sessions.

According to Mr. Schollink the management of changes has been central in his career, and his experience with this project was the greatest change he had to implement. Looking back, Mr. Schollink learned that while there is a risk aversive attitude at the start, people can begin to enjoy change during the process. He also mentioned additional learning points: (1) changes touch people deeply, (2) there is always the question 'what is in it for me', (3) be clear on what the consequences are, (4) many people want to behave as they always do, and (5) not every one is able to see the big picture in the organization.

Other specific experiences. Another experience concerning his role in managing this project involved changing attitudes. To accomplish this Mr. Schollink hired trainers to communicate that the outside environment was changing and that it would be necessary for people to find a fit for their own role within the new framework. Education is increasingly an important priority in the organizational culture of the Etam Group and Etam Retail Services, and since his involvement and initiative of projects related to training and education, people are more and more open to education. Mr. Schollink thinks he has been able to build a team during the process that feels that trust is very important. People who cannot be open to change leave the organization. As well, changing attitude creates a need for new ideas. Mr. Schollink developed criteria for evaluation of personnel: performance, innovation and flexibility. All three are part of everyone's position in relation to change.

"After completing the project, the challenge was to build the organization, and this was different from the project itself. The project was a special case with certain deadlines and a clear focus. Some of the methods that worked for the project do not work now. Building an organization is asking for a continuous process of change and innovation. This process should become a natural part within the organization," says Mr. Schollink. Relevant questions to address these issues involve considering is there time for innovation, what are the private interests, and how serious is a person's willingness to change. It is clear to Mr. Schollink that there should be a personal motivation to change and innovate. Along these lines, Mr. Schollink created small projects to make it feasible for people to be motivated to achieve results. The problem that remains in Mr. Schollink's view is that it is always the same group, about 20%, who initiate things and who put more effort into the projects. To Mr. Schollink, working to motivate the other 80% is a priority. Yet of this 80%, 20% are likely to not change without investing effort.

Message to new entrepreneurs. Mr. Schollink says to new entrepreneurs that usually in the real world, you have to come with a united judgment or decision; macho behaviour will not work. It is about your position in various groups and in various roles.

Entrepreneurship and Spirituality

Role of intuition. Intuition does play an important role in Mr. Schollink's decision making; nearly 80% of his decision making is based on intuition.

Societal contribution. The organization, Etam Retail Services employs 170 people. Together with the other companies of the Etam Group, the company also strives to maintain long-term relations with suppliers and works with an ethical handbook. Continuity of the business is one of the main things in the mission statement. Trust, loyalty, care for each other and care for the environment are organizational values.

Summary Profile John Schollink

Entrepreneurial executive roles	Manager Logistics Tetterode Nederland Manager Dikema & Chabot Manager Logistics / Project manager Construction of new building for Etam Retail Services General Manager Etam Retail Services
Place of organizations / roles	Tetterode Nederland, Amsterdam Dikema & Chabot, Rotterdam Etam Retail Services, Zoetermeer All in the Netherlands
Involvement	Tetterode Nederland: 1987 – 1996 Dikema & Chabot: 1996 – 1998 Etam Retail Services: 1998 – to date
Business sector	Tetterode: graphic industry Dikema: steel Etam Retail Services: retail services
Venture activity	Tetterode: wholesale in graphic equipment and other materials Dikema: wholesale and production of steel Etam Retail Services: retail services
Customers	Tetterode: companies in the graphic sector Dikema: various companies Etam Retail Services: retail companies
International activities	Various German and Japanese and American suppliers for graphic apparatus. For Dikema he did business mainly with Germany For Etam Retail Services he conducts business with countries all over the world
Characteristics of an entrepreneurial executive	Initiation of an innovation which logically lead to the introduction of new working method, breaking taboos, charismatic leadership and designing and implementing a creative idea. Inspiring employees does also apply and international impact although it is less big.

8.7   Thomas Versterre, Smits Vuren

I am managing director at Smits Vuren BV, a production company of Sovion. The company is changing a great deal due to the market situation and because of changing international laws. It has a down to earth mentality, and in the last two years there have been various re-organizations and mergers. I was tasked with managing two locations, and to manage effectively I worked to clearly communicate the main responsibilities and expectations, giving people the freedom to realise plans and I also built a system to control the process and outcomes. As well, I have been busy in developing plans for coping with the new regulations of the European Union. For example, when the US government did not allow gelatin from Europe, I had to develop alternatives and decided to move to other sources of materials, and rebuild the US market again.

Company Profile

Company dynamics. The total company Sovion has a turnover of about approximately 7 million euro; Delft Gelatin, where Mr. Versterre is managing director, has a turnover between 25 and 35 million euro. During his tenure, he has been able to increase the problem solving capacity of the personnel, and some tasks have been centralized, and some positions have been merged. In addition, there is a lot more cooperation with sister companies regarding purchase and sales. "By combining efforts the performance is better," says Mr. Versterre. And, new regulations are brining changes in the type of customers the company deals with.

Strengths, weaknesses and successes. Strengths that Mr. Versterre identified are a high degree of flexibility, low costs, and technical knowledge about techniques and applications. Weaknesses that Mr. Versterre pointed out were environmental issues with the government related to inconvenient smells and waste water. According to Mr. Versterre, the organization is successful based on its performance. The company also manages the changes in rules and regulations and is a frontrunner in its sector.

Defining Opportunities

Evaluation criteria. When Mr. Versterre pursues market opportunities he defines his criteria for success in advance of the process. For Mr. Versterre, the most important criteria to evaluate market opportunities is the possibility of earning money.

Opportunity evaluation techniques. Mr. Versterre practices different techniques as part of his business strategy. Some of these techniques include re-segmentation of the market, the target group or goals and a complete re-design of goals, the market and target groups. He also values discussion with his team about new ideas and perspectives. For example, when considering how to change the production process they use an 'idea pigeon hole' to collect new proposals. "You have to take care of every idea seriously," says Mr. Versterre.

Experiences

Remarkable initial experiences. Reflecting on his experiences, Mr. Versterre says that it is important to realize that you need your stakeholders; and they must be involved in your thinking. He has experienced a positive climate because of the level of enthusiasm and fun within the company, and he sees this as the most important thing for the long-term. Mr. Versterre also noticed that he gained more management freedom when performance was successful. While he works to give a lot of autonomy to people, sometimes it does not work out well and occasionally he had to fire employees. "The company exists for more than 175 years, and it is one of the few production industries. There are people working within the company for a very long time, so it is very important that people are motivated and enjoy their work," notes Mr. Versterre.

Fears and difficult decisions. When he started the results were not positive yet there was a positive pattern. Still, one location needed to be closed and this affected about 85 people. Mr. Versterre went though a social plan to close the factory and building. In the UK, another firm had to be closed, affecting 15 employees. Looking back, Mr. Versterre thinks that the closures were a good decision because now, with one company focusing on the same end-product, they are able to make profit.

Initial learning points. For Mr. Versterre, a key learning point is that you must involve people in the process, explain why some hard decisions have to be taken, and make plans that will lead to profit.

Other specific experiences. He noticed that a top down approach of managing does not work. "Let people come with their own solutions to problems. When they develop an idea, it will work better," says Mr. Versterre.

Message to new entrepreneurs. It is good to be yourself and have fun. When you aren't having fun you better go and search for something else. Working hard is important, but you must have time for enjoyable activities.

Entrepreneurship and Spirituality

Role of intuition. Intuition is Mr. Versterre's starting point and when it feels good he tries to rationalize his decisions by inclusion of numbers. Dealing with people is nearly 80% intuition Mr. Versterre's opinion. Yet when dealing with financial decisions, it's all based on detailed calculation.

Societal contribution. The company is a 100% recycling company; only waste water is left at the end of the production process. And the company creates jobs for nearly 138 people, based on full-time employment it is 117.

Summary Profile Thomas Versterre

Entrepreneurial executive roles	Masterfoods Manager industrial engineering two years, production shift manager three years Bison International Manager operations two years Delft gelatine, Smits Vuren, Global ceramic materials (UK) Managing director seven years
Place of organizations / roles	Smits Vuren, Vuren (The Netherlands) Delft Gelatin, Delft (The Netherlands) Global Ceramic materials in Stoke on Trent, (Great Britain)
Involvement	1998 to present

Business sector	Processing of slaughter by-products
Venture activity	Production of starting material for the pet food industry, feed industry, gelatine industry and ceramic industry from bones derived from healthy animals fit for human consumptions.
Customers	Internal customers for example the gelatine factories from Rousselot. External customers such as the pet food industry, and the ceramic industry, for example Wedgwood etc.
International activities	Sovion has many production companies in the world and they cooperate with each other. The purchase of raw material and sales of all products are international activities.
Characteristics of an entrepreneurial executive	Initiation of an innovation Introduction of new working method Breaking taboos Charismatic leadership Inspiring employees in an unorthodox way The drive to win / to achieve high performances

8.8   Lodewijk de Vink, Warner-Lambert

I held the position of President of Warner-Lambert, a pharmaceutical company. During my tenure, the organization faced many dynamic situations like facing patent expiration of major products, shifting focus to R&D, and marketing of new compounds. A major success was the introduction of Lipitor, a cholesterol lowering pharmaceutical. The company moved to merge with American Home Products, yet eventually after a drawn out process, Warner Lambert was acquired by Pfizer. The company achieved positive financial results during the last three years, and both turnover and employment increased significantly. Warner-Lambert employed 30,000 employees in 1988 and in 2000 about 35,000 employees. Now it is a part of Pfizer.

Company Profile

Company dynamics. From 1980-2000 turnover increased threefold, and market value increased eight-fold. The value of Warner-Lambert at the time of the transaction with Pfizer was $128 billion US. During Mr. De Vink's involvement, the three pillars of Warner-Lambert were dominated by the one-platform company, Parke Davis Pharmaceuticals. Strategically, there was a need to minimize overlap. There was also a dependence on one major successful product which made a merger necessary and unavoidable. Warner-Lambert became part of Pfizer.

Strengths, weaknesses and successes. Strengths are innovative R&D and a very close relationship between R&D and marketing leading to innovative regulatory strategies, and to major successful product introductions. Weaknesses included the fact that too much of the future of Warner-Lambert was dependent on the Lipitor product that had a patent expiration in 2011. According to Mr. De Vink, the company was successful. It was the fastest growing pharmaceutical company in the US during the last four years of his tenure.

Defining Opportunities

Evaluation criteria. When Mr. De Vink pursues market opportunities he defines his criteria for success in advance and during the process he adjusts them when needed. For Mr. De Vink, the most important criteria to evaluate market opportunity are the likelihood of success, the process of the implementation and who is responsible.

Opportunity evaluation techniques. Mr. De Vink practices different techniques as part of his business strategy. "I try to approach decisions from both sides of the spectrum even if I am inclined to lean toward one side," says Mr. De Vink. He mentioned that important diversity strategies were employed to obtain a diverse workforce, and to approach new ideas from different angles. Some other techniques Mr. De Vink uses include the redesign of goals, re-differentiation of goals, re-segmentation of the market related to the goals, completely reconfiguring the market, and developing breakthrough competencies, or areas of competitive strength that create new competitive advantages and market niches; an adjustment of his leadership style and communication style.

Experience with Innovation. Normally R&D comes up with a scientific idea for a new product and then in a further step, marketing starts looking at how to market it. Mr. De Vink decided to give the two groups, Marketing and R&D, anonymous feedback on each others ways of pursuing a new product. This gave rise to a tremendous breakthrough in communication between the two groups as details came out which had never come out before. He thus created a safe atmosphere in which really divergent opinions could be voiced!

He experienced this as inspiring and encouraging dialogue. Even differences in opinion in the discussion between R&D and Marketing created better processes and outcomes in marketing innovative new pharmaceuticals which were effective and profitable. Mr. De Vink was always trying and succeeded in integrating this process.

That is, from the earliest idea of R&D, Marketing is party to the process of what the invention or new product can be used for and how it can be formulated to provide the best benefit to patients and doctors (the clients!). Mr. De Vink also worked to make it possible for both groups to see and understand each other's cultures.

Most important was the radical change in the new product development process so that the process is less about the physical product and more about what it will bring in benefits to the user. This is a revolutionary process in the pharmaceutical industry, where the scientific (inventors) culture is still very much separate from the marketing culture. This often leads to products that are not optimal in their design. In Mr. De Vink's view, a greater integration of development and marketing can vastly increase the value of the product to the customer.

Experiences

Remarkable initial experiences. Deep insight into people and teams and their skills, motivations and knowledge are valuable and necessary. Mr. De Vink realised that when you succeed it builds great teams for product development because functional barriers fall away and it is possible to discuss issues in greater depth. The development of the Lipitor product as a long-term solution and product definition in treatment of patients contributed greatly to its success and thus of the value of Warner Lambert.

Positive factors were: (1) It used to be very frustrating to bridge the cultural gap between marketing and R&D visions of a new product. A new approach bridges this gap; (2) Mr. De Vink even forced a merger of the R&D and Marketing budgets for this product; now both groups share the same budgetary goals!; (3) Used facilitators and case studies to bring the two groups together. Negative factors were: (1) R&D used to be not interested in marketing; (2) Marketing used to be equally uninterested in R&D; (3) It took time and courage and creativity to break this cycle. Looking back on the outcomes, Mr. De Vink was satisfied with the results. The new approach made it possible to move from "invention" orientation to "application" in the market.

Fears and difficult decisions. For Mr. De Vink a fear was realizing that if this intensive people process would not succeed it would further divide R&D from Marketing. He states that there were no really difficult decisions, and that he worked with an experienced outsider to facilitate the process.

Initial learning points. Mr. De Vink learned that breaking up existing paradigms within people and teams is essential for creating change. He also learned that bringing in independent, outside facilitators to help the new common culture grow is important. Furthermore, economic incentives can support a change process and can lead to the desired outcomes of integration and a new culture. Finally, Mr. De Vink feels that solo operators are dangerous in business. If he would have the chance to do this again, he would speed up the process, work more intensively and be less careful.

Message to new entrepreneurs. Mr. De Vink says to new entrepreneurs that it is important to develop a broad vision, to adopt a willingness to learn, and to accept debate. He also feels that you must apply an entrepreneurial attitude to managing your own career at all times.

Entrepreneurship and Spirituality

Role of intuition. Intuition is an important ingredient of decision making for Mr. De Vink; nearly 50-60% in his case!

Societal contribution. Mr. De Vink talks about the desire that, as an executive, your philosophy is the correct one and it is important to convince others of the "common good". In his work at the board of the Pharmaceutical Manufacturers Industry Association, he follows a policy to have people understand "why we are doing what we are doing" and to be very conscious of the industry and as a result to know what needs to change to keep the support of stakeholders and to continue to be healthy in the face of the fact that the pharmaceutical industry has a poor image! Mr. De Vink also views that the company contributes to the creation of jobs and supports charities. As well, the company and the industry deeply influence the quality of life of many people.

Summary Profile Lodewijk de Vink

Entrepreneurial executive roles	Marketing pharmaceuticals Country General Manager President International Warner Lambert President Worldwide-CEO, Chairman, Warner Lambert
Place of organizations / roles	Schering-Plough Warner-Lambert New Jersey, USA and affiliates
Involvement	1969-1988: Schering Plough 1988-2000: Warner-Lambert 2000-present: Private Equity
Business sector	Pharmaceuticals
Venture activity	R&D, manufacturing, Marketing of Pharmaceuticals, OTC and Consumer Products
Customers	Physicians, Pharmacies, Patients worldwide
International activities	Subsidiaries, partnerships, joint ventures Mr. De Vink worked and lived in USA, Canada, Belgium, Switzerland and the Netherlands
Characteristics of an entrepreneurial executive	Initiation of an innovation Introduction of new working methods Breaking taboos Charismatic leadership Inspiration of employees International impact with working method Designing and implementing creative ideas

8.9   Rudolf Deutekom, UNICEF

I was director of UNICEF's Private Sector Division. The Private Sector Division, in collaboration with 37 National Committees, is responsible for contributing about one third ($500 million US) of UNICEF's annual funding needs. When I joined the Private Sector Division of UNICEF, there was a duplication of management and fundraising support activities between NY and Geneva, so I moved all activities to Geneva. Among the goals that I have set, raising funds for child health and care activities in the world is a foremost priority. To realize this goal, I introduced brand management as a concept. Today, there are four brand management groups employing 20 people in a larger fundraising support structure of about 200 international staff.

Defining Opportunities

Evaluation criteria. When Mr. Deutekom pursues opportunities he defines his criteria for success in advance and adjusts them when they seem not to work during the process. For Mr. Deutekom, the most important criteria to evaluate market opportunities is the number of active customer clients.

Opportunity evaluation techniques. Mr. Deutekom practices different techniques as part of his strategy. Some of these techniques include the re-differentiation of products or services, and developing competencies in order to gain competitive advantages.

Experiences with innovation. Mr. Deutekom raises revenue by using brand management techniques systematically. He aims to use his experience in re-organizational development and marketing strategy from private industry for the benefit of UNICEF.

Experiences

Remarkable initial experiences. He observed that there were already people from business backgrounds in the organization, and that at the top people were typically extremely hard working and dedicated. What Mr. Deutekom noted was that 20% of the team was doing the bulk of the work, while the remaining 80% were often not directly supporting the proper organizational goals. This required a rational approach of structure and thinking. Yet, the positive factors that Mr. Deutekom points to were that the Executive Director of UNICEF was committed to change and that his own first lieutenant was extremely capable and experienced in the (politically charged) world of UNICEF and its international support structures. Many of the National Committees were supportive of his work in rationalizing the organization and its goals, but while these important stakeholders formally supported change, directions from the center weren't always appreciated. Every so often, therefore, you had to be bold and decisive, forcing decisions in terms of strategy, structure and working methods. Less positive factors were that National Committees could be rather undermining and the anti-corporate mentality that flared up once in a while mostly within UNICEF's established, programmatically oriented staff.

For Mr. Deutekom, this was a job of facilitating professionalism, innovation and installing procedures. He is most satisfied about the level of innovation achieved, and the level of the people within the organization. As well, the degree of acceptance of new corporate strategies and procedures is high.

Fears and difficult decisions. Political conflicts with regional directors (in the UNICEF's complex matrix-management structure) were difficult moments for Mr. Deutekom. Another challenge was the fact that not all corporate partnership (sponsorship) aspects were entirely under his control, especially in the area of branded (joint) communications. For difficult decisions, Mr. Deutekom would go "upstairs" to get support from superiors for his management decisions throughout the organization. For instance, McDonald's sponsorship had to be reversed because of anti-corporate sentiments in selected markets. According to Mr. Deutekom, "The people problems were the hardest".

Initial learning points. He was pretty tough on certain issues out of principle. Without his "first lieutenant", he would not have been able to do it, says Mr. Deutekom. And looking back, he says he really would not do anything differently. Even in an institutional, not-for-profit organization, there are opportunities but you need the patience to continue looking for creative solutions. As an example, cause related marketing with the UNICEF brand name worked successfully. As well, the organization and the related importance of North / South solidarity proved to be a point where the business community could make a fundamental and structural contribution to improve life in the less developed world.

Other specific experiences. When considering what makes him an entrepreneurial leader, Mr. Deutekom feels that he has been able to apply business principles in an international, inter-governmental organization dedicated to social development. He has worked to break taboos and integrate new concepts and principles within the not-for-profit sector.

Message to new entrepreneurs. To new entrepreneurs Mr. Deutekom says, do your home work thoroughly and in advance! It is also important to talk with players in the sector you are entering, to follow your intuition, and to discuss things with your life partner.

Entrepreneurship and Spirituality

Role of intuition. Intuition isn't something that Mr. Deutekom feels plays an important role in his decision making. Yet, he feels that as he gets older it does play a larger role. He estimates that in his early career, intuition comprised 25% of his decision making process while later on it increased to nearly 55-60%.

Societal contribution. Making the switch in his career from a Levi Strauss executive to UNICEF was a gift. According to Mr. Deutekom, UNICEF contributes in a huge sense to the advancement of a (better) world fit for children. Mr. Deutekom's contributions can be labeled as successful, from his perspective.

Summary Profile Rudolf Deutekom

Entrepreneurial executives roles	His career history includes Unilever and Levi-Strauss Europe. He also ran his own consultancy firm from 1989-1996. Now he is retired from consulting and professional work. His profile will focus on the position at UNICEF.

	1982-1985: President, continental Europe of Levi-Strauss International
	1985-1989: Executive VP for Europe's Development division of Levi-Strauss international
	1996- Director Private sector Division of UNICEF New York and Geneva
	1996-2005 Director Private sector Division of UNICEF New York and Geneva
Place of organizations / roles	Brussels, USA and Switzerland
Involvement	From 1982 to present
Sector	International Social Development
Community activity	UNICEF raises funds for the promotion and protection of children's rights and implements child health and social care activities around the world.
Customers	The general public and corporate customers supportive of the work of UNICEF.
International activities	Has been working in Brussels and USA and Switzerland, MBA degree in USA Organizations where he held positions were all internationally active
Characteristics of an entrepreneurial executive	Introduction of a new working method Breaking taboos

8.10 Harjan van Dam, bv SPORT

I am general manager at bv SPORT. I would describe the organization with the Olympic rings. In the last two years, bv SPORT focused on shaking off the municipality culture. Because of these changes the job satisfaction amongst the employees has increased and is still increasing. My leadership approach started with business like principles of obtaining results. It is about first, getting things straight and second to renew things. When the structure is clear the enjoyable, pleasant sphere amongst employees can flourish because people flourish.

Company Profile

Company dynamics. Since his involvement the organization has achieved positive results. The culture has changed, there are new activities, and there is new confidence from the political government. Strong points are the openness in communication, the responsibility, direct lines with the politics and skills of the employees. Dependence of bv SPORT on politics is a less positive point in Mr. Van Dam's view. Its approach is business like, logical, efficient and financially sound.

Strengths, weaknesses and successes. He was 33 years when he became manager in Univé. He did not have experience but he was totally convinced he could do the job and it worked out very well. Mr. Van Dam told us about his experience as manager of a group of 75 professionals on a fulltime basis at the foundation of legal aid assistance (Stichting Univé Rechtshulp). Aid assistance had to act independently, and in practice it was insufficiently independent. When he started as a manager at this foundation he led a research project to find out how the foundation could work independently from the assurance.

The aim was to find out how to present his plan based on the research and how to implement the plan to ensure the objectivity; he had a business approach for this process. The main focus was building an ICT system to register facts and to focus on obtaining knowledge through knowledge. "The professionals had to get more focused in their work but at the same time let the islands between them disappear," he says. He realized a situation where there was fulltime availability during opening hours and no breaks because the client was central. His task was to make the organization change to make it more commercial and this is where his drive to act as an entrepreneur came into existence.

Defining Opportunities

Evaluation criteria. When Mr. Van Dam pursues opportunities he defines his criteria for success in advance. For Mr. Van Dam, the most important criteria to evaluate market opportunities are concreteness of results, the process of change, and the expected involvement, motivation, skills and experience of employees.

Opportunity evaluation techniques. Mr. Van Dam practices different techniques as part of his strategy. He always searches for the best sounding board. He has round table sessions and internal working visits. Some of these techniques include the re-design of goals, the re-differentiation of products or services, and complete re-definition of markets or target groups, thus breaking through existing lines.

Experiences

Remarkable initial experiences. One of the remarkable things at Univé was that Mr. Van Dam had to give a good explanation to all the professionals backed up with strong arguments. Mr. Van Dam says, "There is some sort of intellectual mask. You come with arguments but what really matters were their feelings and people showed resistance. I believe in a universal approach to leadership, it is a capacity which can be executed everywhere, in every type of organization". His positive approach involved the production of a document in which the plans for changes were written and decisions were taken based on the document. This made it somewhat easier to accept the plans and to produce more openness. He noticed that the lawyers were used to working from their own concerns and less from the general business or customers interests, so the approach was very different for them.

The culture at bv SPORT was very formal and very much like that of the municipality; it was not at all entrepreneurial. bv SPORT obtained the status of self-sufficiency since 1999, and when Mr. Van Dam started he faced an organization and employee culture where they were risk averse, submissive, lacked a customer friendly climate, too much interdependence of employees, and a lack of motivation for new initiative creation. As he had been working with realizing culture change within business for some years, the task given to Mr. Van Dam was to help people find more meaning through their roles at bv SPORT. One of his first steps to work towards much needed change at bv SPORT was to replace about 20 fulltime employees with new people with fresh spirit. Communication was another key task that took a lot of effort. In Mr. Van Dam's view, showing respect for everyone's contribution is a main ingredient for success. Change requires patience, tactical actions, ambition and taking action (discipline) in response to market opportunities.

Fears and difficult decisions. For Mr. Van Dam, the most difficult decisions revolved around staff issues, such as firing personnel and finding ways to keep the working environment and culture open to change.

Initial learning points. "Work ethic differs, and my work ethic differs from others but my speed in acting and my feeling of responsibility is not the norm. Find, and sometimes wait, for the (right) moment," says Mr. Van Dam. He goes on to say that he has learned that searching for diversity in the management team is important. Looking for a copy of yourself or only for a 'yes-man' to mobilize your management team is not the best choice. Through opposition and challenge you learn and start thinking in a creative way. It is important to communicate a lot and to give arguments for decisions or expectations. Acting commercially in an arena where the political government dimension exists is not easy.

Message to new entrepreneurs. "Life is what you make it. Just do it, have self confidence and think independently," says Mr. Van Dam.

Entrepreneurship and Spirituality

Role of intuition. Intuition plays a reasonable role for Mr. Van Dam. Usually 70% of his feelings influence his decisions, and in some cases his decisions are based on a ratio.

Societal contribution. As a provider of sport and exercise facilities, bv SPORT makes a large contribution to the local population of Leeuwarden.

Summary Profile Harjan van Dam

Entrepreneurial executive roles	Harjan van Dam is executive manager at bv SPORT in Leeuwarden, the Netherlands from 2003 to the present. Before he held managerial positions at Univé Zorg and Univé Schade. He is interim director at and chairman at BVO Cambuur-Leeuwarden soccer club.
Place of organizations / roles	Univé, the Netherlands bv SPORT Leeuwarden, The Netherlands St. BVO Cambuur-Leeuwarden, The Netherlands
Involvement	St. BVO sport 2005-present bv SPORT 2003-present Univé 1999-2003
Sector	Sports as part of the municipality of Leeuwarden
Activity	bv SPORT offers facilities for sports such as soccer fields and swimming pool
Customers	Population of Leeuwarden
International activities	None
Characteristics of an entrepreneurial executive	Breaking taboos Charismatic leadership (purpose) Inspiration of employees Adequate communication

8.11 Wim Kok, Former Prime Minister

*I started as chairman of the NVV, some years later of the FNV, the most promi-
nent Dutch Trade Union Confederation. In 1986, I started a career in the politics
and retired in 2002. At the end of the seventies there was a big economic crisis in
the world. Unemployment was very high. I thought deeply to come up with an
agreement with the employer federation in my position of representing employee
interests. This resulted in an agreement which is called 'The Agreement of Wassenaar. The agreement reduced employee working hours in exchange for higher
returns for employers through wage restraints. This agreement was settled only
after substantial pressure from the government. There were frequent strikes those
days. In Dutch history, this agreement marked the beginning of the so-called Polder model, i.e. the necessity of cooperation between parties, originally with totally
different goals and values, after profound discussion and negotiation.*

Defining Opportunities

Evaluation criteria. When Mr. Kok pursues opportunities he defines his criteria as much as possible in advance. During the process he slightly adjusts them when necessary. Afterwards he always evaluates the processes. The most important criteria are feasibility, possibilities to reduce obstacles to realize goals, cohesion amongst people, the skill to create confidence and commitment of people.

Opportunity evaluation techniques. "You need room for reflection in order to get new ideas," stresses Mr. Kok. He practices different techniques as part of his strategy. He organized dialogues between groups of people, especially with 'sparring partners'. Some other techniques included the re-differentiation of goals, developing breakthrough competencies, or areas of competitive strength that create new competitive advantages and winning strategies, and an adjustment of his leadership and communication style.

Experiences with innovation. Mr. Kok knew that it was necessary to modify the national disability law (WAO) in the early nineties but approaching such a critical topic was difficult. "The number of disabled people was approaching one million (some 7 % of the population) and therefore the cost to the state was increasing dramatically. To do nothing was not an option anymore". For Mr. Kok, this was a very hard period especially because earlier in his career he was associated with the social vision of the trade unions. He used "management by speech" to convince others, especially grassroots supporters.

Experiences

Remarkable initial experiences. Mr. Kok believes the changes in the WAO went too fast for his grassroots support. In retrospect, people needed more time to adjust to the required change. Looking back, Mr. Kok says that he should have spent even more time preparing people for these important changes. He noticed that much effort was needed to convince others; to build on the values of democracy and trust. Mr. Kok had to arrange a special congress of his political party. In the end this worked out positively. Gradually people started to become aware of the need for social and economic reforms.

Fears and difficult decisions. The disability law adjustment was one of the most difficult decisions he had to take. During his first period in government in the nineties unemployment was very high, and when he was Minister of Finance his policy of cutting public expenditure was not popular. The emergence of Fortuyn as a new political reality had an impact in the last part of Mr. Kok's political career. Fortuyn started to communicate what a part of the citizenry was already thinking about Islam and the integration of people from different ethnic backgrounds into the Dutch society. Mr. Kok describes those days as "...a variety of storms began to rage, there was a slow down in the economy. There was a rise of the Asian countries and Europe was changing significantly. People were pre-occupied with questions such as the place of the Netherlands within Europe. This all brought big confusion in The Netherlands. The call for good leadership in those days was immense. And then the murder of Fortuyn ..." This was a difficult period for Mr. Kok yet he had a responsibility as a leader to go on, even after the murder of Fortuyn. Creating public support and building trust again became the main priorities.

Initial learning points. "Trust is the key word. It is about gaining and maintaining trust. This requires that you respect others, otherwise you will loose it. Trusting people is also an important part because you have to trust others to delegate tasks," learned Mr. Kok. Further, Mr. Kok says that you must "express your own opinions but put that in the greater context, the common interest. Do not loose your own identity or opinion but try to find common ground with others peoples' interests."

Through different experiences in his career, he has shown that he is an excellent bridge builder "a mediator". "I do have my own opinion on issues. But in my various positions it was always necessary to mediate. I usually start with the question "what unites us." Then the parties involved could easily get a picture of each others' motives which usually results in positive energy. Sometimes you need negative energy to unite but that is not my nature," says Mr. Kok. Another learning point for Mr. Kok was that when you work with a new concept, such as in his case the formation of the cabinet, it is very, very important that you support it totally. As well, a willingness to share was very important.

Other specific experiences. Besides his role in the Agreement of Wassenaar, Mr. Kok has been recognized as a leader when he became Prime Minister leading an exceptional combination of parties (Labour-Conservative) which was very new for the Netherlands. Mr. Kok reflects that, "It was just an extra ordinary cabinet with a remarkable diversity of members. You could say that the psychological barriers that existed between his labour party (the PvdA) and the right wing party (VVD) were broken". The taboos were left to the side of the work and Mr. Kok mentions that, "it was not a natural match but it was a workable unity, a marriage of convenience."

Message to new entrepreneurs. Mr. Kok says simply; make the best of your life.

Entrepreneurship and Spirituality

Role of intuition. "Actually the role of intuition is more than you could expect in advance, when taking important decisions it counts for sure," says Mr. Kok. Because of his responsibilities however, he is mainly focused on taking good decisions for the different parties involved. Many decisions have to be taken quickly in the public domain. Therefore it is not his individual preference only that counts. In his career there were several difficult issues that tempted him to quit his position but because of the responsibility he felt, he could not. He had to persevere also in very difficult situations and to find the positive aspects in it. Mr. Kok adds, "For many people I am boring, because in the public domain things should be explained repeatedly based on rational foundations. Therefore my actions often appeared predictable."

Societal contribution. Through this selection of his experiences it becomes clear that he has acted as a leader with charisma, perseverance, trust, and a great sense of responsibility. Mr. Kok's experience has made him an entrepreneurial leader based on his capacity to mediate, to empower people and groups. Mr. Kok has been able to identify shared goals that are very important to build teams of people that are motivated to work together. The thread throughout his experience is his drive to find synthesis and cooperation to realize a better share for the common good, and his capacity to break taboos by putting the common good in the fore-front and making personal preferences less important.

Mr. Kok thinks a lot about the meaning of life, yet when he was younger he did not spend much time on it. He says that "it suits my character, I am philosophically inspired." Especially environmental issues and the current materialistic thinking trend have caught his interest, and he believes that we still only use a small part of the instruments at our disposal to feel happiness.

When asked if he has been successful, Mr. Kok replies that "the economy was flourishing, the conditions were good, and the starting point was positive, employment increased even if disability was still high. I would not say that I have been successful. Only by making nuances one could say that I have been successful in politics and in the community. I have tried to find the best solutions. Sometimes I succeed and sometimes not. Nothing was really easy." He also admits that he is very demanding of himself and even more than he is towards others. "To start as a politician is difficult. But it is still a nice experience and it gets nicer as your party flourishes. However, leaving is even more difficult. There is no right time to leave politics. You have to announce your departure in advance but the moment you do this, you have already left because than you do not feel you have authority anymore. You always have concerns there are always things that need your attention," he says.

The polder model had a good impact in those days. Internationally the model receives admiration, and Mr. Kok thinks the model is not outdated. Regarding all the community issues that are still active concerning, for example integration of culturally diverse groups, he is convinced that 'Modern Polder Model" will work. Consultation, communication and real contacts between groups do not guarantee success but it is a condition for success.

Summary Profile Wim Kok

Entrepreneurial executive roles	1973-1981: Chairman of the Dutch Confederation of Trade Unions NVV (Nederlands Verbond van Vakverenigingen) 1981-1985: After merger between NVV and the catholic trade union NKV he became chairman of the new trade union confederation, the FNV. (Federatie Nederlandse Vakbeweging) 1986: Member of Parliament for the PvdA (Partij van de Arbeid, Labor Party) 1986: Leader of the PvdA 1989-1994: Minister of Finance, Deputy Prime Minister 1994-1998: in the first cabinet he became Prime Minister of the Netherlands 1998-2002: in the second cabinet he remained in this position. 2002: retired from politics. He is still very active as corporate supervisory board member and in voluntary activities
Place of organizations / roles	The Netherlands
Involvement	His entrepreneurial executive role became dominant during the two cabinets where he had the position of prime minister.
Sector	Public sector
Community activity	Enhancing welfare of citizens by good use of the common interest and resources.
Customers	Citizens
International activities	Experience with international organizations such as the European Union, United Nations, NATO, OECD, IMF
Characteristics of an entrepreneurial executive	Breaking with taboos Charismatic leadership Introduction of a working method with international impact Although a leader-manager, he remarks that there are large differences between the role of an entrepreneurial executive in a corporate organization and in government. The biggest difference is that in politics all processes are highly transparent and the politician is a public person.

9 Venturers

9.1 Introduction

In Chapter 9 we describe eight venturers – Gerard Boskma, Lex Entrop, Jan de Jong, Erik Maassen, Michael Pullens, Bert Reeders, Philip van Rooijen, and Ger Sterken. Generally speaking, the venturers first became aware of business opportunities by working in an existing company. They subsequently started their own firms mainly with the same type of expertise they originally had in their salaried job. They are successful because they are able to apply their ideas, which they usually developed by working in an existing firm, within a new framework to realize new benefits in comparison with the old framework. Venturers are able to reframe existing activities in new ways which benefits their market position.

Mr Boskma introduced interim management activity for helping organizations in economically challenging periods. Mr. Entrop had success with aluminum doors due to his market approach of delivering directly to the builders. Mr. De Jong had to spin out the activities he built within an existing company and he believes that failures often lead to new opportunities. Mr. Maassen joined other business partners focusing on their specific expertise. Mr. Maassen's experience tells him that it is very important to realize a good fit between the different fields of expertise within a company. Another example can be found in the profile description of Mr. Van Rooijen who was an interim manager but decided to do the same type of work in his own firm. By using the network he built in his previous job, Mr. Pullens was able to bring projects into his consultancy. Mr. Reeders benefited from being able to read market trends given his extensive experience with cacao products. Mr. Sterken just proceeded with his work and started his own firm.

Mr. Entrop and Mr. Reeders felt their ventures were very successful. Mr. Boskma, Mr. Van Rooijen and Mr. De Jong also think their ventures were/are successful. Mr. Maassen thinks it is reasonably successful. Also after Mr. De Jong left, the company survived even the most difficult market circumstances. Mr. Pullens believes there is much more to achieve while Mr. Sterken thinks his venture was quite successful, but nowadays results are declining somewhat.

Venturers often face the dilemma of leaning on their previous networks or letting go. For most venturers deciding on intuition is at least as important as reason.

9.2   Gerard Boskma, Boer & Croon

After experience in the consultancy world I started a new venture activity as a spin off of the existing company (Boer & Croon). I was working as a consultant at Boer and Croon when, in 1980, there was a downward economic trend. Many firms needed analysis of their strategic competencies. These analyses resulted in implementation advice, and for some companies it was not easy to implement these recommendations. I came up with the idea to set-up a unit for interim management implementing the advice from these sort of consultancy projects. I was not the first one with such an idea, but in a very short-time Boer & Croon became the market leader in interim management expertise.

Company Profile

Company size indicators. The last three years the financial results were positive, with both headcount and turnover increasing. Turnover for the entire company is more than 50 million euro annually. At present the company has 400 full-time employees.

Company development. The employee positions are more complex nowadays in comparison with the start-up stage. There has been growth in turnover; the structure is very simple with a back office for supporting facilities. In 1980, during the economic recession, many other firms went bankrupt. Through their services of interim management they managed to stay alive. The consultancy firm is ranked high in their category.

Defining Opportunities

Evaluation criteria. When Mr. Boskma pursues a market opportunity he defines criteria in advance. Evaluation criteria he uses include questioning the need to change, assessing the willingness to change within the sector, and evaluating the quality of the directors.

Opportunity evaluation techniques. Mr. Boskma has a systematic approach to stimulate creative processes to uncover new opportunities through centers of competencies. One technique he uses is annually re-designing and re-segmenting all products or services. He continuously develops new competencies to increase their competitive advantage.

Experiences

Remarkable initial experiences. It was remarkable to notice that the financial institutions, such as banks, were not prepared for the required turnarounds that companies faced. This meant that banks were approached to think in a creative way about the financial issues in the turnaround organization. Positive factors from his start-up experience were the objective position of the interim manager being accepted within the turnaround organization. There was also government participation involved and especially then the independent position was useful. By being an outsider it was easier to confront personnel with the hard reality of their situation, and it was also possible to select good interim managers. Less simple factors included that often the supervisory boards were not familiar with the financial reality in their companies and it therefore took time to convince them how serious these situations sometimes were.

Fears and difficult decisions. He did not have fears, and Mr. Boskma's independent mind helped him in dealing with difficulties. Mr. Boskma stressed that he does not easily complain which is a necessary trait for an interim manager.

Initial learning points. Every project was an adventure and this was what was important to him. Mr. Boskma developed respect for the trade unions and works councils in companies who faced turnaround situations as you often need their support and finding quality professionals is not easy. He believes that they should have a stake in the process to ensure commitment.

Case specific experiences. The step to work from an international perspective was very challenging. Mr. Boskma searched for partnership with Egon Zehnder Executive Search who already operated internationally and this turned out to be a good match. Soon he started to work with local people in foreign countries and found it very challenging. It took a lot of effort to find excellent professionals. Another unique experience was the internal crisis in his organization after seven years. At that time he worked with 40 interim managers and about half of them decided to split off from Boer & Croon without any prior announcement; this was a difficult situation to handle. The interim managers who stayed were very loyal to him.

Message to new entrepreneurs. Take time for reflection, observe yourself, and analyze your way of functioning are all tips that Mr. Boskma believes in. Try to find out what gives you energy and what not and make decisions based on these factors are also things that Mr. Boskma works by as a general guide. Being honest with yourself, and having courage and luck on your side are also key.

Entrepreneurship and Spirituality

Role of intuition. Mr. Boskma balances his decision-making with at least 50% of the decision influenced by intuition.

Societal contribution. The company contributes through its projects, and also works in the non-profit sector with clients such as hospitals. Once per year, the company conducts a socially oriented project at a lower fee structure, for example, the supervision and management of Hortus and Sail, a non-profit organization.

Summary Profile Gerard Boskma

Previous venture	Boer & Croon Strategy and Management Group
Place of business	Amsterdam, The Netherlands
Founding year	1973
Involvement	1980 till 2005
Business sector	Services
Venture activity	Management consulting and interim management
Customers	Corporate customers and public sector
International activities	UK, France, Italy, Germany, Spain and USA through minority interests and partnership with Eghon Zender Executive Search
Company strengths	Management of people Good relationship network
Company weaknesses	Virtual organization. There were four directors while the interim managers were not on the payroll. The freelance construction makes the organization vulnerable when resources are not available.

9.3 Lex Entrop, Intal

I was selected in London to run the Shell agency in Surinam in 1955. After some years I became a manager for other agencies as well, namely the Ford and Firestone Agency. During this time I noticed that the country could benefit from entrepreneurial activities, and recognized that there were opportunities for new business. I had some knowledge of tires and I decided to set-up a tire recapping business. At one point I found my tasks for the Shell agency were completed. When I re-emigrated to the Netherlands I became manager of a pump factory where I set-up a new series of pumps for some years. In 1968 I was invited to start Intal (international aluminum corporation). I set-up another company, Entropal in 1989 for the production, delivery and installation of aluminum windows and doors. I started this activity when I was 59 years old.

Company Profile

Company size indicators. The last three years of his involvement at Intal he achieved positive financial results. The turnover was also stable for the last two years, with an increase in employee numbers. The turnover was between 5 and 10 million euro per year. In 1968 he started on his own and by the end of that year he had seven employees. When he left the company in 1988 there were 100 employees.

Company development. In 1968 he was invited to start Intal. Three companies were involved: Lips in Drunen, with expertise in ship propellers and aluminum extrusions, an American company International Aluminum Corporation in Los Angeles (IAC) with expertise in the design of windows, and Eland Brand in Amsterdam, where there was a factory already. IAC and Eland Brand owned 50% and Lips owned the other 50%.

The personnel of Intal changed because of internal education programMs. In the 20 years while Mr. Entrop was director, the company earned about 6 million euro profit after tax. He was the only director working with four commissioners (two of each parent company). The company expanded enormously when it built factories in other locations and even incorporated an ultra modern double-glass production unit.

Concerning their strategic approach, the company worked to deliver standardized measures so they could produce high quantities at lower costs. Later on there were other preferences among the buyers, first a demand for single glazing, and later an increase in demand for double-glazing. The company delivered to the contractors from the beginning. Later on direct deliveries to the builder's merchants for resale to private individuals was organized. The company had to change continuously, adapting their programs for production.

Intal does not exist anymore and the successor of Lips was Alcoa. Alcoa bought the remaining 50% of Intal from IAC and changed the focus of the company towards commercial and industrial building. Mr. Entrop and the other commissioner decided to leave the company because they thought the new focus was not credible. The deal was that Alcoa would pay his salary until he was 65 years old and then they would pay the pension that had accumulated. Alcoa did not succeed and the business was sold in pieces. At that time he was 59 years old and started Entropal with the party that had built the factory. Alcoa found out about this start-up and threatened to end his pension. Mr. Entrop then transferred the business to his brother. In the first two companies, Surufa and Intal, he did not take financial risks but in the third company he did assume some financial risk. After three years he transferred his shares to his brother.

Defining Opportunities

Evaluation criteria. Mr. Entrop mentions that when he pursues a market opportunity he defines the criteria with which to evaluate the opportunity in advance and afterwards he evaluates why it worked or why it didn't work. The most important criteria are turnover, profitability, and feasibility for the organization.

Opportunity evaluation techniques. Mr. Entrop also mentions that there were a lot of stimulators in the market. He had to think originally, and maintain a degree of independence from the current situation. In his company he had personal contacts with everybody in order to stimulate them, for example designers had to work product oriented and sellers had to work market oriented. He used the following techniques often, such as continuously redesigning products with a focus on expansion, re-differentiation of products with a focus on production of series, developing competencies aimed at creating competitive advantages and making assembly simpler through the use of special tools.

Experiences

Remarkable initial experiences. With the company Surufa, he did not possess ownership of any land; eventually three people bought three adjacent plots of land and they built a factory. The ministry of economic affairs helped them as well, and for five years they were free from paying tax.

In Intal he approached several architects who told him that his company would not be able to compete with the wooden windows. Mr. Entrop used advertisement, which was expensive for the company, to convince people their aluminum windows and doors were competitively priced and worth the investment. As a result, he received orders from housing corporations and asked them to pay 40% in advance. After two years all the starting capital costs (50,000 NLG) were earned back.

When he started Intal he rented a factory for production purposes. Some years later he bought land and built a 40,000 square meter factory that he expanded after two years into 60,000 square meters and after another two years he had a factory of 100,000 square meters. There was room for production and distribution. Later on he started a glass factory within the same building in order to expand the production of double glazing.

Fears and difficult decisions. He did not have fears as Mr. Entrop was convinced that it was worth developing the activities he was working on. His father-in-law and administrator were not always easy to work with at the start of the new enterprise, and at times there were difficult discussions.

Initial learning points. Mr. Entrop did not dream of starting and developing businesses. In Surufa his involvement concerned the start-up process and in Intal he continuously was trying to develop new products. In both cases he learned to be very tenacious, to develop continuously, and to think originally. It is very important to decide how to choose a market approach: the builder's merchant or directly through the builders. Mr. Entrop was satisfied with the second option, although he did continue with about 20% of direct business to merchants. Another learning experience occurred during the separation from Intal, which was painful but a reasoned decision. When Alcoa bought it and wanted to move to the utility building he tendered market research. The results predicted that the new focus would not succeed. It was hard to leave the employees that he hired himself but he could not go on with it because his faith in success was lacking.

Case specific experiences. Government policy prescribed the installation of cantilever windows for ventilation. It was only after Intal showed that the ventilation grille that they invented had better testing results than the cantilever window, based on results from the Dutch scientific research office (TNO), that the government altered their regulation. Having seized this new opportunity, Intal penetrated the market successfully.

Message to new entrepreneurs. As a message to new entrepreneurs, Mr. Entrop believes that it is important to persevere and focus, have original thinking, innovate and try to tackle problems in a new way, work with enthusiasm because this will inspire others and work in a goal oriented way.

Entrepreneurship and Spirituality

Role of intuition. Intuition certainly plays a role when approaching certain problems, according to Mr. Entrop.

Societal contribution. With Surufa he contributed to the labor market and savings of foreign currency which was very important for Surinam. In Intal he offered better windows for the same price. And although Entropal was less innovative according to Mr. Entrop, the company did reach a broader market than the other companies.

Summary Profile Lex Entrop

Previous venture	Intal B.V.
Other ventures	Surufa B.V. in Paramaribo, Surinam in 1961 Entropal B.V. in Geldermalsen, The Netherlands
Place of business	Geldermalsen, The Netherlands
Founding year	1968
Involvement	1968 to 1988
Business sector	Metal industry
Venture activity	Design, produce, supply and install aluminum windows and doors with glass for, among others, houses, schools, offices
Customers	Contractors in the housing, schools, offices etc.
International activities	Germany, France, Switzerland and Algeria – Intal windows and doors were exported to Algeria following an earthquake in that country
Company strengths	The company was very competitive especially towards wooden windows and doors; Intal windows were practical and needed no maintenance. Because of production in a company owned factory, the company was very flexible in service and profitable. They had a unique way of assembling. All products had a short delivery time.
	The dependence on contractors for installation when the products including assembly were delivered
Company weaknesses	The company was not equipped for utility building They had to anticipate new requirements from the markets

Company Profile

Company size indicators. The company was profitable last year, and headcount and turnover increased. Turnover varies between 2 and 5 million euro annually. At present he has 25 full-time employees, and in the last three years did not realize positive financial results.

Company development. There are no changes in personnel education or in organization structure, yet there is high growth in turnover. The firm has gone through a professional stage which requires a more funded approach. In some areas the firm is a market leader. Mr. Maassen was involved with the take-over of a databank led by the publishing group Reed Elsevier.

Defining Opportunities

Evaluation criteria. When Mr. Maassen pursues a market opportunity he only evaluates it afterwards. His judgment was always based on feeling and ideas of employees. He currently works with a more procedural approach.

Opportunity evaluation techniques. Mr. Maassen has no systematic approach to stimulate his creative processes. Yet, one technique he uses is to re-differentiate all products or services to improve them. When it is necessary, he re-segments the market. Finally, he develops new competencies to increase his competitive advantage.

Experiences

Remarkable initial experiences. He noticed that receiving a salary every month was no longer a normal thing and he noticed also that when it comes to spending money he was very critical. When he became a business partner the positive thing for him was his working experience within the firm. People there trusted him and he was familiar with the challenges within the firm. In his second entrepreneurial adventure, people he knew were involved and he found that to be a positive experience. The most challenging part was obtaining positive financial results.

Fears and difficult decisions. Mr. Maassen did not have real fears; he started without any business plan, pretty much uninhibited. Difficult decisions involved the dismissal of personnel that didn't meet expectations.

Initial learning points. If he would start-up again he would do it more thoroughly. Mr. Maassen would not only act on the basis of enthusiasm. He has experienced that as an entrepreneur you must face a lot of practical issues he is not familiar with at all, nor has heard about from entrepreneurs, and some of these issues can lead to significant worries.

Case specific experiences. Mr. Maassen was involved with the take-over of a databank from the advice group Elsevier. It was a unique experience for him to work with a professional working group to realize this initiative. Having a good match between the several expertise amongst those involved in the working group was worthwhile.

Message to new entrepreneurs. Entrepreneurship is not only about success stories of Unilever, Ahold or Heineken says Mr. Maassen, entrepreneurship is also about fuss and hassle.

Entrepreneurship and Spirituality

Role of intuition. He makes use of intuition a lot, more than 50%.

Societal contribution. The support Mr. Maassen gives to the small accountancy offices; advice about IT and sale of his market vision are his contributions to society. He is also working on a knowledge platform on accountancy topics.

Summary Profile Erik Maassen

Current venture	Full•Finance Consultants
Place of business	Apeldoorn, The Netherlands
Founding year	End of 1999
Involvement	1999 to the present
Business sector	Services
Venture activity	Consults with accountancy firms and departments on such topics as IT, communication, management and organization, and technical knowledge. Supervision of acquisition and merger processes.
Customers	Accountancy firms
International activities	None
Company strengths	Knowledge of the market
Company weaknesses	Small firm

Company development. Considering the educational quality of the personnel, the company benefited from highly qualified employees. The financial performance, such as turnover, increased as a result of acquisition and expansion over time. And, the company was reconfigured into a holding structure. Considering the strategy, integration occurred both vertically and horizontally. As well, the market share increased a great deal. There were also changes in the customers, with an increase in the number of clients.

Defining Opportunities

Evaluation criteria. Mr. Reeders pursued opportunities defining criteria during the process. Market growth and distinctive product qualities were important.

Opportunity evaluation techniques. Mr. Reeders did not have a systematic approach to stimulate creative processes. Techniques he used included the redesign of products or services (using a methodology called attribute mapping) and developing breakthrough competencies or areas of competitive strength that worked to create new competitive advantages.

Experiences

Remarkable initial experiences. Mr. Reeders always maintained a very independent position when he moved to New York. There were no faxes, poor phone services, and no telex yet when he started his position in New York; communication with the home office was always difficult. In that situation, trust was very important. The most positive factors were that the small trading company in Amsterdam with a new American partner was welcomed in the European community, and he had knowledge of commodity trading techniques which were then novel in Europe which he learned in the US. He also had knowledge of derivatives, term markets, and hedging. Negative factors in the initial phase included the need to break into the local business community, and sourcing raw materials from risky countries.

Fears and difficult decisions. Mr. Reeders didn't have any fears, yet the most difficult time of his life was during WWII. Looking back, he has no regrets whatsoever about his career. Although at times, he worked too hard. Taking over Kupsch in the two years after he returned from New York was very intensive. Initially, the Kupsch people did not like this at all; he was after all one of them originally.

Initial learning points. For Mr. Reeders it is important to have a really inspired team around you at all times and to realize that you cannot do it alone. Using financial leverage is also a valuable tool.

Case specific experiences. A new differentiation of cacao related products and services had to be explored leading to its use in many more products then just chocolate and chocolate milk. For this project it was necessary to take a very broad view of the market to discover new uses and applications for cacao and this also required being able to read market trends. Mr. Reeders became involved in product processing in cacao producing developing countries of origin. There he found that local laws corruption to be difficult factors. In another situation, the 42 shareholders of the company did not desire dividends for 20 years and preferred to invest the profits into the business. That meant that the company was never fully leveraged as there was always plenty of shareholder money available. In retrospect, he intervened in this financing situation too late. Still, the company was sold to Cargill in 1987 for 1.6 billion Dutch Guilders, making shareholders very happy.

Message to new entrepreneurs. Mr. Reeders' message to new entrepreneurs is to learn to tolerate the mistakes you make and to set very clear goals. Also, don't wait too long, it is better to intervene sooner rather than later in a potentially problematic situation. And also of great importance, listen to your spouse or partner, and always work to create an environment of trust.

Entrepreneurship and Spirituality

Role of intuition. Intuition plays a significant role for Mr. Reeders, and he estimates that nearly 70% of his decisions are based on intuition.

Societal contribution. Mr. Reeders contributes to society with the creation of jobs and through the support of environmental issues and charity. He does not like corruption at all, and maintains high values in all his dealings. He also appreciates a broad image of social responsibility from companies, and admires the concept of worker councils in companies.

Summary Profile Bert Reeders

Previous venture	General Cocoa Company Holland B.V.
Place of business	Amsterdam, the Netherlands
Founding year	1962
Involvement	1962 to 1990
Business sector	Food industry
Venture activity	Merchandise and Industry in cacao and coffee
Customers	Chocolate industry, bakeries, and dairy industry
International activities	Almost the whole world for sale and purchase activities Purchase in: Africa, South America and Asia Sale: Europe, Asia, North America and Australia
Company strengths	The entrepreneurial mind, the team spirit, the customer orientation, the control of risks
Company weaknesses	Sometimes there were no successful new initiatives

9.8   Philip van Rooijen, C2Results

I held various positions at Versatel, The Netherlands Railways, and Nauta Dutihl (attorneys) before and after I did my executive MBA at Nyenrode. Some of the positions were in Germany and France. When I was a lawyer I found out that I enjoyed being an entrepreneur and became an interim manager at Versatel. After this position I decided to continue this type of assignment, but as an entrepreneur. I started C2Results for search assignment and coaching, together with four partners.

Company Profile

Company size indicators. During the last three years the financial results were positive. Headcount decreased while turnover increased and turnover is between 2 and 5 million euro per year. Mr. Van Rooijen started alone and at present the firm has a headcount of 5.5 employees, based on full-time employment.

Company development. The structure of the company changed to four partners, and besides interim management, coaching and search services are also offered. Mr. Van Rooijen focuses on medium sized companies and operating divisions of large concerns. The company enjoys a good reputation because of the quality service provided at competitive prices. At present, he deals with multiple customers.

Defining Opportunities

Evaluation criteria. Mr. Van Rooijen mentions that when he pursues a market opportunity he defines the criteria on the go. Criteria used include assessing the level of challenge, type of the company, feasibility of expected results according to the company, the quality of the interim manager, and less important criteria are the fee and the time schedule of the project.

Opportunity evaluation techniques. Mr. Van Rooijen occasionally uses brainstorming as a technique for creative thinking.

Experiences

Remarkable initial experiences. He has an enormous drive to develop and implement, to create new ideas and realize opportunities. Mr. Van Rooijen's first project was for his previous employer, and that made the start-up much easier. In addition, his partners all have complementary competencies. Other stimulators are the network of his business partners and their drive and enthusiasm. Less easy was the fact that the position of interim management does not have a positive image. Finally, C2Results was too small.

Fears and difficult decisions. He never has fears but sometimes things feel awkward. For example, it was difficult to separate one of the partners from the business.

Initial learning points. Mr. Van Rooijen never dreamt of having this kind of business. He is gradually growing into the business and has learned that an integrative approach to management works best for him. He also feels that it is important to realize that it is not only knowledge, and that you must work to bring together the right people to create success. Finally, he stresses that you must be loyal towards your people because you need them for the business.

Case specific experiences. Switching from being a lawyer to becoming an entrepreneur was quite an experience. Mr. Van Rooijen found it important to think over every step carefully because then you can adjust your plans if needed.

Message to new entrepreneurs. Have passion, be enthusiastic, have self confidence and, finally, truly believing in what you are doing are the most important messages Mr. Van Rooijen has for new entrepreneurs.

Entrepreneurship and Spirituality

Role of intuition. He feels that he uses intuition often yet always confirms his decision with rational arguments.

Societal contribution. Mr. Van Rooijen strives to conduct his business in a responsible manner.

Summary Profile Philip van Rooijen

Current venture	C2Results B.V.
Place of business	Baarn, The Netherlands
Founding year	2001
Involvement	2001 to the present
Business sector	Interim-management
Venture activity	Search and recruit executives for interim management and consultancy. The fields of expertise are: finance, human resources, marketing & sales, communication and general management. The name C2Results indicates Committed to Results: no-nonsense, pragmatic, solution driven and implementation driven.
Customers	C2Results executes projects for the media, telecom / ICT, finance, logistics and financial services sectors
International activities	Germany and France Assignments for foreign subsidiaries of Dutch companies
Company strengths	Strong in developing and executing a no-nonsense vision and getting it done
Company weaknesses	Too small Time for acquisition versus time for executing the assignments

9.9   Ger Sterken, Interleaf

I worked for A.L. van Beek N.V., one of the most important European businesses in tobacco, for 10 years in Copenhagen where I lived with my family. Then I moved back to Holland and worked from the head office in Rotterdam. Because of my job responsibilities I had to travel quite a lot and thus built a large network within the tobacco sector. After A.L. van Beek N.V. was taken over by one of the largest (US) dealer companies in the world in 1987, I found myself out of job and my business friends suggested that I start my own tobacco business so I could continue the same type of work. After years working as an entrepreneur, one of my big foreign suppliers asked me to work exclusively for them. For me this was a significant opportunity. Years later this supplier also was taken over by the same US company that took over A.L. van Beek N.V. This offered me the possibility to work with new suppliers and continue the Interleaf business.

Company Profile

Company size indicators. The past three years realized positive financial results and headcount remained stable as turnover decreased. Turnover for the company varies between 2 and 5 million euro annually and at present the company does not employ other personnel.

Company development. The firm has not faced major changes in personnel, financial situation, strategic approach, or position in the market yet the structure changed into a limited company and turnover has decreased somewhat.

Defining Opportunities

Evaluation criteria. When Mr. Sterken pursues a market opportunity he defines criteria during the process.

Opportunity evaluation techniques. Mr. Sterken has no systematic approach to stimulate creative processes to uncover new opportunities. In his view, situations change all the time, therefore a such an approach would not work. Today, he finds himself in a position to harvest opportunities.

Experiences

Remarkable initial experiences. Mr. Sterken started his own venture in order to continue working in a style as during the A.L. van Beek period. As well, several people within his network asked him and he found himself much too young to stop working and too old for looking for a new employer. So he just started his own company. In the start-up stage he had many contacts already. And although the image of cigarette smoking declined in popularity, Mr. Sterken also noticed that in the Far East and in Africa many more people were smoking cigarettes than (in comparison with) the West. But here in Western Europe he saw the explosion of the smoking of roll-your-own.

Fears and difficult decisions. He did not have fears or difficulties, and Mr. Sterken found it was a logical process to continue with his activities, also because he had always liked his work.

Initial learning points. The main reason for many of his business activities in the sector had to do with the possibility to travel, especially to Scandinavia, a part of the world he and his wife liked so much.

Case specific experiences. The most unique experiences for Mr. Sterken were related to his travels. He traveled to 16 African countries, several in South America, the Middle- and also the Far East and throughout all of Europe. From these experiences, history (VOC) became one of his keen interests. Today, his activities concentrate on the Dutch industry, Scandinavia, Belgium and Germany. He knows the requirements of these buyers so he does not need to do a lot of research anymore and relationships are based on trust with his suppliers and buyers.

Message to new entrepreneurs. To new entrepreneurs Mr. Sterken says that before you accept a job think about your own qualities, don't look solely at the short-term material aspects of the job, but judge what your possibilities are on the long run. He also feels that avoiding job hopping can help you find value in the opportunities you have at that moment. In addition, he would encourage people to try to become very good in a field so that people will ultimately seek out your services. And most importantly says Mr. Sterken, "when facing setbacks – don't give up, never!"

Entrepreneurship and Spirituality

Role of intuition. For Mr. Sterken, his decision-making process is a combination of rational thinking and intuition.

Societal contribution. Mr. Sterken does not see his business activities as contributing to society.

Summary Profile Ger Sterken

Current venture	Interleaf B.V.
Place of business	Leersum, The Netherlands
Founding year	1987
Involvement	1987 to the present
Business sector	Wholesale in leaf tobacco
Venture activity	Trading between suppliers and industry
Customers	Producers of cigarettes, hand rolling (shag) tobacco and cigars
International activities	The manufacturers are in Scandinavia, Holland, Belgium and Germany
Company strengths	Personal contacts with suppliers and customers
Company weaknesses	As a solo operator, he does not work with the very largest producers. Those do their business directly with the three big suppliers (US) in the world.

10 Re-launchers

10.1 Introduction

In Chapter 10 we describe eight re-launchers – Britt Blomsma, Erik Brink, Dick Houtman, Wim de Knoop, Michael Moore, Peter Ruigrok, Marjon Velthuis, and Evert Versluis. The re-launchers bought or took over a company in order to develop it further based on their own efforts and vision.

Questioning how these re-launchers realize success is the focus of this chapter. Ms. Blomsma and her business partner, Mulder, bought part of a firm heading towards bankruptcy. With their systematic approach towards marketing the firm flourished. Mr. Brink was pressured to develop new concepts when he noticed that the agreement he thought he had with the mother company, did not work out. His self confidence and the support of his business partner Hiemstra, also motivated his new approach to the market. Mr. Houtman was asked by a friend to get into a new venture where his systematic approach to collecting performance-based data works because it provides a base line for focusing on new markets. Another profile in this chapter is Mr. De Knoop who buys unprofitable businesses in order to turn them around and make them profitable. Mr. Moore has been able to completely reorganize the firm he bought and is achieving positive results. Focusing activities of the company was a key strategy in his approach.

Mr. Ruigrok's description gives an example of managing unmet expectations in a sector that faced many diseases such as BSE, or foot-and mouth disease.

Ms. Velthuis' profile gives an example of how to put extra effort into realizing growth by buying a firm and spinning out more activities Mr. Versluis experienced what can go wrong in a firm that was bought and faced many difficulties from day one.

It seems that one of the main characteristics of a re-launcher is the marketing approach and adopting a pro-active approach to market trends and needs. These entrepreneurs have to deal with the dilemma of putting aside the history of the previous firm or previous activities and networks. Former employees sometimes resist changes that seem necessary in the judgment of the re-launcher. The majority of the re-launchers use intuition as an important tool in the decision-making processes.

On the question 'is your company successful?' Ms. Blomsma answered as follows: Considering the saturated boat market and the poor economy, very successful Mr. Brink's answer was: from 2001 until 2003 the emphasis was on product development, with innovation and renewal as the main themes. With a hardworking team and through taking risks, we were able to develop new products for new markets. When the products proved successful in the market, this strengthened the organization commercially and professionally. Important themes are now market development and client retention. Management made the right choices at the right moment. According to Mr. Houtman his venture is successful, considering the circumstances. According to Mr. De Knoop his venture is also successful but could still do much better. Mr. Moore and Ms. Velthuis judged their ventures successful. Mr. Ruigrok answered as follows: success is a process, not an outcome. So, it depends on the picture that you look at in a given moment of time. Success of a venture is based on efforts of a whole team. According to him his company is successful if it is making a contribution to the well-being of society. That is not the case yet. Making profit is a necessary condition to fulfill that mission. The process is more important than the result, is one of his favorite quotes. Mr. Versluis judges his work as reasonably successful and he adds that he can really live with the successes.

10.2 Britt Blomsma, GeuzenBoats

I studied Social and Cultural Sciences, with a concentration in culture, organization and management at the Free University, Amsterdam and completed an International MBA at Nyenrode (2001-2002). From 1996-2001 I worked as a recruitment consultant. Living in Scotland and Oman as a child, I also spent time in South Africa to complete my studies and for work (1994-1996). After my MBA graduation, I found myself in a consultancy position that I did not enjoy and after six months I quit. At that moment, together with my boyfriend Titus Mulder, there was an opportunity to buy the boat building part of a larger company. The company was facing bankruptcy, and we both felt it was a good opportunity. For Mulder coming from an entrepreneurial family, starting a business was a dream.

Company Profile

Company size indicators. The company was profitable last year, with both the total number of employees and turnover increasing. Turnover is less than 1 million euro annually. When Ms. Blomsma joined the company there were four full-time employees and when she left the company last year it had eight full-time employees and positive financial results.

Company development. Ms. Blomsma details that the start-up phase was very hectic yet soon the first steps for forming a professional organization came into place. The business focus shifted from product orientation towards market orientation, and marketing and sales became central to the strategic approach. During this initial period of development, Ms. Blomsma noted that the position of the company in the market moved from third place to a shared first place. In addition, the customer profile changed as well, reaching from the private market into the business market and extending beyond just Friesland. The business image changed as well. It is also important to note that the core personnel within the company are craftsmen. In addition, the part of the company that was taken over had a turnover of about 250.000 euro annually, later in the first fiscal year of GeuzenBoats (2004); the turnover was almost 1 million euro.

Defining Opportunities

Evaluation criteria. To Ms. Blomsma, pursuing a market opportunity means defining the criteria in advance and evaluating the on-going process. Her evaluation criteria include focusing on what the benefits might be, what profits are possible, what time is involved, the feasibility, and understanding what the opportunity costs are.

Opportunity evaluation techniques. Ms. Blomsma had a systematic approach to stimulate creative processes to uncover new opportunities via internet research, and talking with other entrepreneurs, customers and friends. One technique she and Mulder used in the business involved re-designing all products or services to improve them. When necessary, Ms. Blomsma re-segmented or re-defined the market, deliberately crossing established boundaries. Finally, Ms. Blomsma continuously sought to develop new competencies to increase their competitive advantage.

Experiences

Remarkable initial experiences. Ms. Blomsma was convinced they could improve the product and do things better to develop the part of the company they bought. She noticed that the shipbuilding industry was very informal compared to the more formal interaction of other business sectors in larger cities she was used to. In Friesland, business was more locally oriented and deals were made on a very informal basis. Factors that contributed to making their start-up easier were based on the business, marketing and financial knowledge they had. In Ms. Blomsma's opinion, this was also their competitive advantage in comparison with other companies. Yet they did face challenges that included a lack of specific industry knowledge, limited experience with the production and maintenance of boats and taking over a bankrupt venture also means taking over the chaos. There were 40 boats in the port yet nobody knew who the owners were, what appointments had been made with these owners, and there were no contact details associated with any of the boats.

Fears and difficult decisions. Ms. Blomsma could not list any real fears yet she did have stress when thinking about the new business. She questioned whether their activities and energies would produce what they intended, and would they realize success. The most difficult decision Ms. Blomsma faced was accepting a high degree of risk by approaching a bank and a business angel for money to invest and to expand the business.

Initial learning points. Looking back on her experience, Ms. Blomsma emphasizes that one must think seriously about starting a company with a partner. It is crucial to know the person that you intend to work with and also consider the consequences if the working relationship fails. Ms. Blomsma also feels that this applies to working with a business angel, and stresses that it is important to understand what expectations that person or group might have. Given the opportunity to start another company, Ms. Blomsma knows she would begin by developing more specific, written agreements and that especially the financial arrangements must be thoroughly documented and in professional order.

Case specific experiences. As an alternative solution when faced with no advertising budget, Ms. Blomsma encourages visiting professional fairs and events. In one year Ms. Blomsma was able to win 10 business clients by visiting fairs. And, the message about the business continued to spread beyond the boundaries of any one fair, working in favor of the business. Another strategy Ms. Blomsma employed was creating a list of water sports companies from the telephone book and calling them. As a follow up, Ms. Blomsma mailed them offers and cards to ensure that she could establish name recognition with GeuzenBoats among potential clients. She also submitted editorial pieces to selected publications and magazines as a method to increase their visibility. Another effort included approaching the Olympic sailing team with the possibility of sailing the national Dutch Matchrace championships in boats built by GeuzenBoats. Ms. Blomsma also designed a brochure for the company, and that was a true innovation within the sector.

Message to new entrepreneurs. Being an entrepreneur is a very nice experience and she believes that in the very near future she will start again. Her key messages to new entrepreneurs: Just do it, Give it a chance. Don't think you first need a very brilliant unique idea to start. Try to do things better than your competitors and then you will have results. A good team is very important.

Entrepreneurship and Spirituality

Role of intuition. Ms. Blomsma bases her decision-making process more on rational thinking (80%) and less on intuitive feeling (20%).

Societal contribution. Until the end of 2004, Ms. Blomsma was involved with the business, and her company offered jobs in the local community and contributed to charities.

Summary Profile Britt Blomsma

Previous venture	GeuzenBoats B.V.
Other ventures	Happy Ambition, a company which was a partner in GeuzenBoats
Place of business	Sneek, Friesland, The Netherlands
Founding year	2003
Involvement	2003-2005
Business sector	Shipbuilding industry and watersports
Venture activity	GeuzenBoats builds sells and leases sailboats. Current models are Geuzenvalk and Tirion 'One Design'.
Customers	Individual customers and water sport companies such as boat rentals, sailing schools and outdoor and camping parks, 80% The Netherlands, 20% International
International activities	Germany, Belgium and eventually other countries. Through boat shows and other marketing such as websites, magazines and dealers.
Company strengths	Network Angel network Loyal and adaptable staff Strategically competitive, professional, efficient production, economies of scale, creative marketing Active sales strategy, administrative and financial control, complementary personalities of owners
Company weaknesses	Initial lack of production know-how and experience. Relatively less professional in terms of costing, business and strategic planning Conflicting characters of owners-entrepreneurs

10.3 Erik Brink, WeerOnline

I started my company in 2001 through a management buy-out. Now I am owner /
managing director together with Gerrit Hiemstra, my business partner. I became
an entrepreneur because of my drive to achieve, to be my own boss, to take my
own decisions and to establish my own vision. Hiemstra is the expert in meteorol-
ogy and I am the business developer.

Company Profile

Company size indicators. The turnover is less than 1 million euro. When Mr. Brink
started the firm, it had six employees, and currently there are 12. Turnover has increased and during the last three years positive financial results were achieved.

Company development. The average employee education level is somewhat lower now, at the start the average level of education was college and graduate education. In the beginning stage, new product development requiring a high level of training was necessary and now that more tasks are standardized, fewer experts are needed. Turnover doubled in the last four years. Standardization was implemented in four departments; the weather room, IT, sales and marketing, and management. In the coming years investments are necessary in middle management and in a shift from product to market development.

Defining Opportunities

Evaluation criteria. When Mr. Brink pursues an opportunity he evaluates afterwards if the criteria were appropriate. Criteria he uses frequently include assessing the bottom line, a key! To meet this need, the company looks closely at the ability to segment and differentiate, market position, gross margin, and investment in marketing and sales.

Opportunity evaluation techniques. Mr. Brink approaches stimulating creative processes systematically. He visits fairs and seminars, talks with other entrepreneurs, uses the Internet often and reads newspapers and journals. He applies the following techniques as well: redesign of products, annual product re-segmentation, redefining market boundaries and creating competitive advantages.

Experiences

Remarkable initial experiences. The start-up of the company was easy in Mr. Brink's opinion. They prepared a business plan and found a source of finance. Just after that initial period the real experience started, and according to Mr. Brink they had to go through the school of hard knocks. The positive factor was that they got finance for their plans. On the challenge side they did not have enough resources when they started, and because of the management buyout there was some basic turnover guaranteed but within one month they lost 30% of the turnover. Things went differently than expected. They agreed that the parent company from whom the activities were bought would act as a preferred supplier for them but instead the parent company went ahead working with Mr. Brink's biggest competitor. This resulted in a lawsuit which Mr. Brink won.

Fears and difficult decisions. The big fear was the uncertainty. There was no money to pay the costs and there were times when Mr. Brink thought he would not succeed. The difficult decisions he had to take was the dismissal of personnel.

Initial learning points. As a boy, Mr. Brink dreamt of having his own business. After having experienced a somewhat difficult start-up, looking back Mr. Brink says that he would start smaller, simpler and collect more finance to start with. He has learned to make better written agreements, and that trust is not enough. Afterwards he reflected that although it was difficult, it worked out well because they had to be innovative from the beginning.

Case specific experiences. The most unique experience is that every day he is an entrepreneur. A manager manages a business for someone else, but as an entrepreneur you do it for yourself. Things can be enjoyable yet when you make false decisions you cannot blame others and your decisions have immediate consequences for your bank account and this makes you more cautious.

Message to new entrepreneurs. Mr. Brink believes that not every one is suitable for entrepreneurship, it is a lonely activity. If you are an entrepreneur then you don't think in terms of barriers and this perspective gives you the possibility to be creative; you can put a lot of effort in it.

Entrepreneurship and Spirituality

Role of intuition. Intuition does play a role for Mr. Brink; about 70%, and it is always a dominant influence in a small firm.

Societal contribution. Doing business in an ethical fashion is one of the values of their venture. Care for safety in bad weather is another value. When bad weather is expected WeatherOnline inform their customers directly and accurately, and this information is offered as a free service at the moment.

Summary Profile Erik Brink

Current venture	Company: WeerOnline B.V. (WeatherOnline)
Place of business	Arnhem, The Netherlands
Founding year	2001
Involvement	2001 to date
Business sector	Publisher / media
Venture activity	WeerOnline publishes weather reports
Customers	Consumers, newspapers, broadcasters, internet publishers, travel agencies, government, farmers, construction companies, insurance companies, recreation companies, water companies
International activities	WeerOnline works closely with WetterOnline in Germany, WeatherOnline in the U.K., and t7online in China. The cooperation is focusing on creating meteorological knowledge and product development.
Company strengths	Innovative Flexibility, IT driven
Company weaknesses	Experience Vulnerable in terms of size

10.4 Dick Houtman, Gooiconsult

I completed a MBA and got used to the adrenaline level that comes from business experience. Additionally, I became acquainted with viewing an entrepreneurial world that couldn't be matched by working at a bank. I was asked by a friend to get into a new venture and that made the transition easier. I am too much of an entrepreneur not to have direct influence on my environment. Thus, in a corporate environment, I do not function very well as I feel I would have to leave too much of my creativity and decisiveness behind. Finally, I do not feel at home in an environment where it is necessary to be preoccupied with shareholders value as I find that too restricting to stay enthusiastic over time.

Company Profile

Company size indicators. The company was profitable last year, and both head-count and turnover increased. Turnover varies between 2 and 5 million euro annually. At present the company has 35 full-time employees and since his involvement, financial results have shown average marginal profitability.

Company development. Staff members usually have backgrounds in psychology or sociology. Mr. Houtman started to employ people from the business sector to add another dimension to their services. He would like to focus more on strategic advice for improving performance. Financial growth is steady and slowly they are acquiring assignments with larger customers. All activities have been put under one umbrella and there is one director with a staff supporting the primary processes. Compared with other firms in the sector that offer the same expertise the difference is, according to Mr. Houtman, that his group offers more practical oriented advice while competitors have a more theoretical orientation. Also, projects are much more framed by strategic topics.

Defining Opportunities

Evaluation criteria. When Mr. Houtman pursues a market opportunity he defines criteria in advance and during the process evaluates them. Evaluation criteria question if there is a fit with business and personal values, can they be profitable and what are the requirements for that, is it manageable and, finally does it contribute to fun and new experiences.

Opportunity evaluation techniques. Mr. Houtman has a systematic approach to stimulate creative processes to uncover new opportunities, so seven times per year he organizes 'office days' to enhance creativity. This is the inside-out approach, according to Mr. Houtman. They also have an outside-in approach to identify what concerns preoccupy customers. On a weekly basis they talk about customer questions. One technique Mr. Houtman uses is to annually re-design all products or services. Once a year he also re-differentiates all products or services. When deemed necessary, he re-segments or redefines the market, crossing established boundaries. Finally, Mr. Houtman continuously develops new competencies to increase competitive advantage and they strive to practice what they preach.

Experiences

Remarkable initial experiences. Realizing that the corporate world takes good care of you in terms of salary and benefits was a discovery for Mr. Houtman. He welcomed the fact that you are in a position to make many decision on your own and that a bad decision impacts you directly and immediately. Stimulators during the start-up phase of the venture were completing his MBA, and experiencing how conservative and frugal banks can be. Mr. Houtman was paid two salary grades below the actual position level, and was greatly annoyed by this and ultimately decided to leave that position to start his own business. Some of the difficult factors related to starting the business included the lack of money available and a feeling of risk aversion from home.

Fears and difficult decisions. Mr. Houtman was faced with many questions, among them he worked to answer whether he had the big picture in view, what his financial situation was, and how would his family react to business development. He was very frugal and when things were difficult he tried it again and he was very determined not to go bankrupt. Mr. Houtman was always concerned that he would perhaps not succeed and he couldn't stand the idea of having to return to the corporate world. In his opinion, all decisions have pros and cons. Once you become an entrepreneur you cannot cover risks the way you were used to. And Mr. Houtman feels that you must learn to live with uncertainty as an entrepreneur.

Initial learning points. Among his initial learning points, Mr. Houtman learned that he would look for a better developed plan and he would be more careful with whom to go into a venture. As well, it is important to balance optimistic thinking with realities and to share experiences and results when it is possible.

Case specific experiences. Mr. Houtman mentions that his work concentrates on three characteristics: competencies (including knowledge and skills), performance and results orientation. Of course, these are linked with each other. Even in a low innovation sector it is possible to realize measurable results. Mr. Houtman starts his work with collection of data, and he finds that many of the current trainers resist this approach. Yet, he has invested in his business formula now for four years and feels that many trainers are not very business oriented. As a result, Mr. Houtman teaches them to focus more on the goals of the customers and to become more market oriented.

Message to new entrepreneurs. Mr. Houtman's message to new entrepreneurs is just do it and be economical with your reputation.

Entrepreneurship and Spirituality

Role of intuition. He makes use of his intuition about 50% of the time. And to Mr. Houtman, his intuition is his most important tool.

Societal contribution. Mr. Houtman contributes most to the creation of new jobs in the labor market. His company is seeking opportunities for offering services to projects on a pro-bono basis (volunteer work). A precondition is that the talent of his people is put to work and is not wasted. The delivery of a standard for performance measurement is a more daily and commercial objective.

Summary Profile Dick Houtman

Current name	Gooiconsult Advies & Training B.V.
Other ventures	In 1999 he founded Earthwalk B.V., and held shares in Trip Productions B.V., Lisse, in Samaritan Holdings LLC, Minneapolis and currently in Gooiconsult Groep B.V. (mother company of Gooiconsult Advies & Training B.V.
Place of business	Huizen, The Netherlands
Founding year	1985
Involvement	2003 to the present (a management buy in)
Business sector	Education and training
Venture activity	Gooiconsult offers custom designed training and HR development programs for performance improvement. They measure the effectiveness of projects with performance related metrics to gauge organizational effectiveness.
Customers	Profit and not-for-profit organizations such as the ABN AMRO Bank, Peugeot, Medtronic, Casema, UPC, Tax Authorities, Radbout Hospital, Feenstra / NUON, Government Ministries
International activities	None
Company strengths	Balance between the human and the business perspectives is one of the strongest aspects of the company's approach. This means listening to personal concerns and letting employees take responsibility. Thus, the strategic goals of the organization are combined with intervention as required to realize what is best for the client organization.
Company weaknesses	The operation is relatively small and therefore relatively vulnerable from a financial point of view. Market developments on the other hand make this a preferable position to be in as opposed to the big development firms.

10.5 Wim de Knoop, Amcom

*I held corporate positions for 12 years and subsequently I started Flucom in 1965.
My son and daughter are also entrepreneurs. I took over the business that hired
me as a part-time general manager for one year. My personal business was then
buying unprofitable businesses. I have a technical background.*

Company Profile

Company size indicators. The company achieved positive financial results in the last
three years. Since the take-over the headcount grew from four to eight employees. In
2004, there were fewer personnel than in 2003 and the turnover decreased as well in
that period. Turnover ranges between 2 and 5 million euro per year.

Company development. Employee education levels now fit the required tasks better. The strategic approach also changed and the company now works much more with dealers as well as with European importers. As a result, a stronger market position has been achieved. Currently the firm is the market leader in maritime communications. In land mobile communications the firm is one of the top eight suppliers, and to service this sector a new department and dealer network was established.

Defining Opportunities

Evaluation criteria. Mr. De Knoop mentions that when a market opportunity is pursued, success criteria are defined in advance. Criteria he uses are figures and results from prior experience.

Opportunity evaluation techniques. Mr. De Knoop uses the discussion of progress to judge and analyze the position of the firm in comparison with competitors. Techniques used frequently track how European importers inform the manufacturer in Japan of their new equipment specifications and which adjustments are required for the order. The manufacturers in Japan tend to focus more on the needs of American companies. Currently there are European market leaders which can influence this process according to European norms.

Experiences

Remarkable initial experiences. For this type of business it is very important first to listen, and then to change. Gaining trust and showing interest are also very important. Stimulators for Mr. De Knoop were his location in Aalsmeer, a pleasure cruising center well known among customers, and also opportunities to work together with partners. Factors that hindered further development of the firm were the sabotage and fear of employees, and the unprofitable financial status of the company.

Fears and difficult decisions. Mr. De Knoop did not have fears, yet it was hard to understand that the Japanese manufacturer initially did not trust Amcom. He found it difficult to take risks in spending money and to be dependent on suppliers.

Initial learning points. Approaching problems with an open and unbiased mind is something that Mr. De Knoop learned early on. Also he observed that when employees are not motivated that the work usually does not go well. And he feels that the only thing you can do better than the previous owner is to buy a company at a lower price. Mr. De Knoop also says that based on his experience, research done by accountants is not sufficient for valuation.

Case specific experiences. The companies he previously acquired all offered unique experiences. One take-over was successful, and the other he closed down after three years. He also took over another firm that he later sold. With Amcom he finds a high level of synergy.

Message to new entrepreneurs. Although he is satisfied with his position, Mr. De Knoop feels that it is important to be aware that once you start a new venture, the work is never done and there are a lot of rules and regulations to follow.

Entrepreneurship and Spirituality

Role of intuition. Mr. De Knoop uses intuition infrequently; he is more of a rational thinker. In the case of hiring new employees, he feels that he does rely on his intuitive feeling of the person.

Societal contribution. His contributions to society are focused on the labor market, environmental issues and charity. Mr. De Knoop also offers students traineeships to give them opportunities in the business world.

Summary Profile Wim de Knoop

Current venture	Amcom
Other ventures	1965 Flucom (is now a part of Hillvast) Various take-overs: Te-el Plafondsystemen – Hoogeveen, The Netherlands, Postma Electronics Telecom, Cafe Sport B.V., Doeven Electronica & Meteo
Place of business	Nieuw-Vennep, The Netherlands
Founding year	1979
Involvement	1986 to the present
Business sector	Import, export and Wholesale
Venture activity	Equipment for radio communications (for example for the maritime applications)
Customers	Shipping, inland shipping, pleasure cruising, off shore, police, fire brigade, ambulance and defense.
International activities	Western Europe
Company strengths	Highly motivated personnel Guaranteed very fast delivery
Company weaknesses	Not enough stock is fatal, order forecasts made monthly, goods are delivered six months later, accurate forecast are a challenge. Too much dependency on key employees is a weak point. Product knowledge cannot be learned quickly. Difficult to replace employees on short notice.

10.6 Michael Moore, Merison Groep

I was born in Northern Ireland. I am currently CEO of Merison. I worked for Monitor and for Razorfish, and have started companies among which include Conduit and Capital Change, a private equity firm. After these experiences I bought Merison and restarted that company, completely reorganizing it. I was motivated by a desire to return to operations oriented activities, after intensive focus on strategy and finance, and reworking an entire company. Through Fred Lachotzki, a professor at Nyenrode, I found Merison and bought it in 2004.

Company Profile

Company size indicators. The last three years Merison achieved positive financial results, making a profit last year yet turnover was flat. The company currently has 37 employees.

Company development. In the first year the turnover grew 40%, though more growth was expected. There have been some structural changes but not radical ones. For instance, changes in the strategic approach. There is also much more value added focus related to brands and licensing and there is more international orientation. Marketing is increasingly internationally oriented and aims at products and also offers comprehensive retail solutions.

Defining Opportunities

Evaluation criteria. When Mr. Moore pursues a market opportunity he defines the criteria with which to evaluate the opportunity in advance. The most important being the level of financial resources needed, management resources required, time to success and the number of uncontrollable success factors.

Opportunity evaluation techniques. Mr. Moore's approach to stimulating creative processes within the company involves redesign of products and re-differentiation of products, re-segmentation of products once a year, redefining the market crossing established boundaries every year or two and creating competitive advantages.

Experiences

Remarkable initial experiences. Mersion manages the design, sourcing and distribution of food related and non-food items for Albert Heijn. The relationship between Merison and Albert Heijn is based on open communication, and Mr. Moore was able to establish new routines including monthly meetings, and reporting to them in terms of the level of Albert Heijn sales, rather than Merison's sales to Albert Heijn. What made the startup process difficult was largely related to internal resistance to organizational change from employees.

Fears and difficult decisions. Working with one very large client such as Albert Heijn was a concern. And when he bought the company outright he found it difficult to decide not to use leverage (loans) at that point, although the possibility still exists for opportunities in the future.

Initial learning points. Start afresh, Mr. Moore would make changes faster, and focus mostly on human resource issues. In his previous work experience he worked with this type of purchase and turnaround for others (companies) and discovered that it is much easier when he is doing it on his own account. Mr. Moore also feels that he is at his best surrounded by people and operations. He knows his people skills are very important! You have to understand the key metrics of the business, or value chain of the client. And forward projection of the client's sales numbers is necessary as well (as opposed to your sales number to them).

Case specific experiences. Building sophisticated planning into the IT system at Merison allowed easy and quite accurate forward projection of client sales. This upgrade has been of great benefit in working with the client as many of the products in their line of non-food items are designed, and redesigned by the company and then specified for manufacture and supply from Chinese sources. Even so, the client is very set in their ways and initially resisted this proposed change. In hindsight he would have switched earlier to reporting to the client based on their sales numbers! He would also have retained the direct connection he had with the commercial director at his client, had not the manager restricted him.

Message to new entrepreneurs. Mr. Moore's message to young entrepreneurs is to keep your ego in check, don't be afraid of failure and to realize that it is not all about luck. Also, don't underestimate yourself and be careful in the route you take into entrepreneurship, always keeping in mind low cost, low cost, and low cost!

Entrepreneurship and Spirituality

Role of intuition. For Mr. Moore, intuition is a guiding force in his decision-making and he makes strong use of it, accounting for about 65% of his decisions.

Societal contribution. The role in society is an integral part of Merison's place in the market and they work to give something back to the community. The company contributes to society by creating jobs; by helping charity and social volunteering that help handicapped children. Mr. Moore also contributes a substantial sum annually to a hospital ship in India, and contributes to the Kruif Foundation as well as helping to commercialize Amerpoort pieces.

Summary Profile Michael Moore

Current venture	Merison Groep B.V.
Others ventures	Conduit Communications Benelux Razorfish Capital Change B.V.
Place of business	Bunschoten, the Netherlands
Founding year	1896, acquired by Mr. Moore in 2003
Involvement	2002 to the present, since December 2004 as CEO
Business sector	Retail/wholesale
Venture activity	Creation, design, development and sourcing of household solutions and products for sale via supermarket outlets.
Customers	Large retail chains
International activities	For sales in Germany, UK, Belgium and Ireland and for purchasing worldwide but especially in Hong Kong/China.
Company strengths	Knowledge, sourcing skills, internal processes, creativity in creating total concepts and selling these rather than products.
Company weaknesses	Focus is too local Purchasing, not selling, mentality

10.7 Peter Ruigrok, H₂R Invest

Starting a venture in 1998 was an idea that I had for many years, yet first I had opportunities to start a corporate career and that was the better alternative at that time. After completing my MBA in 1995 the drive to run and own a venture returned. In that year, I was asked to manage the turnaround of Heras, the place where I started my career as a trainee in 1981. When Heras was back on track, I left the company together with two partners I worked with during the turnaround to start my own venture. H₂R Invest BV was launched and I changed from a corporate manager into an entrepreneur. I have worked and lived in the USA, South Africa and Saudi Arabia.

Company Profile

Company size indicators. The company was profitable last year and the number of employees decreased and turnover remained stable. At present the company has 115 full-time employees. In the previous two years the firm was not profitable.

Company development. The shift from a production company to a sales and con-tracting company was significant. Ensuring that employees become more client oriented, and have better communication skills is also a major focus issue.

Defining Opportunities

Evaluation criteria. When Mr. Ruigrok pursues a market opportunity the activity must fit into his personal vision, making a contribution to a peaceful world. Prod-ucts that thrive on the waves of greed and fear do not all fit into this category.

Opportunity evaluation techniques. Mr. Ruigrok has a systematic approach to stimulate creative processes to uncover new opportunities. Once a year he attends a meditation retreat, and he regularly practices yoga and meditation. He believes that these activities allow him to think more creatively and openly. For the com-pany, he uses other techniques that include the re-differentiation of products, re-definition of markets, and crossing established boundaries.

Experiences

Remarkable initial experiences. The start-up went well, and Mr. Ruigrok accom-plished what he had aimed for yet there were difficulties later on. He and his part-ners decided to hire a managing director to run the daily business; Mr. Ruigrok himself does not have a formal title. He takes on projects that can enhance the growth of the venture, rather than being involved in every single detail. For Mr. Ruigrok, this is the best way to keep time for entrepreneurial activities.

Fears and difficult decisions. Although Mr. Ruigrok couldn't identify any fears, it was a difficult decision to cease production in the Netherlands and start-up pro-duction in India almost simultaneously. The reorganization had many impacts, and among them was the loss of employment for a few people. All things considered, he believes it is not the entrepreneur's duty to offer lifetime employment.

Initial learning points. Mr. Ruigrok has learned to deal with unfulfilled expecta-tions. He is consciously working on the mental processes of coping with the dif-ference between his expectations and the real outcomes. The main activity of the venture when his team first bought the company, was building cold storage facili-ties for large meat processors. Due to the on-going diseases in this sector (BSE, the foot-and mouth disease, swine fever, fowl pest), sales dropped substantially. To find answers to these challenges was a major learning point.

Case specific experiences. Mr. Ruigrok believes that his approach to business is less performance driven than the average entrepreneur because he is convinced that good performance will follow a good process. When his venture was too de-pendent on one big customer the team shifted to work for a competitor. Although he was very happy with this breakthrough, his customer was even happier.

Message to new entrepreneurs. His message to new entrepreneurs is the same message he shares with his children. Mr. Ruigrok believes that a good education, including the development of cognitive skills, communication skills and emotional skills is valuable. Do whatever you do with respect for others. However, his most important advice is to "listen to your heart."

Entrepreneurship and Spirituality

Role of intuition. Intuition does play a role in Mr. Ruigrok's business life. Nearly 75% of his actions are based on intuitive feelings and he uses analytic information as well to understand processes but not to reach targets.

Societal contribution. Entrepreneurs play an important role in society. They have the power to make things happen, though not everybody may notice it. Mr. Ruigrok did not become an entrepreneur to become rich. Entrepreneurs are leaders who have the power to create a better world for our children. Also in the less affluent parts of this globe. How much one earns or how many jobs are created by a venture are less relevant to him. He quotes Arie de Geus "Profit is for a company, what oxygen is for a human being. One cannot live without it, but life would be poor if it's only purpose was for breathing." Just imagine that we all have a mission to complete while we are hanging out here? Then why not work on it while working. In all fairness, he feels he has not yet succeeded in this respect.

Summary Profile Peter Ruigrok

Current venture	H$_2$R Invest B.V. with subsidiaries Markus Hermetische Deuren (bought in 2000), Metaflex Isosystems (bought in 1999).
Place of business	Krimpen aan de IJssel, Aalten, The Netherlands
Founding year	1998
Involvement	1998 to the present
Business sector	Industrial construction
Venture activity	Sale and production of hermetically sealing sliding doors for operating rooms, theaters and sound studios Sales, designs and engineering, manufacturing and construction of conditioned areas such as clean rooms, cold storage facilities, production facilities for food, special stations for uranium enrichment
Customers	Food industry, producers of enriched uranium, hospitals, pharmaceutical industry.
International activities	Export to European countries, production in India
Company strengths	Fighting spirit and creativity to overcome disaster Superior engineering and production capabilities
Company weaknesses	Too slow response to external threats Sense of urgency is missing

10.8 Marjon Velthuis, SRT International

I completed a BBA / MBA, with internships in the US, Spain, South Africa. I started in 1984 as a trainee at Burhmann Tetterode with Esveha, a wholesaler in office products and stationery. In 1989, I transferred within Burhmann Tetterode to the publishing company Succes in the position of Marketing Manager. When I heard about the decision of the holding company to sell some of the companies I considered buying one of the companies myself because I felt that it was a one-time chance, a sort of now or never. At that time I worked at Succes as a marketing manager and in the 11 years I worked there I learned a lot about the business. In 2001 I took over the company, actually buying seven companies with a business partner.

Company Profile

Company size indicators. The company was profitable last year and headcount decreased but turnover remained stable. Turnover varies between 10 and 25 million euro annually. When she came into the company in 2001 it had 65 full-time employees and at present the company has 56 full-time employees. During the last three years positive financial results were achieved.

Company development. There are no changes in the education level of personnel. She took the company over when the economy was booming, after a period of slow growth. After the take-over only one company remained with departments in The Netherlands, Belgium and Germany; this presented a need for centralized management with one single strategy and vision. The new approach results in more synergy, efficiency and a stronger market position.

Defining Opportunities

Evaluation criteria. When Ms. Velthuis pursues a market opportunity she defines the criteria in advance and during the process evaluates them. She uses the following criteria to assess opportunities: the risk, the quality, the distribution channels, the turnover, and long-term possibilities. She judges opportunities intuitively.

Opportunity evaluation techniques. Ms. Velthuis has a systematic approach to stimulate creative processes within her. Now and then she disassociates from a subject, and finds that she talks a lot with her business partner when they are on business tours. For the company she uses the following techniques of annually re-designing products, and re-differentiating products.

Experiences

Remarkable initial experiences. Ms. Velthuis thinks people took her far more seriously because she was not alone in the process and because she was familiar with the company. Therefore things went fast. She knew the company Succes very well and together with the other six companies she bought, it was a challenging situation. Her business partner had also experienced a management buy-out and he was actually the director of one of the companies that acted as a supplier of Succes. Another positive aspect is that she can work very well with her business partner. More difficult factors were that it was a situation with a lot of politics and professional jealousies. Also the board of directors was willing to buy the company.

Fears and difficult decisions. Fear is a big word according to Ms. Velthuis. Indeed it was a great risk that she took because of the external investment, and her personal situation became more uncertain with the shift away from salaried employment. Ms. Velthuis also felt a responsibility for herself and her employees, making it difficult to put the seven companies together, some employees having to leave.

Initial learning points. One thing that Ms. Velthuis realizes is that she was very busy developing a structure that would work for her company and less focused on market developments. And according to Ms. Velthuis this process was very time consuming, especially in terms of implementation.

Case specific experiences. Ms. Velthuis bought the company in good economic times and found it difficult to predict the future development of the company. In five of the companies there were a lot of inefficiencies. In every company Ms. Velthuis had the same sort of departments and that was not efficient when things were grouped into one company. The big concern was how to organize it all. The employees were not so keen on changes, and she felt that successful change can only happen if the employees are willing to change. In one situation, a number of employees decided to leave the company and this was difficult for her but she learned to have faith in her own competencies. It was remarkable that after three years, four of the artist that had previously left came back looking for work with her. In the end, she rehired only one of them. Ms. Velthuis also feels that surviving is counting on your own strengths, and you should not build a company on specific people because employees often seem to leave at just the wrong time.

Message to new entrepreneurs. To new entrepreneurs Ms. Velthuis says it is important to start from your own strengths. This sort of a start enriches you as a person and it is good for you curriculum vitae as well.

Entrepreneurship and Spirituality

Role of intuition. In her branch very little information is documented, but she often tries to work with lists. Only when it feels good, she takes the decision.

Societal contribution. Ms. Velthuis contributes to society by creating jobs for 60 full-time employees. She also contributes to society through her products.

Summary Profile Marjon Velthuis

Current venture	SRT International B.V.
Place of business	Rijswijk, The Netherlands
Founding year	1927, Management Buy-out 2001
Involvement	1989 to the present
Business sector	Stationery Publishing
Venture activity	Development, production, marketing and sales of Succes and Ryam agendas, stationary, Papillion agendas and calendars and Bosboom bags and other leather goods.
Customers	Resellers such as office product distributors, department stores, stationers, importers and distributors
International activities	Company branches in Belgium and Germany. Distributors in Switzerland, Austria, Greece, Great Britain, Rumania, Australia and Canada
Company strengths	Strong brands, good name recognition, high quality, consistent strategy, complete product range, motivated employees
Company weaknesses	Significant dependence on sector agendas, high price points, high inventory risks

10.9 Evert Versluis, Van Egmond Mechanism Transport

After my military service I worked in a logistics firm. A headhunter alerted me to another logistics firm which needed help badly. Later, I managed to find the funding to buy the company and became the owner in December 1982. I have purchased two companies during my career and founded two ventures as well.

Company Profile

Company size indicators. The company has been profitable in recent years. Headcount and turnover were level during the last two years, and turnover is between 5-10 million euro. Mr. Versluis started the firm with 26 employees and at present there are 17 full-time employees.

Company development. His firm is achieving an increasing level of professionalism with sales skills based on product knowledge. The original company faced difficulties in 1982 and after a turn-around exercise it managed to develop and grow again. There have not been big changes in the organizational structure. The strategic approach of the firm changed from a product focus to a market focus. The company now has a complete product assortment and there is also a more conscious approach to market segmentation and more specialties.

Defining Opportunities

Evaluation criteria. When Mr. Versluis pursues a market opportunity he defines the criteria in advance. He uses the following criteria: the performance of the products, the profitability and efforts.

Opportunity evaluation techniques. Mr. Versluis has a systematic approach to stimulate creative processes by continuously making 'pictures' of the logistic processes when he visits companies or potential clients. He actively thinks and fantasizes about improvements that can be realized within the hardware or within processes. His slogan is "change today what may be done better tomorrow." Techniques used include the redesign and re-differentiation of products or services and regular market re-segmentation. Additionally, the company monitors areas of competitive strength which can create new competitive advantages.

Experiences

Remarkable initial experiences. As the new owner, the first obstacle Mr. Versluis encountered was that the banks told him they would no longer finance the company. He found nothing easy along the way. It seemed as if everything went wrong with this company the day he bought it, yet fortunately, he found a new bank after searching. Other factors that made things difficult were the biggest supplier refusing to deliver and two of his sales people leaving to a new competitor.

Fears and difficult decisions. Mr. Versluis does not call them fears, instead he talks about very serious events, or heavy weather because suddenly your life is only about the venture, and that is nearly all there is, yet he is certain he would have done it anyway! Firing 10 people and later another four because he did not have the funds to pay them was a very difficult decision. He also had to make a very difficult deal with the tax inspector, lacking the money to pay back taxes.

Initial learning points. Today, Mr. Versluis would be far less naive in starting or taking over a business. He would be much harder in dealing with the bank, as he feels he was mistreated. Still, the opportunity was enormous. There was no process of logistics thinking in the health sector and he saw the possibilities. He defined these opportunities very tightly and documented the processes. It turned out to be very good lessons for his following ventures; that is, building logistics know-how into products and services for the health sector. Mr. Versluis never dreamed of becoming an entrepreneur, but had considered the option. He started a few other firms meanwhile as well and still owns them. Taking more time before and during negotiations is the main lesson he learned.

Case specific experiences. Mr. Versluis acquired NVA Systems which was a company in the nursing home market and used this venture to apply his logistics know-how from his first company to enter that market with new logistics based products. This know-how helped the venture enormously. There were no significant difficulties, Mr. Versluis experienced more the need to make product adjustments and understand soothe new cultural.

Message to new entrepreneurs. For new entrepreneurs, Mr. Versluis says imagine working in the mud for quite a while, in heavy mud, but you see the goals … and forget the executive image with the BMW. He heard a motto recently which he wanted to share, "managers do things well, entrepreneurs do good things."

Entrepreneurship and Spirituality

Role of intuition. Mr. Versluis uses intuition as a major part of his decision-making, possibly as much as 70%.

Societal contribution. Mr. Versluis does a lot of volunteer work in the business community on boards of industrial associations. His company has contributed to society through job creation, through working on environmental issues and to societal welfare initiatives and charity. Societal contributions can be a lot of fun too!

Summary Profile Evert Versluis

Current name	Van Egmond Mechanisch Transport B.V.
Other ventures	Mr. Versluis took over the current business and afterwards he founded: InterMetro Nederland B.V. –1986 and HW Logistics 2004. Additionally he purchased NVA Systems in 2001.
Place of business	Nijkerk, The Netherlands
Founding year	1925
Involvement	1982 to present
Business sector	Wholesale
Venture activity	Sale of transportation products and logistic advice
Customers	Retail, catering industry, healthcare
International activities	On a small scale direct sale: Belgium, France, England, Germany
Company strengths	Flexibility and specialization
Company weaknesses	Too broad an approach

11 Trend Entrepreneurs

11.1 Introduction

Trend entrepreneurs are founders of new ventures dedicated to the triple bottom line stakeholder orientation as a comprehensive and logical part of their business strategy.

Chapter 11 presents the profiles of Ariane Inden, Carel Jongbloed, Christian Mayorga, Jack Spoorenberg, John Verstraaten and Han Ypes. After studying their profiles we concluded they can be categorized as entrepreneurs who deal with activities that have impact on the larger community. We call them trend entrepreneurs because it is more a trend nowadays to be aware of finding a balance between people, planet and profit. Although there is an overlap with other groups such as Mr. Mayorga, who could also be categorized as a start-up and Mr. Spoorenberg as a venturer, we want to present these entrepreneurs separately.

Their activities have an impact on environmental issues with activities related to people, planet and profit; the three elements of sustainable entrepreneurship. The entrepreneurs themselves might not consider this in the first place but because of their approach not specifically stressing sustainability while still acting in a sustainable way, we think these entrepreneurs are good examples of this category. The activities they undertake can not easily be copied by others, usually technical or special knowledge have been obtained by Research and Development. For example Ms. Inden products are not tested on animals and there are no animal-derived ingredients used in the products. Mr. Jongbloed focuses on helping people realize business activities or re-developing business. His current activities concentrate on helping those who have less, for example in less developed countries. Mr. Mayorga sources wood from Latin America to help develop local economies in countries in central and South America; a sort of giving back to his home country. Running his business includes adopting a sustainability perspective (by applying the Forest Stewardship Council protocols). Mr. Spoorenberg's company is a model of resource reutilization and waste reduction which makes it a sustainable activity. Mr. Verstraaten focuses on environmental issues and solutions that are important for society such as removal of asbestos and he supports innovations in workplace safety by setting up a foundation. Mr. Ypes is another example of a trend entrepreneur selling products for waste handling and disposal.

We can conclude that sometimes the products themselves have a sustainable impact (Mr. Spoorenberg, Mr. Jongbloed, Mr. Verstraaten and Mr. Ypes) and sometimes the way of approaching business activities makes them a trend entrepreneur dealing with sustainability (Ms. Inden, Mr. Mayorga).

Reading their stories resulted in the conclusion that the trend entrepreneurs are successful at the scale they are operating now. A dilemma might occur regarding scale when they want to grow and therefore need financial support from i.e. banks. Mr. Verstraaten moved his business simply to reduce the number of competitors and he is operating on a smaller scale. Mr. Spoorenberg mentions that the scale of his operation is small even at the international level. To survive Mr. Ypes has developed new activities almost exclusively with big, industrial customers instead of small companies that hire his machines.

Trend entrepreneurs deal with the question of what scale is needed to remain successful in dealing with the bigger picture of entrepreneurship in relation to community, ecology and economics. For the trend entrepreneurs described in this chapter, intuition could not be ignored. It often played a dominant role and for a few of them the importance of intuition depended on the type involved.

The question 'is your company successful' was answered as follows by Ms. Inden: yes, it is a special concept that combines quality of the product and in-store service. The company offers a line of 1,000 different cosmetic products of high quality ingredients, salon treatments for skin rejuvenation, and make-up workshops. Mr Jongbloed did not answered this question. According to Mr. Mayorga it is too early to tell, they started trading only quite recently. Mr. Verstraaten and Mr. Spoorenberg judge their ventures successful. Mr. Ypes thinks it is successful in surviving the economic crisis and it has strong long-term prospects.

11.2 Ariane Inden, Ariane Inden Cosmetics

After my career experiences at Lancaster, Biodermal, L'Oreal and MBA studies at Thunderbird in the US and Nyenrode, I started my own cosmetic company together with my husband Erik Boertje whom I met at Nyenrode. The drive to creativity, opportunities and high objectives were the most important reasons for me to start a venture. I had a lot of energy and was very eager to put a lot of effort into the venture.

Company Profile

Company size indicators. Last year the company was profitable. The company has been profitable over the last 11 years. The firm has ten employees, and some are hired for research and development, but they are not fixed personnel. There have been no changes in headcount but turnover increased in the past two years. The company achieved positive financial results during the last three years.

Company development. There have been no changes in the education level of personnel, strategic approach or type of customers or market. Turnover shows an upward trend. The market for her products is growing.

Defining Opportunities

Evaluation criteria. When Ms. Inden pursues a market opportunity she settles on the criteria in advance. According to her, these criteria are quality and image.

Opportunity evaluation techniques. She has no systematic approach to stimulate creative processes herself. For the company, she comes up with new initiatives frequently, developing new competencies to increase competitive advantage.

Experiences

Remarkable initial experiences. Ms. Inden worked very hard to do what was needed. She worked 18 hours a day, seven days a week. She says that in the beginning stage, life concentrated on work and sleep, and they had to invest a lot in products. Stimulators in the start-up phase were starting the company together with someone she knew very well, her husband Erik Boertje, who at the time had a good job so there was good financial back-up. She also learned a lot when she was studying in the USA (Thunderbird, Phoenix Arizona) for her Master of International Management, and she established trust with producers nationally and also internationally. A factor that was less easy involved an advertisement office sending false invoices, which took a lot of negative energy to rectify. Ms. Inden says that looking back, everything was difficult yet it wasn't disturbing because she expected it, otherwise several others would have done the same thing already.

Fears and difficult decisions. Officially you have to deal with many difficult decisions, for Ms. Inden she perceived these issues as interesting and not difficult. What was a challenge in the start-up phase was the feeling that she had to take difficult decisions when personnel did not meet her expectations.

Initial learning points. As a child, Ms. Inden dreamed of having her own business. The company is very involved in new product development and sources supplies from countries like the USA, Switzerland and Italy as well as from Spain, Great Britain and France. This diversity in product sources tells Ms. Inden that there are great possibilities, unlimited possibilities! If she would start again, she would be tougher and listen more to her intuition from the start. Ms. Inden also learned without very hard work your company won't succeed. After a few years it may be possible to manage time more efficiently, yet you must continue to deliver high quality work. She looks back with fond memories on the early, pioneering years.

Case specific experiences. A new fragrance concept is something that Ms. Inden was working on. A fragrance for mothers and fathers of babies and small children was the basis of the new fragrance concept. Developing a soft fragrance with special ingredients that small children experience as pleasant, not overwhelming was the aim of Ms. Inden's project. This innovation was discussed in the press and on television. Inspiration behind the idea came because Ms. Inden was expecting her first child, and found herself a member of her own target market. At that time, she looked closely and critically at product specifications. It turned out to be a rather large project for that period in her life but certainly a fine challenge. Ms. Inden enjoyed that it was all new and also realized that it could have easily not worked out so well. This concept has been in the market for quite a long time now.

Message to new entrepreneurs. Ms. Inden says to new entrepreneurs, take responsibility and feel that! Focus on what you know, less on what you think you can or cannot do, is her advice. Many people think too much about all possible outcomes and start to doubt their abilities. She also says that you can not be too young to be an entrepreneur! When you get older it gets more difficult to make a start when you consider the risks and the hours you can spend in your venture.

Entrepreneurship and Spirituality

Role of intuition. Ms. Inden uses intuition a great deal in her business dealings. For her, both reason and intuition are involved in her decision-making process.

Societal contribution. Ms. Inden's products are not tested on animals, and there are no animal-derived ingredients used in the products. She frequently uses plant materials that are much better for the skin anyway. These are the basic requirements to guarantee good quality. Ms. Inden also contributes to charity, but she is not sure if the money reaches the people who need it the most.

Summary Profile Ariane Inden

Current venture	Ariane Inden Cosmetics
Place of business	Amsterdam, The Netherlands
Founding year	1992
Involvement	1992 to the present
Business sector	Cosmetics
Venture activity	Develop and market exclusive cosmetic brand products through Ariane Inden specialty stores
Customers	Independent entrepreneurs / retailers Consumers
International activities	Stores in Belgium, Germany, Luxembourg, Scandinavia, France, Portugal, starting up in Switzerland and Australia
Company strengths	Quality of the products
Company weaknesses	Strong competitors in the international cosmetic market

11.3 Carel Jongbloed, Base Group

I was born in the Belgian Congo. I graduated with a Masters in International business from Thunderbird (Arizona). After my graduation I worked for several medium and big companies in the technical industry, textile and printing industry. I worked for a few larger companies and concluded I had no patience for the 'politics' in those companies. In 1990, I moved from the USA to Switzerland, and until 1992 worked for companies. Then I worked as an interim manager in Austria and Germany, which I did not like. I think as an entrepreneur you can set your own direction, and exploit your vision and concepts; whereas in a larger company these processes can take a long time as opposed to in a small company where you have a better picture of the processes. In 1995, I started my own management assistance firm. I have founded different ventures. I use the term general manager in order to stay invisible to people when I own a company.

Company Profile

Company size indicators. The company made a profit during the last year. The last three years achieved positive financial results and the personnel headcount and turnover increased during the last two years. The level of turnover is 5-10 million euro. Mr. Jongbloed started the firm on his own and at present has 22 full-time employees.

Company development. Since Mr. Jongbloed started the company, he has endeavored to find people who are dedicated to their field of work; education is of less importance. In his opinion, sometimes it looks like people with higher education are more focused on themselves and less committed to the venture. Turnover has grown dramatically, which he feels is not such a difficult result for a start-up as it will become more demanding in later stages as more expense is involved to propel growth. At that point, Mr. Jongbloed says that it is necessary to concentrate on core activities.

Mr. Jongbloed sees himself as a micro manager, intimately involved in all facets while viewing the big picture to develop strategy and implement change where it is required. The strategy of the company has not changed, although adjustments to the initial strategy developed when key members of the team convinced each other of the need and found the enthusiasm to implement the new strategy. Market leadership is not that relevant in the start-up context for Mr. Jongbloed. More important to him is tapping into a good niche in the market, and he finds that long-term planning is largely irrelevant. The first goal is to define a plateau from which recovery activities can be developed and build a basis for additional funding.

Defining Opportunities

Evaluation criteria. According to Mr. Jongbloed you need criteria to start pursuing a market opportunity. The criteria he uses include all the necessary elements for a successful start. After the start a reflection stage occurs and at that time, according to Mr. Jongbloed, you evaluate the beginning criteria to see what worked. Often radical changes are needed in the basic plan.

Opportunity evaluation techniques. Mr. Jongbloed refers to the approach mentioned above when looking at opportunity evaluation. It is important to respect others with different feelings thoughts and insights as well, instead of just being the 'boss', says Mr. Jongbloed. The motto he works by is that there are no favorite employees. Within his company he uses the following techniques to stimulate creativity: every 4-6 months evaluate possible redesign of products / services; every 4-6 months consider re-differentiation of products / services; maybe once a year re-segmentation of the market; When necessary redefining the market, crossing established boundaries. Mr. Jongbloed's company is continually working to develop competencies or strengths aimed at improving their competitive position. And they strive to maintain contact with other players in the market, and seek new opportunities and relationships.

Experiences

Remarkable initial experiences. For Mr. Jongbloed there were a number of issues that made the start-up process easier for him. He had a lot of experience from living in different countries, and also experience working in different sectors that turned out to be applicable to his new situation, and he had a strong network. He found that people like to lend a hand when they can. Mr. Jongbloed learned that good preparation, before starting a project, is very important. His advice is to focus on the engine of the company, and think conceptually. A more challenging factor for Mr. Jongbloed was that he thought he was not good at networking and deemed this to be a necessity for an entrepreneur.

Fears and difficult decisions. One of the fears for Mr. Jongbloed was the need to have access to investment funds as an entrepreneur. He used a lot of his own resources, yet found that as he was in consultancy the investments were not that high. In his opinion, it is important to first gain results and then to invest. The most difficult decision for Mr. Jongbloed was in 2002, when Base Group became a subordinate to other bigger projects that he was involved in with business partners. From that time forward he had an increase in responsibilities. Recently, he is working on larger scale projects together with seven partners, and for big decisions he needs consensus to operate.

Initial learning points. Mr. Jongbloed learned that if you do your best, you will see results and that not focusing on success is important. With a balance of emotions, intuition and guts you can operate without stress, says Mr. Jongbloed. One of the biggest advantages that Mr. Jongbloed created was that he did not have to report his performances to anybody, except of course the banks. In his view, operating as an entrepreneur with financial resources of others can be a dangerous step; referring to the 1.5 billion euro he raised together with six business partners for financing their various commercial activities.

Case specific experiences. In his approach to turnaround management, Mr. Jongbloed does not work with a set fee structure. When he works with a company they pay for his travel costs and any consultancy invoices are submitted at the time that the client is making money again. On average Mr. Jongbloed works on a project anywhere from two months up to one year. For him, this is a good way to help a company that is in distress. And, when he has been able to help, he finds that companies are willing to pay him more than what he would ask as a fee.

Recently, Mr. Jongbloed has been busy preparing 12 projects for a simultaneous launch. He is negotiating capital to invest in inventions with the intention that these new products will be launched in the market; some of these products are projected to have a high impact on the community and a business plan is in place.

Base Group is familiar with providing advice to smaller size businesses, and this requires a different approach. Initially, Mr. Jongbloed thought he worked better as an independent consultant. Although he earned good salaries in his earlier career, as an entrepreneur he can now take some big steps financially. And, he realizes he was not a team player, even though today he has changed a little bit.

Message to new entrepreneurs. Mr. Jongbloed feels that the world does not consist of numbers but of people, and it is important to listen to older people with experience as you can learn a lot from them. In business life, a good business ethic is an essential part of operations, and for Mr. Jongbloed this is very important. As well, he stresses that you must be honest with people.

Entrepreneurship and Spirituality

Role of intuition. During his corporate career he has recruited thousands of people, and to a great degree these decisions were based on intuition. Today Mr. Jongbloed is also faced with staffing decisions, yet he does not rely on headhunters, instead he invests his own time in learning about people and relying on his own intuition.

Societal contribution. Mr. Jongbloed says that he likes to help people that have less. His experiences in Africa and the Far East left a lasting impression and many of the projects he wants to start involve inventions for markets in the third world, such as Burma or Thailand. In his view, people there can benefit from the projects so they can gain access to the means to meet basic needs and therefore become less dependent on others. Intrinsic values are very valuable to Mr. Jongbloed. Also, he helps students interested in becoming entrepreneurs by mentoring them as they develop their business plans.

Summary Profile Carel Jongbloed

Current venture	Base Group AG
Other ventures	Electronic products in Taiwan Clothing in Bangladesh, Mexico, USA CD production in Poland Agri-tourism and olive oil production in Italy Laser Technology for the Film industry
Place of business	Zug, Switzerland
Founding year	1995
Involvement	1995 to present
Business sector	Advise on strategic planning, buying and selling companies
Venture activity	Advice in marketing and strategy, also advice on buying and selling companies that go bankrupt or almost go bankrupt. The goal is to redevelop the firm and then develop management buyouts.
Customers	Big as well as small firms that do not have a clear picture of their international market strategy or business processes to realize achievable plans – 30% for Banks (with impending bankruptcy), 60% existing management of companies, 10% owners that want to sell their company.

International activities	Activities in Europe – Germany, Austria, Italy, and Poland, USA, Middle East – Dubai, Israel, Africa – Kenya, Senegal, Asia – Hong Kong, Thailand, Indonesia, Brunei. He works in a highly international market where there is a need for intervention to supervise, and help existing companies and where new concepts and products can be developed but where the use of existing channels is very difficult for the new entrepreneur. He has lived in Africa, in Canada, Middle East and various European countries, and in the USA.
Company strengths	The network of people that put their effort and commitment and good ideas into practice. Therefore a variety of projects can be initiated. There is a business culture where projects and activities are evaluated from a perspective of high reality and consciousness.
Company weaknesses	Sometimes activities worked out too splintered. The main aim is to found new projects, and less the management of a particular project.

11.4 Christian Mayorga, Globex International

I was born in Peru, completed a bachelor degree in computer science, and then graduated from Nyenrode. I held positions in the computer and phone industry. I come from an entrepreneurial family. I started my company with two members from my MBA class, Rutger Buys and Jorge Garcia-Cruz. Buys is VP for Sales and I am VP of Operations. Garcia-Cruz is a member of the supervisory body. A big motivation was to be my own boss. I acquired the necessary knowledge during the MBA at Nyenrode and therefore I took the step to become an entrepreneur.

Company Profile

Company size indicators. Buys and Mr. Mayorga are the only employees of the company, and they do not earn a salary from the company at this point. Turnover is less than 1 million euro per year, yet the turnover has grown since the start of the venture.

Company development. The company is a Dutch corporation with Dutch / American, Peruvian and Guatemalan founders. The venture was founded over two years ago, and in the first year of operation the business was fully dedicated to research. Globex International is a company that sources, processes, and exports / imports sustainably grown and harvested hard, tropical timber. The sustainable timber is sourced in Guatemala and marketed in The Netherlands. Globex timber comes from sustainable forests that are kept and harvested under the protocols of the FSC (Forest Stewardship Council), mainly by local communities in Guatemala. Globex has a close partner in Guatemala, GMB &Westwoods. S.A. This corporation has two partners / shareholders that are involved in daily operations. GMB & Westwoods S.A. has one additional full-time employee, all other tasks are outsourced, allowing for low, fixed overheads and costs, and creating a lean and flexible operating structure. Globex has active and on-going contracts in place both on the marketing side in The Netherlands and on the supply side in Guatemala.

The company is also strongly dedicated to research for new hard tropical species that show favorable growing characteristics and that satisfy needs for FSC woods in the Dutch market. The research efforts are meant to improve productivity and availability and to decrease prices, contributing to both ends of the supply chain. The firm delivered its first container of product in mid-2005. The company then worked to broaden the product offering during 2005, thus realizing a change in the type of customer they were selling to. It took time to locate a niche within the market where they could fit in, so they started with one customer and through a partnership strategy introduced a new product in the market. In the meantime, they are developing partnerships with other companies to introduce other products; some of them are already in the market and others are totally new. The intention is to diversify the portfolio to reduce risk and increase the market base.

Defining Opportunities

Evaluation criteria. Mr. Mayorga pursues market opportunities by defining the objective criteria in advance. He uses market size, margin per product, potential growth, marketing and sales requirements as assessment tools.

Opportunity evaluation techniques. Mr. Mayorga uses brain storming as the main approach to creative thinking within the company. Techniques that he uses include re-differentiation of products and developing breakthrough competencies, or areas of competitive strength, that can create new, competitive advantages.

Experiences

Remarkable initial experiences. In the beginning, they realized that they did not really know the wood industry culture. For example Mr. Mayorga says that within this industry in The Netherlands, not many people speak English. There were also incredible Visa issues with The Netherlands. Factors that did make the start easier

12 Family Business Entrepreneurs

12.1 Introduction

In Chapter 12, family business entrepreneur profiles of Annelies Damen, Annemarie Dekker, Christel Hodes and Jorrit van Kraaikamp are presented. With the exception of Mr. Van Kraaikamp, all have founded another firm by themselves in addition to their involvement in the family business. In comparison with Ms. Hodes, who founded a holding structure for all the activities of the family business including new ones. The ventures of Ms. Damen and Ms. Dekker were less related to the family business.

Mr. Van Kraaikamp expanded on his father's original firm with a broad range of new activities. All four entrepreneurs have shown how their entrepreneurial spirit drives them in achieving results for their activities.

Turnover and personnel headcount varies between these profiles. We can conclude that they all have to deal with acquired rights of previous employees and emotions of the previous owners when implementing changes or when totally rebuilding the organization. These situations can lead to facing different dilemmas. In addition, these entrepreneurs must prove to the family their business actions are sound and value adding.

Mr. Van Kraaikamp and Ms. Damen judge their venture as successful. According to Ms. Hodes the venture is successful in a market where rationalization and economy of scale is critical, the company is still growing in terms of turnover and points of sale. On the question if her venture is successful, Ms. Dekker answered: "yes, even though in this market it is not easy to realize good cash flow".

In family businesses the dilemma of keeping other family members at a distance from business activities might occur. They might also face the problem of putting aside the past. Family business entrepreneurs face expectations from family members. This might occasionally raise tensions if they feel these cannot meet these. Family business entrepreneurs often make use of intuition in their decision-making processes.

12.2 Annelies Damen, Damen Shipyards

After graduation, I went to work in Gabon, New York, The Dutch Antilles and Spain. When I returned to The Netherlands, my father asked me to run the real estate part of the family business which was founded by my grandfather. In Gabon I had already led a project for our family business and I did not want to work for a boss. As I did not have a job yet, I accepted the offer. The real estate business is a men's world, yet I like the flexibility and the possibility to implement new ideas. Additionally I have started my own real estate venture in Spain with a business partner. We both thought there was a good opportunity to design houses in the Barcelona area; through this experience I have become familiar with the culture and language.

Company Profile

Company size indicators. In the business of Damen shipyards, the Company was profitable last year. Headcount and turnover remained stable with turnover about 25 million euro annually. At present there are 10,000 full-time employees. During the prior two years the firm was not profitable. With her business, Amarillo Tres, the venture was profitable last year. Ms. Damen's business partner now lives in Spain. Amarillo Tres has no personnel, and both partners have spent time in developing the business. The turnover has increased, varying from 1-2 million euro annually.

Company development. Since Ms. Damen joined Damen Shipyards there have been no major changes in personnel education, turnover level, in strategic approach, in the type of customers or in the type of market. The structure has been changed to a model that involves a board of directors. With Amarillo Tres, experience has taught Ms. Damen what type of people she is best suited to work with. The venture is developing because there are more projects now then at the start-up. As well, her business partner has the technical know-how and together they make decisions on important aspects of the venture. The work processes are more structured now, and Ms. Damen feels that projects are better planned and processes are thus more predictable.

Defining Opportunities

Evaluation criteria. When Ms. Damen pursues a market opportunity she defines criteria in advance. Among the usual criteria, Ms. Damen ranks creativity as the most important.

Opportunity evaluation techniques. Ms. Damen uses a systematic approach to stimulate creative processes to uncover new opportunities. She uses insights from her study in photography for inspiration.

Experiences

Remarkable initial experiences. When Ms. Damen started in the family real estate business she researched the opportunities and developed a file on what were important criteria in evaluating real estate. Ms. Damen learned a great deal from someone who had a lot of real estate experience; her father had asked him to mentor her in this new field. At first, it was a strange feeling to work in her father's company. It was also difficult to develop a place at the holding level. Ms. Damen believes that as the daughter of the boss, people had a different attitude towards her. Taking the decision to start Amarillo Tres was not at all easy. For Ms. Damen, the most remarkable experience was already at the notary; people in Spain still tend to want to make changes in the prepared documents and that made it difficult to predict how things would go.

Fears and difficult decisions. Among her fears was the thought that she would not be able to sell a ship. The sales processes were difficult, and the business line was new for the company. That made it difficult to establish a good position at the holding level. Following a reconstruction of the company, it was then that Ms. Damen felt everyone was really prepared to be involved. In her venture in Spain, Ms. Damen faced a lot of unpredictable situations that had to do with cultural differences.

Initial learning points. Ms. Damen is more confident now and knows the real estate field much better. In Spain, she has learned a lot that makes processes somehow more predictable than when she first began.

Case specific experiences. It was a unique experience to help manage the family business. In Africa they owned Ship Company, a business supporting oil companies. She had to speak French in order to better understand how a small business could be run in Africa. Ms. Damen was responsible for some projects of the company there, and it was a challenging period with difficulties but there were also adventurous moments. She was forced to think differently and Ms. Damen became very creative and learned a great deal; for instance the importance of staying calm in very stressful situations. She also discovered that doing business in Africa requires a certain degree of humour and also frequent interaction with people.

Message to new entrepreneurs. Ms. Damen says to new entrepreneurs that using intuition in combination with the knowledge and skills you learned at Nyenrode is the key.

Entrepreneurship and Spirituality

Role of intuition. For Ms. Damen, intuition does play a big role in the real estate world. In her decisions, Ms. Damen estimates that intuition accounts for 80% of her total decision. And she believes that as a woman, you have an extra advantage in this respect.

Societal contribution. The family business has created many jobs, in the Ukraine alone there are about 2,500 employees. Ms. Damen Shipyards also sponsored the Dutch Olympic Sailing Team. As well, the company operates in accordance with Dutch environmental regulations.

Summary Profile Annelies Damen

Current ventures	Amarillo Tres Damen Shipyards
Place of business	Damen Shipyards is the family business in Gorinchem, The Netherlands Amarillo Tres, her new business is in Barcelona, Spain
Founding year	Damen Shipyards: 1933 Amarillo Tres: 2000
Involvement	In both ventures she is involved since 2000
Business sector	In both ventures she deals with real estate
Venture activity	Damen shipyards build and repairs ships Amarillo Tres is a real estate development company and venture buys land, designs and markets houses. Amarillo Tres cooperates with an architectural firm and a construction company
Customers	Damen Shipyards: companies and governments
International activities	Damen Shipyards sells all over the world. Company establishments in China, Cuba, Singapore, Poland, Ukraine and Romania.
Company strengths	Damen Shipyards: part of the production is done in lower cost countries. Strength is the building of ships in series. Amarillo Tres: exploits a niche in the market. The houses differ from those designed and built by Spanish real estate developers. People from Northern Europe tend to prefer Amarilles Tres houses. Ms. Damen speaks Spanish which makes doing business in Spain easier. She has lived in Spain and is familiar with the culture.
Company weaknesses	Damen shipyards: some acquisitions such as in Ukraine Amarillo Tres: Damen is not located on site. Her business partner has now moved to Spain. Big cultural differences makes doing business difficult. It takes too much time and money to build up a venture in a foreign country.

12.3 Annemarie Dekker, Remmert Dekker

I am the third generation of the family business Remmert Dekker. After my studies, I went to Switzerland to become a ski teacher. My father called me back to face me with the situation of the family business; the decision was either to sell it or to continue as a family business. At that time I was 20 years old and thought of building my own career. My brother and sister were not interested to be involved, and my father was the technical managing director. There was a commercial managing director who recruited his son to prepare him as a successor, and my father noticed this and preferred me as the successor. Both directors thought me together with the other candidate would be the best team to carry on with the management of the company. I felt it was a challenge to join my father's company, although it was not something I had planned to do. Subsequently, I started two ventures on my own, both related to activities of the family business. For a short period of time I owned another venture I started in Romania.

Company Profile

Company size indicators. In the last three years, the company did not achieve positive financial results, although last year was profitable. The headcount remained stable from 2003-2004, with an increase in turnover. Turnover ranges from 10-25 million euro per year. When Ms. Dekker took over the company there were 62 full-time employees and at present there are 82.

Company development. There are no changes in the education level of the employees. The company has grown since the period she was involved and turnover shows an upward trend. The structure also changed and is more decentralized now. Nowadays the company focuses on other markets as well, and the reputation of the company has grown. Remmert has become a recognized brand in the sector, and customers today are bigger and the market is more industry oriented.

Defining Opportunities

Evaluation criteria. Ms. Dekker mentions that when a market opportunity is pursued, her criteria for success are defined in advance. Criteria she uses include looking at the return on investment and the possibility to repay investments.

Opportunity evaluation techniques. Ms. Dekker does not have a specific approach to stimulating creative processes for herself. In the company she uses a team, the so called crea-team, and regular meetings. Techniques include re-differentiation and developing areas of competencies aimed at competitive advantages.

Experiences

Remarkable initial experiences. She found it all very challenging, especially the processes that were involved in getting to know the company better. Started as an entrepreneur in her father's business was not easy, but she learned a lot. It took her five years to establish a good position in the company and to work with her management partner, though in the end things did not work out with him. From the beginning the match was not good. When both her father and his colleague were in the position to retire, they hired an interim manager, and set a time period of three months to determine who the more suitable candidate was. The final decision was Ms. Dekker, yet on the condition that she would take four years to build experience outside of the company. Ms. Dekker refused and this created a crisis. Due to intervention by her mother and Ms. Dekker's husband, her father decided to give her a chance and also hired a person to help run the company from 1994 - 2002. It was a chance for her to learn from this person and to build experience.

Fears and difficult decisions. She had no fears. She realized that if this plan did not work, she would go for something else. And for herself, she knew that when she was convinced of her purpose, she could really make a go of it.

Initial learning points. Initially trust yourself only and gradually learn to trust others. Doing business in Eastern Europe is very different to Western Europe. It is good to have a variety of experience in your portfolio.

Case specific experiences. When Ms. Dekker started a company in Romania together with a business partner, each had 50% of the shares. The business was a factory in clay and marzipan. It did not work out with this partner, who was Romanian, and Ms. Dekker says it was a challenging time. First it was necessary to build up a network of local people that you could also trust. She also experienced that there were too many regulations and rules for an entrepreneur in Romania, it was too bureaucratic. She discovered that to get things done it helps to give people a bottle of whisky, chocolates, cigarettes and even money; this is simply how it works. After two years, Ms. Dekker found a Dutch business partner who was willing to go to Romania to oversee things three weeks a month there. The company grew fast and she was able to afford a new office space for the 70 employees. Later, she sold the company and her business partner sold his shares as well.

Message to new entrepreneurs. You must follow your heart, have faith in yourself, and give it a chance when you start something. Be persistent.

Entrepreneurship and Spirituality

Role of intuition. Intuition is something that Ms. Dekker makes use of a lot. For her, it plays a big role yet when there is a possibility to use hard figures for important decisions, she gives the numbers the priority.

Societal contribution. Ms. Dekker's companies contribute to society by creating jobs. She uses environmentally friendly material to construct her new office.

Summary Profile Annemarie Dekker

Current venture	Remmert Dekker Alphenaar Chromos
Others ventures	Promaron (1998)
Place of business	Remmert Dekker: Wormer, The Netherlands Alphenaar: Wormer, The Netherlands Chromos: Krommenie, The Netherlands
Founding year	In 1896: Remmert Dekker In 2004: Alphenaar In 2005: Chromos
Involvement	1990 to the present
Business sector	Production and printing of packaging materials
Venture activity	Design and production of cardboard packaging materials
Customers	Consumer product packaging for the food industry
International activities	None
Company strengths	Employee commitment and know-how, innovation, flexibility
Company weaknesses	Difficult to maintain growth rates

12.4 Cristel Hodes, Hodes® Verenigde Bedrijven

I come from an entrepreneurial family. After graduation I joined my parents' company and in 2000 me and my brother took over the family business. I am the director of Hodes® Verenigde Bedrijven Ltd. I have also started two companies related to the family business. I wanted to be independent and aimed to establish my own vision to achieve direct results in the family business together with my brother.

Company Profile

Company size indicators. The company was profitable in the last three years, and both headcount and turnover increased. Turnover varied between 10-25 million euro annually. The company now has 120 full-time employees, growing from only 30 employees at 1997. It is a fast growing company in a fast growing market.

Company development. The company has changed a lot in relation to the changes within the medical sector, which transitioned from a traditional sector to a more commercial and community oriented sector. Personnel are more qualified today and investments have led to turnover growth. The organization is also more structured, and currently obtained an ISO 9001:2000 certification. The company is ranked within the top five in the sector, and customers are more professional and demanding.

Defining Opportunities

Evaluation criteria. When Ms. Hodes pursues an opportunity she defines the criteria in advance, and afterwards evaluates if the criteria were appropriate. Criteria she uses include identifying realistic objectives that are reachable and she believes in individual responsibility for objectives.

Opportunity evaluation techniques. Ms. Hodes has a systematic approach to stimulating creative processes within her company, according to her, production personnel know how processes can be improved and what works best and therefore responsibilities should be distributed among the personnel. Within the company she uses the following techniques of redesign of the products, re-segmentation of products, redefinition of the market, and crossing established boundaries. Ms. Hodes continuously works to develop new competencies to increase competitive advantages. Finally, she thinks employees should adjust to her leadership style and she should adjust her communication style to better reach the employees involved in the business. And when objectives are not met, Ms. Hodes assesses the reasons why not.

Experiences

Remarkable initial experiences. Since the reorganization, Ms. Hodes has been able to bring her ideas into practice. Initially she found it difficult to delegate tasks to others and that also, with a family business there are a lot of issues to deal with. The market was changing rapidly and they had to be flexible in order to face the struggle. Communication with personnel was very important in this stage, as they needed to be a strong team to face the challenges.

Fears and difficult decisions. According to Ms. Hodes, she was very convinced of her competencies so she did not have fears. It took her two years to get familiar with the organization, to learn the market and to become accepted within the organization. The older personnel, who worked for 25 years in the organization, did have difficulty with the younger management and there was a high turnover in personnel during the first three years, as well she had to dismiss some employees.

Initial learning points. It was not a dream to become active in this particular field; Ms. Hodes developed a positive attitude as she gained experience in it.

Case specific experiences. When she and her brother joined the company, they were facing a new stage in development with a lot of changes that were necessary to adjust the organization to fit their vision. Ms. Hodes noticed that experience with the change process has made her a more patient manager, and she is also much more direct in her communication. Also of importance, Ms. Hodes learned to listen to the organization. She also appreciates that it takes time to build good relationships within the company and to gain acceptance from employees.

Message to new entrepreneurs. It takes guts to start says Ms. Hodes. She found it is also important to try to find a balance between your interests, and that without drive and perseverance you will not be successful.

Entrepreneurship and Spirituality

Role of intuition. Intuition plays a big role in spotting and exploiting opportunities in the market for Ms. Hodes. Negotiation plays a role as well, and there is a balance between the two. Intuition accounts for nearly 70% of her decision-making.

Societal contribution. Ms. Hodes contributes to charities, helps to develop innovations and therefore contributes to the quality of life for people.

Summary Profile Cristel Hodes

Current venture	Hodes® Verenigde Bedrijven Ltd.
Other ventures	Hodes® Group, six subsidiaries in 2005 Hodes® Verenigde Bedrijven Ltd. in 2004. This is a holding company in capital venturing.
Place of business	Main office in Arnhem, establishments in Ede, Zwolle, Meppel, Rozendaal, Heerlen, Maastricht, Zuthpen and Rotterdam Airport, all in the Netherlands.
Founding year	1965
Involvement	1998 to date
Business sector	Healthcare, medical technology, capital venturing
Venture activity	The companies deliver medical aids, such as prosthesis, orthodics, medical supplies, homecare, rehabilitation products and workplace adjustments in The Netherlands.
Customers	Consumers, prescribing medical professionals, insurance companies and "end users"
International activities	Oppo Medical Inc., import and production of orthopedic products for: Belgium, The Netherlands and Luxembourg.
Company strengths	Personal treatment and attention inside as well as externally
Company weaknesses	The structure of the isolated individual parts of the company has been eliminated

12.5 Jorrit van Kraaikamp, MB-ALL

I had a corporate career when my father was asked to consult the municipality and therefore he set-up a consultancy firm in 1996. In 2002, I noticed there was a demand in consultancy in the public sector and I got involved in the firm. After seven years as strategic manager at Deloitte Consulting and at Nuon, I took over the business of my father and developed it further. Yet I felt that the time was right and there was an opportunity.

Company Profile

Company size indicators. The company was profitable last year. Headcount and turnover increased, with turnover less than 1 million euro annually. When Mr. Van Kraaikamp took over the company there were five full-time employees, at present there are 12 employees. The last three years saw positive financial results.

Company development. Since 2004 he has upgraded the strength of the staff involved in the supervision of buildings, housing and zoning plans and added new services such as public policy and legal advice. The turnover, the number of customers and profit has doubled. The number of assignments per customer has grown 50%. Two joint ventures have been added to the firm that uses the brand name MB-ALL. Currently, there is a transition going on from a supervision company towards a maintenance company. Supervision is only 50% of maintenance and by combining juridical advice, policy development and maintenance more synergy is possible. The company name is widely known, and for this reason it is easier for customers to come into contact with the business. The company also has worked to build trust amongst municipalities and knowledge has been transferred to the new market; the housing and building sector has seen an increase in acceptance of new working methods.

Defining Opportunities

Evaluation criteria. When Mr. Van Kraaikamp pursues an opportunity he evaluates afterwards if his approach worked well. Criteria he uses include looking at the needs in the market, how to fulfill promises, and assessing what the benefits are.

Opportunity evaluation techniques. Mr. Van Kraaikamp also has a systematic approach to stimulating creative processes within himself. He finds that talking with customers about how to improve services is valuable. Usually, he finds new solutions and approaches to offering improved services to his customers. For the company, there isn't an established routine to look at creative processes due to the busy working schedule they are experiencing. In the past the company worked with some re-differentiation and developed new competencies to increase competitive advantages. Finally, Mr. Van Kraaikamp continuously transports knowledge and skills to other business units of existing customers.

Experiences

Remarkable initial experiences. It was remarkable to notice the openness with his father when he began working with the company, says Mr. Van Kraaikamp. For a short period of time there were two captains on board, and the intention was for him to take over the business when his father departed. Factors that stimulated his involvement centered on the fact that there was a product already, there were customers already and there were some personnel on a temporary basis. Factors that made his involvement in the company less easy were finding that negotiation with family is not easy, there was no structure, he paid for goodwill but it was not clear for what, customers realized he was the son and had to re-establish relationships with the company, and often he found that he had to ask his father's advice because he was not familiar with the sector.

Fears and difficult decisions. For Mr. Van Kraaikamp it was a difficult decision to end his corporate career at Nuon where he held a position in the management team.

Initial learning points. Mr. Van Kraaikamp dreamt of becoming an entrepreneur, but not in this sector. When he took the decision to start in the company, he had to invest a lot in familiarizing himself with the sector and in this process developed a great affinity with it. Mr. Van Kraaikamp feels that he is still in the initial phase. Looking back, he thinks that taking on more risk by hiring more people to grow faster would have been a good decision. He also believes there is a big demand for the services of the company.

Case specific experiences. *The first assignment was the biggest one in the firm's history and he was proud of it. To win new projects, Mr. Van Kraaikamp has a specific approach through which he sees all the tenders and usually prepares them himself. He is also involved in all acquisition of new projects. When dealing with acquisition, Mr. Van Kraaikamp feels it is good to know who in the company will decide to work with you, and you have to ask yourself what the customer needs to make a decision to choose the company over a competitor.

Message to new entrepreneurs. Mr. Van Kraaikamp feels it is important to listen carefully to your own intuition in order to evaluate if you are doing things well. And he says that you can learn a lot from failure.

Entrepreneurship and Spirituality

Role of intuition. Intuition plays a role in Mr. Van Kraaikamp's decision-making. Nearly 50% of his decision is based on intuition, although he feels that each person must find their own balance.

Societal contribution. He contributes to society by creating jobs. Mr. Van Kraaikamp also contributes to charity and feels it is important to work by the rules and legislation established in The Netherlands. He also says that it is important to go back to your own basic values and to remember your roots, and to seek a balance in your life.

Summary Profile Jorrit van Kraaikamp

Current venture	MB-ALL B.V. MB-ALL Analyse B.V. MB-ALL Recherche B.V.
Place of business	Maarssen, The Netherlands
Founding year	MB-ALL B.V. 1996, Jorrit took it over in 2003 MB-ALL Analyse BV en MB-ALL Recherche B.V. were founded as Joint Ventures in 2004
Involvement	2001 to the present
Business sector	Professional services for governments
Venture activity	Maintenance and management of regulations and legislation for municipalities and provinces concerning building codes, environmental regulations, tax and other policies. Maintenance and management of regulations for home and rental property construction.
Customers	Municipalities, 90%: supervision of public places, policy and legal services Construction companies: services concerning avoidance of illegal renting and other practices in the housing sector
International activities	None
Company strengths	Flexible due to small size Good and ambitious working climate facilitates attraction of qualified personnel Innovative products to manage the growing building maintenance market Efficient working methods facilitating subcontracting by clients rather than doing it themselves
Company weaknesses	Growth problems: supervision, recruitment and selection of qualified staff required much time and money

13 Significant Business Entrepreneurs

13.1 Introduction

Significant businesses have founders who have been able to create a business that is relatively important in terms of personnel, turnover and innovativeness. In Chapter 13 we present the profiles of ten entrepreneurs who have significant businesses or a firm which has grown rapidly. These businesses also typically employ more than 20 employees.

Turnover varies from 2 to 250 million euro annually and the personnel head-count varies from 25 to 520. Bruce Kindler has a glove import and wholesale business and he noticed this opportunity in the company he was working for previously. He faces the dilemma of fighting for big clients. Norbert Mutsaerts has a wholesale textile business. H did not enjoy his prior job and started to search for other opportunities.

Rob van Rozendaal has a firm in the entertainment sector. Just as Mr. Mutsaerts, he searched for an opportunity to become an entrepreneur. Arnold van Tuinenburg developed a company in internet applications and he started when he unexpectedly lost his job. Edmée Vitzthum was told by a head-hunter that she could easily be an entrepreneur and started a firm in telecommunications. Hans Mr. Van Well has a retail company. Except for Mr. Van Well, every significant business entrepreneur in this chapter has an international orientation in their activities. Mr. Van Well is oriented locally and successful in providing employment to about 100 people. Herman Westendorp runs a firm in chemicals and his specific chemistry knowledge was of great help to him. Frank van Wezel was very ambitious from the start and early on too significant risks which helped him in realizing the success he now enjoys. Deo van Wijk has started quite a number of ventures s. He was eager to start his own business rather than applying his expertise in a sala-ried position. He took risks similar to Mr. Van Wezel early during the develop-mental process of the venture. Another profile characterizing risk taking and ambi-tion is provided by Arnold de Wolf. These, risk-taking and ambition, intent, appear to be the main characteristics of the significant and growth entrepreneurs to grow and succeed.

Mr. Kindler thinks his venture has been successful, but no companies are im-mune to down cycles, and there is always fear that things will go awry while one is financially stretched during growth periods. "It's like riding a bike. If you stop pedaling, you'll fall over", he added. Mr. Mutsaerts thinks his venture is successful. According to Mr. Rozendaal his venture is reasonably successful "but we aren't there yet", he says. Mr. Tuinenburg thinks his venture is very successful while Vitzthum is not sure of the answer. Success for whom, the shareholders, the market, herself? And what is success? Mr. Van Well thinks his venture is successful, especially considering intensive price competition among supermarkets. Could be even better, he added. My company is successful yet I am not satisfied, said Mr. Westendorp. He wants to set-up a R&D center with some partners. Mr. Van Wezel thinks his company is successful but there is more work to do. Mr. Van Wijk thinks his company is successful. The venture of Mr. De Wolf was according to him very profitable, had grown enormously and during the last 5 years of his involvement the turnover grew remarkably.

Significant businesses frequently have been searching for external finance. They even might have had a need to deal with fast growth as a consequence of their innovative actions. For the majority of the participants described in this chapter the intuition factor was at least as important as reasoning in their decision-making process.

13.2 Bruce Kindler, Kinco International

I studied the NOIB at Nyenrode. Originally working at a new trading company, gloves were being haphazardly handled by someone else in the small firm. When that person left, I approached my boss about importing the gloves and warehousing them in my garage at home to distribute them locally instead of acting as a broker. I never actually wanted or even dreamed of starting my own venture, but when my boss didn't agree, I felt that I had to do it or I would lose my brief yet close contact with the Hong Kong glove factory. It also helped that I had great trust from my Hong Kong supplier.

Company Profile

Company size indicators. The company achieved positive financial results during the last three years, and employment and turnover both increased. The turnover is over 15 million euro per year and the company employs 30 people.

Company development. Over the years there has been an increase in turnover and the number of employees, yet the education and skill levels of employees has remained the same. Mr. Kindler has shifted from general marketing to targeting more non-industrial accounts. He transitioned the business from a minor player in the supply of industrial gloves to a major player in other retail markets. This emphasis evolved from a narrow focus on gloves for industrial use, mainly the welding industry, to providing a large variety of work and garden gloves.

Defining Opportunities

Evaluation criteria. When the Dutch-speaking Mr. Kindler pursues market opportunities, he defines his criteria for success during the process. He stimulates his own creative processes by integrating physical exercise into his fairly regular routine, and enjoys bicycling and alpine skiing as his primary sports. He says the business is always on his mind, but he finds it amazing how many seemingly good ideas occur outside the office while exercising. Although like US President Johnson once said, "I try not to think about politics more than 16 hours a day."

Opportunity evaluation techniques. Mr. Kindler practices different techniques as part of his business strategy. Some of these techniques include the redesign of products or services, re-differentiation of products or services, re-segmentation of the market, completely reconfiguring the market, and developing breakthrough competencies, or areas of competitive strengths that create new competitive advantages and market niches.

Experiences

Remarkable initial experiences. "We started on a very small scale," said Mr. Kindler, doing everything possible himself with the exception of accounting. Accounting was the biggest challenge, so his wife Sherie and a friend took over this aspect. Things were difficult yet it was still a pleasant experience to start the business and seeing results immediately was rewarding.

Fears and difficult decisions. At the time, Mr. Kindler feels he was too young (27 years old) to be aware of any fears of failure. His most difficult decisions involved hiring his first employee and the constant need to his bank for more money to finance inventory.

Initial learning points. Mr. Kindler did not see a path to evolve from a 'Mom & Pop' venture to a comparatively large glove company. His early key to survival was his focus on the small retail stores, since his inventory was limited. Looking back, he is certain that he would focus both on larger retail and industrial customers, if he could have afforded it and could do it all again.

Case specific experiences. During the growth of the company, it was necessary for a change in leadership style, or leadership succession. In this line, Mr. Kindler's son (27) is taking over the management of the company. As they make the leadership transition, Mr. Kindler's son is taking on more and more responsibility while Mr. Kindler increasingly assumes a backseat role. To see this transition through, it has been a costly endeavor for Mr. Kindler. Legal and accounting fees were expensive. And for the business, the transition must be cleanly organized (especially as it concerns family business), as it is important to ensure a solid ownership succession and secure financial transition.

Message to new entrepreneurs. To new entrepreneurs, Mr. Kindler says it is important to start, if possible, even when only limited financial resources are available and to just go for it. It is also important to establish your own personal level of quality time in your life so you control the balance between your business and family and not have the business control you. *Carpe diem* is his motto.

Entrepreneurship and Spirituality

Role of intuition. Intuition is very important to Mr. Kindler. He relies on it as much as 40% in his decisions. However, intuition is always combined with some facts, although intuitional decisions are always 'contaminated' with facts.

Societal contribution. For Mr. Kindler, ethics for business and personal values are and must be the same! In his business, he contributes to the development for solutions of environmental problems and sponsors charitable organizations. As an example, he traveled to Indonesia to help out after the tsunami. The firm also donated 10,000 pairs of gloves for the clean-up of US Gulf storm Katrina in 2005.

Summary Profile Bruce Kindler

Current venture	Kinco International
Place of business	Portland, Oregon, USA
Founding year	1975
Involvement	1975 to present
Business sector	Import/wholesale
Venture activity	Importing work gloves from Asia, primarily China and marketing these primarily in North America.
Customers	Various retail stores and chains including safety supply, ranch farm supply, grocery chains.
International activities	Minor, but growing. About 5% of total sales in New Zealand and Central America.
Company strengths	Value for money Tried ski and bicycle gloves which were a failure but learned a great deal from modern marketing techniques
Company weaknesses	Sales management supervising the sales force

13.3 Norbert Mutsaerts, Noppies

At the end of 1990, I resigned from my job at Ceteco. At that time I had a position in Moscow and I found life less enjoyable there. My wife wished to come back to the Netherlands after having lived in Guatemala, Africa and Russia and I agreed. Yet, I found working for Ceteco in the Netherlands insufficiently challenging and therefore I resigned. At that point I started to think about starting my own firm and becoming an entrepreneur. The time was right, but I did not have any idea or business plan. I knew financially I could take the risk and I explored products such as teak wood from Chili, but decided with help from a construction company in Germany that it was too technical and that I did not have the expertise. It was very much a process of trial and error. Then I came upon the idea of diapers and at that time there was a trend to separate different types of waste. I thought using cotton diapers would fit with this trend and I had seen them in the USA in those days.

Company Profile

Company size indicators. The company has made profit from the beginning and the number of employees and turnover increased every year since the start. The level of turnover is between 10-25 million euro. Mr. Mutsaerts started the firm alone and at present employs 29 fulltime people. The company achieved positive financial results every year since the business started.

Company development. Over the course of a few years, more specific knowledge entered the company via hiring designers, financial experts, agents, and people experienced with ready made clothing. Since the start, the company achieved positive financial results, and the company is experiencing organic growth. Logical steps in developing the organization, like the creation of separate sections with their own responsibilities have been taken. Concerning the position in the market there has been growth on a geographic scale and growth amongst existing buyers. The strategy of Mr. Mutsaerts stayed more or less the same since the start. The buyers market did change in 2001 a little bit in comparison with the start in 1991.

Defining Opportunities

Evaluation criteria. Only after the fact does Mr. Mutsaerts investigate why something did or did not succeed. His most important criteria to evaluate market opportunity is profitability.

Opportunity evaluation techniques. Mr. Mutsaerts encourages innovation within his company by continuously redesigning his products, and all the time he works to re-segment the market in order to find new markets for his products.

Experiences

Remarkable initial experiences. As a first step he approached suppliers of diapers in the USA; the diaper washing service was a normal thing there. As he was visiting suppliers of diapers he accidentally came in contact with companies that distributed maternity clothing. So he started with two different business activities. First, he rented cotton diapers to childcare institutes, organizing that at the end of each day the diapers were picked up for washing. Because this activity fit well with the waste reduction trend he received a great deal of publicity through radio and newspaper. Mr. Mutsaerts' second activity was importing maternity clothes into the Netherlands, Germany, England and Belgium.

After a time the development of new product lines in the USA came to a stop and he decided to design the clothes himself. For the diapers he used the name Noppies and for marketing reasons also branded the clothes with the same name, Noppies Maternity. At the end of 1995 he stopped the business with diapers as it was not challenging anymore, and there were no innovations in that product line.

At that time there were five employees. He hired a maternity clothes designer and began to put more effort into the maternity clothes business.

Starting the business was supported by the fact that the maternity clothes were designed by a well known movie star, he was not in a hurry to realize profits, he was not starting his firm under any pressure and he was only 26 and knew that in the case he wasn't successful he could always find another job. The most important thing was for Mr. Mutsaerts was to try and discover what he enjoyed the most. The factors that were less easy in the starting period included the loneliness of working as an entrepreneur, a huge difference from working in a larger organization. The first year (1991) he worked alone and then from 1992 to1995, his wife joined him in his company. Still, it took Mr. Mutsaerts four or five years to find peers that shared his business interests.

Fears and difficult decisions. Mr. Mutsaerts did not have fears; he saw only challenges and his only uncertainty was related to failure. His true motivation was the drive to just 'let me try it' he says. In the beginning, he avoided taking difficult decisions.

Initial learning points. "The starting process was trial and error. I had a lot of patience. I was responsive to buyers and suppliers and to other business partners. And for the firm it is good to have stable growth." Mr. Mutsaerts did not use external finance for his investments.

Case specific experiences. When he started he did not have much affinity with diapers, yet Mr. Mutsaerts found that he liked the clothing business. He works on an international level and he can actually design and create things. Four times a year his firm launches a new baby clothes collection and twice a year a maternity clothes collection is launched. Recently he moved to a new building that allows his firm the opportunity to grow further.

Message to new entrepreneurs. For new entrepreneurs Mr. Mutsaerts says it is important to be reliable and patient. He also believes it is important to have passion for what you do; otherwise it will not be a success.

Entrepreneurship and Spirituality

Role of intuition. Mr. Mutsaerts makes good use of intuition, and estimates that intuition influences 50% of his decision-making.

Societal contribution. As one matures, Mr. Mutsaerts thinks that he or she is more aware of the contribution they he make to society. He does participate in some charity work, yet thinks it is not enough.

Summary Profile Norbert Mutsaerts

Current venture	Noppies Inc – 2002
Other ventures	Miller & Matter / EZ Bizz – 1999
Place of business	Lelystad, The Netherlands
Founding Year	1991
Involvement	1991-present
Business sector	Wholesale trade in textile
Venture activity	Design, sale, distribute maternity and new born clothes under the brand name, Noppies.
Customers	Retailers of clothes from all over the world
International activities	In 45 countries. He has a company in the USA (Noppies Inc), he has agents in many countries (especially in the USA and Europe) and he has distributors in the Netherlands and Germany.
Company strengths	The creativity in designs, the reliability in deliveries, the commercial supply, the international approach.
Company weaknesses	According to Mr. Mutsaerts, he is not that good in the recruitment of qualified personnel.

13.4 Rob van Rozendaal, The Music Marketeers

Since I was a boy, I dreamt of becoming an entrepreneur. As a kid I sold nuts in my neighborhood, and at 13 years old I wanted to go to Nyenrode. First I was in the military service, and then took a six month break. After graduating from Nyenrode, I worked for a TV producer for a few years. At one point I realized that both the music industry and being an entrepreneur was more 'my thing' so I decided to start a business where I could enjoy working again.

Company Profile

Company size indicators. In the last three years the company was profitable, with headcount and turnover increasing in the last two years. Turnover is around 2 million euro. Mr. Van Rozendaal started the firm by himself, later on he built international offices with his business partner Lorenz van der Stam and at present employs a fulltime staff of over 30.

Company development. The current team is composed of highly-educated people. Turnover is not stable and fluctuates in large part due to the dynamics of the market. The organizational structure has changed from a one-man venture into a corporation and now there are long-term customers, whereas in the beginning they dealt mostly with one-time customers. The company's market position also changed as Mr. Van Rozendaal started to explore other markets and products. The firm focuses on developing software, media network operation and, very recently, the management of advertising services. This combination will enable the company increase its sales.

Defining Opportunities

Evaluation criteria. For Mr. Van Rozendaal the most important criteria to evaluate market opportunity is intuition.

Opportunity evaluation techniques. Mr. Van Rozendaal works to encourage employees in his company to be creative with a focus on continuously redesigning products, re-differentiating products annually, and all the time re-segmenting the market to find new markets for products. During 2001-2003, Mr. Van Rozendaal redefined the market and crossed established boundaries. Today the company also produces software for background music and images.

Experiences

Remarkable initial experiences. After he made the decision to start, it was not easy to decide what to do exactly. It took one year to find a project, as creativity was important for him. Soon Mr. Van Rozendaal started to focus on acquisition of bigger projects. In this way, he found the initial phase to be easier, and subsequently he had money to invest in buying material and for marketing purpose. A factor that made the start somewhat difficult was trying to identify the first project for the company. As well, Mr. Van Rozendaal started on his own, so he had to do everything himself. This required that he become familiar with different facets of starting a business, and his earlier network of contacts was not helpful.

Fears and difficult decisions. Mr. Van Rozendaal did not have fears but uncertainty, and he was told by people around him that it was time to stop with the new business and get a job. Certainly, there were difficult moments and it was a continuous struggle for Mr. Van Rozendaal not to have debts. It took three and a half years until the firm began to exist.

Initial learning points. Perseverance is very important, says Mr. Van Rozendaal. After a while you don't recognize yourself because it is learning by doing. Mr. Van

Rozendaal also said that working on your own with so much responsibility can be very lonely. When he had the opportunity to hire people, he found work to be less lonely. Yet one important insight for Mr. Van Rozendaal was the fact that as an entrepreneur he didn't have the frustration of being an employee.

Case specific experiences. According to Mr. Van Rozendaal there is a huge difference between doing business in the Netherlands and doing business in the Eastern European countries. Specifically, the mentality towards integrity is different and he feels that people from former Czechoslovakia are envious of the Western European society. In Poland and the Ukraine he found this the opposite, yet corruption was rife. In working in Central Eastern countries, his local associates received menacing letters from, among others, competitors. And in one situation, a local director was followed by people in a car with lights turned off. Yet, Mr. Van Rozendaal was determined to not yield to threats and went on with his work. Today, his office in Poland is doing well and the technical department that develops Music Marketeers' software is located there.

Mr. Van Rozendaal also worked through a situation whereby he discovered that his accounting was not right. He had based important decisions more or less only on his intuition and drive for creativity, and it was painful afterwards to face the negative financial situation that resulted from these decisions. In the period of 2001-2002, he was forced to reduce headcount from 40 to 20. Now he has 30 employees, and he has a sound financial picture of the company.

Message to new entrepreneurs. When you are involved in foreign business, it is important to work with people that you can trust says Mr. Van Rozendaal. Working with local people is needed, yet it is necessary to maintain a close overview of the daily business operations. In his opinion, it is good to give shares to employees, but authority is another matter. For Mr. Van Rozendaal the need for creativity is a strong drive in him and he finds that working with someone else to assess what investments are worthwhile is valuable, at present his brother has taken on that role. Mr. Van Rozendaal also says, "…start with something that you are familiar with, and be willing to take high risks both on the social dimension and on the financial dimension."

Entrepreneurship and Spirituality

Role of intuition. Too much use of intuition is dangerous, feels Mr. Van Rozendaal. During the last one and a half years, he discovered that the use of analytic research in combination with intuition works better.

Societal contribution. Mr. Van Rozendaal creates jobs opportunities with his company and he enjoys that some employees choose to stay on with the company for extended periods of time. His philosophy is that people perform best if they are happy and enjoy what they do.

Summary Profile Rob van Rozendaal

Current venture	The Music Marketeers B.V.
Other ventures	1995, Creative Interaction B.V. 2001, TMM International B.V. + daughters 2004, IDS Polen
Place of business	Amsterdam, The Netherlands
Founding year	1992
Involvement	1992 to present
Business sector	Entertainment
Venture activity	All-in-one Background Music, Narrow Casting and Content services. Special product CD's and DVD's.
Customers	Various types of companies
International activities	Primarily in Spain, Poland and The Baltics, offices in Spain and Poland, customers and agencies worldwide.
Company Strengths	Innovative, creative and flexible
Company Weaknesses	The company depends too much on him, and as the company matures, this dependency decreases.

13.5 Arnold Tuinenburg, Apcare

I have a technical background, with experience working for Honeywell, Electric Engineering, (Getronics Installation Services), Datapoint, Grandhill Multimedia, Internet Connect Centre (Worldcom), Agency.com, and with KPN Housing & Hosting I helped establish new departments or services. Based on my earlier experience, I knew that my primary expertise was in hosting internet applications. Previously I worked for several companies in the internet and telecommunication sector and in 1996 I decided to start a venture with a business partner, but that did not work out. In a second attempt, I started a firm building on my internet activities while I held a salaried position. In 2001, I officially started Apcare after being with KPN. And a half year later I found a business partner, Michael de van der Scheuren.

Company Profile

Company size indicators. The company was profitable last year. Turnover was 2 million euro last year and grows over 40% annually. At present the company has 15 fulltime employees and is growing. For the last three years financial results were positive with only the first two years not realizing a profit.

Company development. Mr. Tuinenburg points out that no strategic changes have occurred since the start. Turnover and profitability are good and they have capital to realize growth. There was a shift from a solo entrepreneurship to an internet management organization. In the early days, when he worked for KPN, he borrowed money to build a small workshop offering services yet with the recession during the start period he did not have enough projects, and ran out of money. At that point he approached a business partner with money who became the second owner of Apcare. Overall, the market for hosting is difficult, but because of the economy of scale Apcare experiences, they can afford a highly educated, 24-hour a day team. Now, even well known companies are becoming customers.

Defining Opportunities

Evaluation criteria. Mr. Tuinenburg feels that one must be very alert at all times, and it is important to define criteria in advance. At the same time, it is important to realize that entrepreneurship is a dynamic process and new insights and situations quickly influence initial criteria or objectives.

Opportunity evaluation techniques. For Mr. Tuinenburg each prospect or customer is a new challenge in meeting the needs of the customer. There are no standardized procedures for a start-up so you need to improvise all the time.

Experiences

Remarkable initial experiences. Unexpectedly, he lost his job with KPN and saw the moment as an opportunity to start out on his own. Other factors that pushed the start of Apcare along included Mr. Tuinenburg receiving some work assignments, with one project requiring the design of software for reading emails. Yet it was always a challenge to win new customers.

Fears and difficult decisions. In all stages of the start-up, Mr. Tuinenburg feared bankruptcy, and not being able to create a successful venture. The amount of time it took to start the company and the costs involved were also not encouraging. It was difficult to gain new customers, and at the same time there was great pressure to secure new projects in order to stabilize the working situation and decrease the level of uncertainty related to the new venture.

Initial learning points. For Mr. Tuinenburg, a salaried position or choosing to be an entrepreneur are not significantly different propositions. He thinks you can act with an entrepreneur's spirit as an employee as well, and this is how he felt when he was an employee. The primary difference from his perspective is that as an entrepreneur you are your own boss and nobody can kick you out of the company.

Case specific experiences. Starting Apcare took a lot of time, and in the beginning years he could not take any holidays. Now Mr. Tuinenburg can easily leave the business for a week. Also initially, he had no time for reflection as the start-up situation was very dynamic and energy intensive. Mr. Tuinenburg often hears of procedures and standardization in the automation sector which means that highly educated people are forced to adjust to these procedures and standards. He believes this does not work as his staff's intellectual capacity is not used optimally.

Message to new entrepreneurs. Try to keep it simple, watch the company numbers, and ensure that your head is on right!

Entrepreneurship and Spirituality

Role of intuition. When making decisions, Mr. Tuinenburg does make use of intuition and finds it especially important concerning big decisions.

Societal contribution. Mr. Tuinenburg contributes to society through his firm which enables people to work from home offices, saving traveling costs and time, and promoting efficiency. Mr. Tuinenburg also feels that your own norms and values predict your actions and it is therefore good to take time for reflection.

Summary Profile Arnold Tuinenburg

Current venture	Apcare B.V.
Other ventures	Grandhill Multimedia, together with a business partner. However, he indicates that the market was not ready yet (1996). Tourist Nederland, for his own internet activities to earn some money in the past.
Place of business	Oude Meer, The Netherlands
Founding year	2001
Involvement	2001 to the present
Business sector	Internet
Venture activity	Apcare is a hosting provider and manages internet applications
Customers	Customers who have time constraints but can afford paying a high price. They find availability of services very important.
International activities	Apcare has customers from Norway to Singapore

Company strengths	Expertise, satisfied customers, starting to get a familiar name in the market. Cash flow stability because customers with annual contracts monthly. Working in the data centers, for example KPN and Interxion, it can respond very quickly.
Company weaknesses	Low capitalization, his own and outside investors, was difficult
	The newness of the venture did work against it in the past
	The company is never closed, causing on-going personal pressure
	It continues to require intensive management
	A small mistake can have dire consequences
	Few investors for a slow but stable firm, but banks like it.

13.6 Edmée Vitzthum, Switchtrax Telecom

I started three companies after graduation at Nyenrode. I have working experience in Europe and the USA, and live in France. I was formally an investment banker and eventually I wanted more freedom. Initially, I did not realize I could be an entrepreneur and my entrepreneurial career came totally unexpected. A headhunter told me that I might not easily find a position in business that fit my desires with the profile of an investment banker and suggested I consider becoming an entrepreneur. With that advice, I started a small firm after my career with two investment banks.

Company Profile

Company size indicators. The total number of employees decreased and turnover increased during the last two years. The company made no profit during the last three years of Ms. Vitzthum's involvement, and the level of turnover was between

5 and 10 million euro. At the time she left the company there were 20 fulltime employees.

Company development. The company did not face major changes since start-up in terms of strategic approach or organizational structure. There were changes in the market position, as Switchtrax became a competitor with larger telecom companies and average customer spending increased.

Defining Opportunities

Evaluation criteria. Ms. Vitzthum worked to define market evaluation criteria in advance and used the following points for evaluation: size of the expected market, expected growth, SWOT analyses of the competitors, market research among potential customers, developments of subcontractors and the effects on margins. Additionally, competitor pricing and the relation to margins and, finally affiliation with distributors are also things she considers.

Opportunity evaluation techniques. Within the company, Ms. Vitzthum used various tools for management, including defining a description of the business concept, and detailing important trends related to the concept. Key data important to the business was also collected, for example, recording specifics of an opportunity by linking the concepts to numbers. Ms. Vitzthum kept notes of the company position that included things like particular competencies, skills, or resources within the company that might make the business concept particularly attractive or defensible. She also maintained an analysis of the competition including the relevant competitors and their likely response to her business proposition. This made it possible to determine and record what type of opportunity was being pursued.

Experiences

Remarkable initial experiences. Ms. Vitzthum says that the key ingredients for start-up are a good and committed team and investors, and in her experience, creating and tapping into your network is a key success factor. After four attempts she found the correct business partner and they went forward with the venture. In the start-up process there were challenging factors, like the vicious circle of no money – no team, and no team – no money! And it took a long time to start the business. Ms. Vitzthum also thinks that it might be more difficult for a woman to find a business partner.

Fears and difficult decisions. In the beginning she did not perceive any fear and simply believed in her venture, pushing forward at all times. It was in the later phases of the venture that she found herself bluffing her way around fears. Among the difficult decisions was inviting a third partner into her venture, in order to resolve the bottleneck that they were experiencing.

Initial learning points. Among her initial learning from the business, Ms. Vitzthum lists the most significant points: So much depends on coincidence or even luck;

You have to be more skeptical in all aspects of defining your opportunity, checking the match in values and objectives with all potential partners; Be more opportunistic; Less passion and more opportunism.

Case specific experiences. At one point, Ms. Vitzthum proposed a new strategy to promote growth which was a service to the small and medium sized business sector. They wanted to capitalize on the first mover advantage to push a new telephone service into the market. But, the service offering turned out to be too complicated to easily convey in a sales call for the existing sales force, and in her opinion the opportunity was ahead of its time in the market.

Message to new entrepreneurs. To new entrepreneurs Ms. Vitzthum says to look for funding with business angels over bank or venture capital. In her experience it is more important to get a committed financing partner rather than to go for the highest valuation of the business at the initial funding stage. And taking too much risk under pressure can be a grave mistake.

Entrepreneurship and Spirituality

Role of intuition. In her estimate, Ms. Vitzthum uses more than 50% intuition when making a decision.

Societal contribution. Primarily, the values and norms she works by in her business activities reflect her contributions to society.

Summary Profile Edmée Vitzthum

Current venture	Switchtrax Telecom Limited
Other ventures	2000: S.a.r.l. Coffee Unlimited 2002: Inside Track Tours Inc.
Place of business	London
Founding year	Switchtrax in 1997
Involvement	1997-2001
Business sector	Telecommunications
Venture activity	Provider of innovative telecom services
Customers	Small and medium sized businesses
International activities	The Netherlands and United Kingdom
Company strengths	Technology, the capacity to negotiate with suppliers, and independence
Company weaknesses	Sales channels, recruitment of personnel, no brand name

13.7 Hans van Well, Foodwell

Following my study, I worked for my family food wholesalers business. I did my MBA in Florida. The family business in which I was a third generation owner was sold. Following this, I started my own company, a supermarket so I could pursue my ambition to be an entrepreneur.

Company Profile

Company size indicators. During the last three years the financial results were positive while the total number of employees decreased over the last two years. Turnover is between 10 and 25 million euro per year and when Mr. Van Well started there were 15 employees, at present there are nearly 100 people working for the business.

Company development. In 1987 when he started, employee education levels were roughly the same as they are now. Of note are the executive management courses on offer that can serve as continuing education. Financially, the firm has grown very fast. Mr. Van Well started out on his own and after two years incorporated the company. One important development has been a focus on better price positioning which is influencing turnover. He is also working to delegate more tasks and responsibilities to employees. As well, the company's position has been strengthened by an increase in square meters of floor space, by expanding the assortment and as a result they have captured a greater market share. Mr. Van Well also noted that occasionally the customer base grows and the level of regular customers continues to increase.

Defining Opportunities

Evaluation criteria. Mr. Van Well only pursues market opportunities that are well defined in advance, and he looks most closely at the possibility for increased turnover to realize increased profitability.

Opportunity evaluation techniques. He does not use any specific approach to stimulating creative processes for himself or for the company, yet he does develop skills aimed at increasing competitive advantages.

Experiences

Remarkable initial experiences. For Mr. Van Well it was most remarkable that everything that happened was immediately measurable which meant it was possible to manage things from the beginning. As part of this management, he found it important to walk in the supermarket and bookstore with a customer's perspective. Also of importance, his leadership was appreciated and for him working in the store and thinking with his employees about strategic issues is a valuable experience. Factors that made the start-up difficult were perceptions of others from Nyenrode related to a negative image of becoming a grocer. At that time, going into a retail business was not a priority or optimal choice for a career. In fact this worked to motivate him to strive for success. Otherwise, there were no real setbacks and after 13 years from the start-up of his supermarket he launched a bookstore next door.

Fears and difficult decisions. Very challenging for Mr. Van Well was his limited knowledge about the practical aspects of running a supermarket. After studying things, he questioned how he could create a more structured management approach. On the other hand, he experienced the purchasing process as quite exciting.

Initial learning points. Mr. Van Well did not dream of starting his own business as it was expected that he would succeed in the family business. When the decision was taken to sell the family business, he took the opportunity to start on his own business. Given the chance to start over again, he would try to buy the building instead of renting. And he notes that he has learned to let people find their own solutions to problems. He also thinks that when it comes to people, it is essential to let them know they are a valuable part of the success of the business!

Case specific experiences. A strategy to realize growth involved moving into another sector by starting a bookstore. His philosophy on this matter is based on his thinking that if he can not do it, who can do it. Mr. Van Well prefers to discuss opportunities with others and he works closely with his employees to face the supermarket challenge of 'pricing wars'.

Message to new entrepreneurs. Keep your spirits up is Mr. Van Well's message to entrepreneurs. And he believes that it is important to encourage people to find their own solutions to issues.

Entrepreneurship and Spirituality

Role of intuition. Mr. Van Well does not believe he makes much use of intuition. Perhaps 30% of the time he relies on his intuition when making a decision.

Societal contribution. Mr. Van Well mentions his leadership style that is based on letting people learn and develop themselves as well as encouraging employees to enjoy what they do in their work. Motivating people to develop their skills and apply these in the workplace is another contribution that Mr. Van Well strives to make. And through his business he may create more job opportunities.

Summary Profile Hans van Well

Current venture	Foodwell B.V.
Place of business	Houten, The Netherlands
Founding year	1987
Involvement	1987 to the present
Business sector	Retail
Venture activity	Foodwell B.V. is the holding company and there are two subsidiary companies: Van Well Supermarket B.V. (a C1000 franchise), and Bookwell B.V. (a Bruna franchise).
Customers	Consumers in the Woerden region of The Netherlands
International activities	None
Company strengths	High turnover per square meter, highly motivated employees. Big market share.
Company weaknesses	Situated in a disadvantaged area

13.8 Walter Herman Westendorp, TLP International

I was born in the Netherlands, I am an owner of the company I founded in 1988. After my Nyenrode study I studied chemistry in Germany. I had a corporate career before I started my own firm and also worked for the family business for seven years. I have lived and worked in Germany and Hong Kong for some years. I used to be a marketing director in the Far East where I first discovered that entrepreneurship was for me. There were bureaucratic and political issues at the company I worked for that led to my resignation in 1987 from Ciba-Geigy. Following that, I started my own venture.

Company Profile

Company size indicators. Mr. Westendorp started on his own and at present has 12 employees. The company has realized positive financial results since it began.

Company development. Within the company the education level of employees has risen through special training programs offered on production preparation, application of products, marketing and sales. In terms of turnover, each year has seen a substantial increase in turnover. And the company changed from a proprietorship to a corporation. On the marketing and sales front, agents are frequently used so there is less direct contact with the end user of the products. In the beginning TLP was a newcomer and now it is an internationally accepted supplier. Due to the closing of some of his customers' businesses, Mr. Westendorp shifted his activities to low income countries.

Defining Opportunities

Evaluation criteria. When Mr. Westendorp pursues a market opportunity he defines the criteria in advance and if needed he formulates new tools during the working process.

Opportunity evaluation techniques. Mr. Westendorp has a systematic approach to work with market analysis that involves analyzing and registering developments in the fashion sector together with international companies. These activities contribute to developments leading to new effects and new products. Within his company he uses brainstorming, business fair visits, and contact with merchandisers of important companies in the branch to explore new opportunities. As well, he sometimes redesigns the products, re-segments the market and continuously develops new competencies aimed at creating competitive advantages.

Experiences

Remarkable initial experiences. The first orders came only three or four years later, with the first order placed by Levi Strauss. This was a great motivation for the business and the company gained a positive image from this project. His chemistry studies helped him a great deal and he was able to initially not hire anyone and save money. His wife was also a great source of support. Thus, the lack of resources was initially the main difficulty.

Fears and difficult decisions. Clients going bankrupt was a real possibility and he constantly feared that. He also had to deal with a few bad agents in different countries, so under these circumstances it was difficult to visit customers over and over again. The decision to keep going was a challenging one for Mr. Westendorp. Early on, he almost lost a great deal of money yet maintained his strong sense of perseverance.

Initial learning points. Mr. Westendorp always dreamt of becoming an entrepreneur as both his father and grandfather were entrepreneurs. Given the chance to start again he would prepare things earlier and stay calmer so that he could take more time to deal with challenges. Mr. Westendorp also learned to work with big companies and discovered how important it is to thoroughly explain innovations to customers who only then, can implement them further. Building a reputation as an innovator can only be based on the success of winning new business.

Case specific experiences. His innovation in bleached jeans was successful, and as it was his invention he patented the concept. Mr. Westendorp did experience technical problems in the beginning, with the bleaching process sometimes resulting in a yellow color.

Message to new entrepreneurs. The keywords that Mr. Westendorp would share with new entrepreneurs are "working hard". And it is also important to be very good in your profession!

Entrepreneurship and Spirituality

Role of intuition. Intuition plays an important role for Mr. Westendorp and he estimates that as much as 50% of his decisions are based on intuition.

Societal contribution. He tries to be a trusting individual and contributes to the countries were he does business through job creation and supporting the development of solutions to environmental issues (for example, using non-toxic and non flammable materials). Also Mr. Westendorp contributes to charity and, in general to the economy through his business activities.

Summary Profile Walter Herman Westendorp

Current venture	TLP international B.V.
Place of business	Loon op Zand, The Netherlands
Founding year	1988
Involvement	1988 to the present
Business sector	Chemicals
Venture activity	Production of chemical preparations for the textile and the jeans industries
Customers	Jean producers, industrial jean laundries and textile companies.
International activities	Eastern Europe, South East Asia, Africa and South America. The products are being delivered directly to the import agents or other customers in the various countries.
Company strengths	Innovation, quality is high, reliability, and service
Company weaknesses	Long delivery time

13.9 Frank van Wezel, Hi-Tec Sports

Ever since I was a boy, I dreamt of having my own business. Ten years into my ca-reer I moved to London where I often played squash. In the locker room my play-mates often complained about their shoes and this inspired me with the idea to cre-ate specific footwear for this sport. In those days there were no specific shoes for squash. In 1974 I founded Hi-Tec Sports Plc, in Essex, UK, originally as a distribu-tor of squash shoes. Now, my company designs, markets and distributes about 800 different types of sport and leisure footwear per annum. In the overall global sneaker companies league my business is the 13th largest. In the golf market the company is 2nd in the UK and in the outdoor market, the company 4th in the world.

Company Profile

Company size indicators. The company was profitable last year. Headcount and turnover remained stable. Annual turnover is in excess of 250 million euro annually.

At present the company has 520 full and part-time employees. When Mr. Van Wezel started there were five employees.

Company development. The company is hiring more personnel compared with the earlier years. As the industry has grown, there is more focus on individual segments in the global market. There are fewer customers in the retail sector as large customers are getting larger and smaller customers are disappearing. The larger customers need a lot of attention worldwide.

Defining Opportunities

Evaluation criteria. When Mr. Van Wezel pursues a market opportunity he defines criteria in advance. The primary opportunity evaluation criterion he uses is instant profitability.

Opportunity evaluation techniques. Mr. Van Wezel uncovers new opportunities for the company by continuously working on product innovation, re-branding and studying new geographic markets. One technique he uses is to quickly redesign products or services and when necessary, he re-segments markets.

Experiences

Remarkable initial experiences. "I didn't know anything about the shoe business. Founding the business felt somehow romantic. When I came up with the idea I met the right people; a bank manager, a sales director, a warehouse manager and an accountant, all living in my street in England. This business is extremely competitive. Competition manifests itself through marketing. It's all about image because all the shoes, including the famous brand names, are produced in the same factories by the same people and under the same conditions," says Mr. Van Wezel.

Fears and difficult decisions. It was a challenge to find good quality squash shoes. The difficulty was to get familiar with the industry and for that he had to learn a lot about the products. For example, the shoe sizes used in the industry were all new to him. It was also obvious very quickly that having just one product does not work as customers requested different shoes for other sports. Therefore, he had to move on to other product designs immediately.

Initial learning points. Mr. Van Wezel learned that when you start you must have a variety of products, and talk with potential customers before you have developed the product, as they always come with specific wishes and ideas. Hire the best people from the start who can rapidly interpret these customer demands.

Case specific experiences. In one instance, his daughter came in contact with an American girl whose parents were in the UK for a teacher exchange program. The father asked Mr. Van Wezel if he could sell his shoes in America. He was living in Modesto, California. At first Mr. Van Wezel hesitated because he did not know if there was a market for his squash shoes in the USA but then he thought it might turn out to be a unique opportunity. The problem however was that the American had no money to invest whatsoever, so all risks were with Mr. Van Wezel. He ended up giving him a container with 10,000 pairs of shoes, covered freight and import costs, and made advance payments as investment in the US market. It was a big investment for Mr. Van Wezel since at that point in time his own company had been in existence only three years and to risk a total of over 150.000 GBP on a market he did not know with a person he had just met who came from California where he had never been demanded courage and faith. After a month he heard that there was no real market for squash shoes and that US customers where asking for light-weight outdoor boots instead. Mr. Van Wezel had the squash shoes returned to the UK and started to produce outdoor shoes for the US market. Now, almost 30 years later, his company is still in Modesto and has an annual turnover of US $ 100 million (3 million pairs) in the USA. The gamble paid off!

Message to new entrepreneurs. When considering what message to share with new entrepreneurs, Mr. Van Wezel believes that fortune favors the bold!

Entrepreneurship and Spirituality

Role of intuition. Intuition is very important and it accounts for nearly 80% of his decision-making process. He engages in an investment only when it feels good.

Societal contribution. Mr. Van Wezel feels that through his company he contributes to society by creating jobs and by giving to charities and sport organizations. For his services to the game of squash he was made a life vice-president of the English Squash Association.

Summary Profile Frank van Wezel

Current venture	Hi-Tec Sports PLC
Other ventures	Subsidiaries and investment companies
Place of business	Southend-on-sea-Essex, Great Britain
Founding year	1974
Involvement	1974 to the present
Business sector	Sport shoes and sports wear
Venture activity	Design, marketing and distribution of about 800 different types of sport shoes and 500 items of sports clothing annually.
Customers	Sports stores, department stores, shoes stores, uniform stores
International activities	Sales in over 100 countries through distributors and subsidiaries
Company strengths	Easy to deal with; Can react quickly to the market; Global approach with up to date collections; Competitive prices
Company weaknesses	Information systems; Little fashion appeal for performance products; Marketing budget too small

13.10 Deo van Wijk, Saturn Methanol Conversion Company

I have started various companies. I wanted to create and build something lasting in order to leave something behind. Methanol is my specialty and I thought that what I could do for a company, I could just as well do for myself, adding that I can do creative financing.

Company Profile

Company size indicators. The turnover of the Houston, Texas based company is in the $5-10 million range (4 – 8 million euro) and there are 12 employees. In the Trinidad operation turnover is 20-35 million Trinidad dollars (3 – 5 million euro) and there are 22 employees.

Company development. Mr. Van Wijk was behind the development of the first Saturn company in Houston, Texas. Trinidad followed later, offering an opportunity to realize lower wages and new financial partnerships.

Defining Opportunities

Evaluation criteria. Mr. Van Wijk pursues a market opportunity by defining the conditions for success in advance. His criteria are looking forward and planning for a five year horizon.

Opportunity evaluation techniques. Mr. Van Wijk does have a systematic approach to stimulate creative processes and uses brain storming sessions as well as techniques that focus on creating new competencies, or areas of competitive strength that can lead to the creation of new competitive advantages

Experiences

Remarkable initial experiences. The most remarkable thing for Mr. Van Wijk was that private individuals without any money can start a $300 million company with loans. When he started, nothing was easy, absolutely nothing. There were a few things that helped the start-up process and they included persistence, and pursuing the right contacts through all partners. Factors that were difficult involved everything cost related coming out of his pocket.

Fears and difficult decisions. Of course there were fears for Mr. Van Wijk; however in his opinion you can never show that you have fears. In the case that it was necessary to fire an employee, Mr. Van Wijk found this very challenging. And not feeling that he could take vacations was a difficult thing.

Initial learning points. The fact that Mr. Van Wijk was fired from his previous company, MetallGesellschaft, together with some other 40,000 employees, helped a lot in terms of learning. At one point in his career Mr. Van Wijk generously shared his company shares with his employees, and as a result this structure later forced him to sell a venture he had wanted to keep. It is important to be an 'all-round entrepreneur' and keep the big picture in view, Mr. Van Wijk found in his experience. And at all times keep an updated vision in your head of where you are and where you want to go.

Case specific experiences. Following his previous ventures, Mr. Van Wijk saw early on an opportunity in the growing world-wide methanol market and used his substantial network to garner resources to start the Houston, Texas company. That venture was a success and Trinidad was a logical next step.

Message to new entrepreneurs. Mr. Van Wijk's advice to new entrepreneurs: asking for what you want is always more difficult than you think and it costs more time than what you think is. Knowing every process in detail is critical as well.

Entrepreneurship and Spirituality

Role of intuition. Certainly intuition always played a role in Mr. Van Wijk's decision-making, and he estimates that it accounts for nearly 50% of his final decision.

Societal contribution. Mr. Van Wijk wants to leave something behind for the community and for example, regularly donates computers to elementary schools. The companies he owns also create jobs and contribute to environmental solutions, social welfare and charity.

Summary Profile Deo van Wijk

Current venture	Saturn Methanol Conversion Company
Others ventures	Petrolab
	Methanex
	Saturn Methanol Co
	Titan
	Altas
	Pipe Services International in Houston
	Pipe Services International in T.T.
	Micro Chemie
	Body Armor
	AutoBySite
Place of business	USA, Germany, The Netherlands
Founding year	1991
Involvement	1991 to present
Business sector	Methanol
Venture activity	Company focuses on innovations in the areas of water and fuels
Customers	BASF, Shell, Hoechst and other chemical companies
International activities	USA, Trinidad, Europe
Company strengths	Analytical and visionary entrepreneurial approach
Company weaknesses	People management, lay-offs

13.11 Arnold de Wolf, Wolco Holland

I spent a part of my education in the USA and in England. I started several small companies with a variety of products. With an enormous drive for freedom, I could not bear criticism easy especially when I did not agree with ideas that came from other persons and I see myself as a pigheaded person. These characteristics made me a natural entrepreneur, and I have since started four ventures. The company where I worked initially was selling upholstery fabric and my boss wanted to expand and asked me to sell silk flowers and products to drugstores. I received shares of this new venture that had a market for upholstery fabric in Europe and for the new products in the Netherlands. After a few years I bought the drugstore business from my boss.

Company Profile

Company size indicators. The last three years of his involvement, turnover varied between 2 and 5 million euro annually. In 1970, there were four employees (including himself and his wife), in 1980 the level of employees had risen to 95 in four companies with total turnover of approximately 14 million euro. And by the end of 2000 three companies had been sold and the company continued on a small profitable basis of five employees.

Company development. Wolco employees represented educational levels related to the tasks to be carried out. During the first year the turnover was 500.000 euro and later due to expansions the turnover increased to 14 million euro for all four firms. In the end, other companies were sold and Mr. De Wolf maintained a small company with a turnover of 2, 5 million euro. First the risks were low but eventually soon it became an import / export company and a factory. The supply to wholesalers changed into the supply of products to department store chains and supermarkets. Another big change was the new export business in 1975 to Scandinavia and Germany. As well, Mr. De Wolf noted that participation in large fairs abroad became important for the company.

Defining Opportunities

Evaluation criteria. When Mr. De Wolf pursued a market opportunity he defined criteria during the process and evaluated them as well. His evaluation criteria included understanding the need for the product, expected profitability, power of competitors, structure of the market, and questioning whether there were private labels or not.

Opportunity evaluation techniques. Mr. De Wolf used the following techniques within his company to keep the level of creativity high: continuously re-designing the products or services, and when possible re-differentiating the products and services.

Experiences

Remarkable initial experiences. It was Mr. De Wolf's wife that suggested he choose between starting a company or salaried employment. Having some shares in the company he worked for was not enough because of his drive to work hard, so when he chose to become an entrepreneur his wife supported him totally. Negotiating with his boss to buy the company was something that was difficult for Mr. De Wolf. In part because, in a way it was already his company and the discussions felt strange. However, in complete harmony agreement was reached to buy part of the drugstore business. Money was always a problem, and in the initial stage he lost some money because he was swindled and due to planned expansions he needed money. For Mr. De Wolf, it was a good decision to start exporting products as he was convinced at an early stage that the Netherlands was too small of a market.

Fears and difficult decisions. Mr. De Wolf's biggest fear was that he would go bankrupt. He found that he was constantly working to convince himself of his decisions, especially in the case of employee related choices like hiring and firing.

Initial learning points. When he was young, Mr. De Wolf knew he had an affinity with entrepreneurship, and after reflection he mentioned that more concentration on his entrepreneurial activities would have been better. His approach was too broad, and through this experience he learned to be more focused. Mr. De Wolf also stressed that integrity is very, very, important and that for him it is possible to do business with integrity.

Case specific experiences. Mr. De Wolf mentioned several unique experiences, among which a drugstore chain in England complained unfairly about the cotton buds delivered. Mr. De Wolf agreed to recall all delivered products and re-supply a different (more expensive) product. The other supplier of the drugstore refused to do this because it was clear the complaints were not fair. The result was that the drugstore asked Mr. De Wolf to become their only supplier because of the good experience they had with his quality assurance and service.

In another case, a big customer complained about the panty shields his firm delivered. The customer told him they would stop doing business with him and suggested they use up all the remaining packed materials. Mr. De Wolf refused this offer, stating a customer should have faith in their product. Mr. De Wolf then suggested to take back all stock in the shops en supply the newer better product instead of using up the packed goods in a quality the customer did not believe in. This was a success that resulted in turnover increasing four times over. Mr. De Wolf's philosophy was when the customer does not have trust in your product; you better stop delivering it immediately. This attitude takes courage because you cannot predict if the customer will continue doing business with you regardless of your actions. Still, as an entrepreneur it is important to believe in the products you offer and when you have faith in your own competencies you have to act otherwise you risk loosing credibility which will costs you more in the long run.

Message to new entrepreneurs. Mr. De Wolf believes that being stubborn is important as an entrepreneur. And that you must have a strong belief in what you are doing. Also, when you start something, usually the initial start ideas are not successful. You must also be aware that usually people you counted on to start your business let you down at the critical moment. Also you always need to know your figures in order to have a healthy business. For Mr. De Wolf, knowing the daily performance of a company leads to the best insights and without these insights you cannot take the best decisions. And last, do not forget to make arrangements for your pension in an early stage of the business because you never know how you will end.

Entrepreneurship and Spirituality

Role of intuition. Intuition plays a very big role in decisions for Mr. De Wolf; about 70-80% of his decisions are influenced by intuition combined with rational reasoning (calculated risks).

Societal contribution. His contributions to society have come through job creation within his business and private funding to welfare organizations.

Summary Profile Arnold de Wolf

Current venture	Wolco Holland B.V.
Other ventures	Amarco B.V. Apco B.V. – 1972 (Factory in cotton buds.) De Wolf Holding B.V. (holding for pensions.) Eurodecor B.V. – 1977 (venture in silk flowers and other products for florist business) Intermaco B.V. – 1973 (import of watches, closed in 1981) Wolco Holland B.V. – 1969
Place of business	Almere, The Netherlands
Founding year	September 1969
Involvement	1970 – 2001
Business sector	From 1984: 98%-sales of razor blades as private label, 2% a variety of drugstore products
Venture activity	Import of razor blades from one producer who had factories in USA and Israel. The razor blades were packed in the Netherlands with the generic branding of the customers.
Customers	Chains of big department stores, drugstores and supermarkets
International activities	Supplier of products mainly to Germany, the Netherlands and Scandinavia
Company strengths	The venture offered consumer products for low prices and high turnover The price, quality and service were key in the venture. The company was therefore known as interesting and very reliable.
Company weaknesses	Because the venture was small, it depended too much on him. In the last years of his involvement he prepared the company for a take-over and did not have the motivation to start a new initiative. The logistics and packaging were not executed in the Netherlands anymore after the company was sold. The venture became a sales office with focus on the existing contacts mainly.

14 Small Business Entrepreneurs

14.1 Introduction

In Chapter 14, the profiles of six entrepreneurs with small businesses are described. The number of employees ranges from two to nine, and the turnover of these businesses varies from less than 1 million to 5 million euro per year. Jaap Bellingwout and Marco van Schaik are former entrepreneurs and Hans Klok, Jurrian te Gussinklo Ohmann, Roel Wolbrink and Bart Zieleman are still entrepreneurs. Mr. Bellingwout's firm is positioned in the metal industry, Mr. Klok's and Mr. Te Gussinklo Ohmann's firms are in the services sector, Mr. Van Schaik is in telecommunications, Mr. Wolbrink in clothing, and Mr. Zieleman in wholesale.

These small businesses also demonstrate how innovation plays a dominant role in operations as shown by Mr. Bellingwout, Mr. Te Gussinklo Ohmann, Mr. Klok and Mr. Zieleman. Mr. Wolbrink is an example of a duo-entrepreneur; he started a firm with another Nyenrodian and the firm flourishes because of the complementary capabilities of they each bring to the venture.

Delegation did not work well in the case of Zethameta; the company Mr. Bellingwout set up with his father-in-law. Being present and available turned out to be a success factor in his business.

Mr. Klok became an entrepreneur at an older than average age after a long, salaried career. He learned the differences that exist between being an entrepreneur and being a manager in a corporation. Maybe one of the main characteristics of small business entrepreneurs is the dilemma of delegation. Their firms are too small to have more than one person per position, and in case of an illness it is difficult to delegate and this can create a great deal of pressure. Ultimately, for the small business entrepreneur this requires that the entrepreneur has expertise in many areas. Mr. Van Schaik mentioned that in a start-up process you rarely have enough money and cannot afford to make mistakes. Not having enough money to maintain his position as a dominant player was what Mr. Wolbrink experienced.

All the participants of this chapter perceived their business as successful. Mr. Wolbrink would give his venture a 7 on a 10 point scale. Half of the participants made increased use of their intuition in the process of decision-making. For others if felt better to maintain a balance between reasoning and intuition.

14.2 Jaap Bellingwout, Robelco

I am a former entrepreneur and grew up in Indonesia until the age of 18. My fa-
ther-in-law had a venture in used and scrap iron and I started working for him af-
ter completing my studies in the Netherlands. It was a steel company (Zethameta
BV) where scrap iron was remanufactured for use in the State Mines. After the
first world war there was an increased need for iron, for example construction
beams for building houses. Old buildings that were being demolished offered steel
beams suitable for reuse, and the company became involved in buying this iron
and preparing it for re-use. In 1966, the business in used iron ceased as the mines
were then closed so my company had to concentrate on first class iron. I then
started Robelco in 1966 with my father-in-law in order to concentrate on these
new activities, at the same time Zethameta continued business in scrap metal
waste. A few years later my father-in-law sold his shares in Robelco to me.

Company Profile

Company size indicators. In the last three years of Mr. Bellingwout's involvement in the company, the firm was profitable and the number of employees, approximately seven, and turnover remained stable.

Company development. Over the years, the company did not make big changes concerning the personnel, and the turnover, the structure, and the strategic approach were stable. Among the innovations, adding engraver activity to the business portfolio was notable; leading to changes in the customer base and markets.

Defining Opportunities

Evaluation criteria. When Mr. Bellingwout pursued a market opportunity he defined his criteria in advance, looking most closely at the implications on service to customers related to the expansion in service and product assortment.

Opportunity evaluation techniques. Mr. Bellingwout relied on maintaining the same approach to business over the years, therefore, identifying new opportunities is part of this formula.

Experiences

Remarkable initial experiences. Very often no useful material for the scrap iron business was available for purchase. Therefore it was very important to be physically present when the iron was purchased to ensure the quality of the material. As Robelco was a daughter company of Zethameta BV, finance was available. Still, challenging factors during the start-up were his father-in-law breaking his hip in 1972 with the consequence that Mr. Bellingwout had to take over running Zethameta, and the business was scrap metal (a product for with which he did not have any affinity). Together these factors created a situation where Mr. Bellingwout was forced to allocate a great deal of his time to run Zethameta along with his own company Robelco. As a solution, he delegated too much of the work to others which did not produce the results he hoped for. At some point, he decided to sell Zethameta BV.

Fears and difficult decisions. Mr. Bellingwout did not have specific fears, yet there were challenges. Starting in the business as the son-in-law of the boss was not easy. And while there were no real difficult decisions to be taken in the business of Zethameta, within Robelco there was a high degree of pressure on him. For example, he was the only person on staff that could draw and he also learned all the facets of the cutting machine to ensure the work could continue even in the situation of illness or absence of other employees.

Initial learning points. Mr. Bellingwout learned to work very hard, and to do the dirty work as well. Every evening he was covered with soot, yet it was a part of the job. There were also a few dangerous situations when he was forced to work alone in a big pilot station due to sickness of personnel. Mr. Bellingwout also learned along the way that you need to maintain good administration, and that this can help to avoid the possibility of corruption and abuse of the business, which he experienced within his company.

Case specific experiences. One innovation that Mr. Bellingwout brought to his company was the use of the cutting machine for steel plates. This innovation evolved from a request for Mr. Bellingwout's company to begin using the cutting torch for jobs from a local business. The result was a new service that Mr. Bellingwout could offer for producing tailor made steel plates for customers. After one year it was clear that one machine was not enough as Mr. Bellingwout was the only one offering this service in the area of Schiedam. In another situation, Mr. Bellingwout became very involved in daily operations when employing Turkish guest workers. The task of weighing material was a difficult process due to the lack of familiarity with the Dutch language. As a result, several technical issues had to be explained to them and Mr. Bellingwout became involved in every step of the very detailed process. In another situation, Robelco became a specialist in the production of rolled metal plates used as steel planking.

Message to new entrepreneurs. Mr. Bellingwout's message is "Express your values in the tasks you have set yourself, both in private life and in business."

Entrepreneurship and Spirituality

Role of intuition. Dealing with people gives you an intuitive feeling and this guides your own behavior, says Mr. Bellingwout. Still he feels that it is necessary to depend on purchasing and sales to achieve financial results.

Societal contribution. And Mr. Bellingwout feels that he makes a small contribution to society by creating jobs for people. For himself, he now has more time to reflect on the meaning of life and enjoys reading and learning.

Summary Profile Jaap Bellingwout

Previous venture name	Robelco B.V.
Other ventures	Holding Ferbecon BV of which Robelco BV was a part
Place of business	Vlaardingen, The Netherlands
Founding year	1966
Involvement	1966-1990

Business sector	Metal industry
Venture activity	Construction steel, metal cutting and fabricating
Customers	Construction companies, maintenance and repair companies and machining factories
International activities	Germany, Belgium and France
Company strengths	Reliability, keep appointments and obligations Broad array of customers, many small buyers Big assortment of products Independent, no bank financing
Company weaknesses	Limited personnel is a risk in case of sickness etc.

14.3 Hans Klok, Marmont Film Financing

After my corporate career of nearly 30 years, I launched my own venture. I was already familiar with the creative industry and was interested to move into the film industry. To make the first step, I attended film courses at UCLA that ultimately led to my first position in the industry. It was during this experience that I observed conflicts with shareholders of a pay television venture and decided I did not want to stay on as the team captain. In 1996 I started as a free-lancer and in 2003 began Marmont film financing, aiming to stay small. My prior experience includes: 1964-73 Procter & Gamble, Belgium, Netherlands, USA; 1973-93 FHV / BBDO (The Netherlands-Europe); 1993-96 FilmNet Television Europe; and 1996-2003 Independent film producer.

Company Profile

Company size indicators. The company was profitable last year and employee numbers remained stable as turnover increased (turnover varies between 2 and 5 million euro / annually). At present the company has six full-time employees. During the previous three years the firm was not profitable.

Company development. Most of Mr. Klok's employees represent diverse commercial backgrounds. His venture has grown and now has a turnover of 5 million euro, with recent activities focusing on international networks of companies in France, Germany and the UK. In this approach, Mr. Klok's company is a market leader.

Defining Opportunities

Evaluation criteria. When Mr. Klok pursues a market opportunity he defines criteria during the evaluation process, assessing the market response and the potential returns for the business.

Opportunity evaluation techniques. Looking at on-going opportunities is a matter of using a technique to redesign and redefine the products his company offers.

Experiences

Remarkable initial experiences. Mr. Klok is certain that he was somewhat naïve when he stepped into the film world. Not knowing how to approach things, Mr. Klok learned by doing. At the same time, he was able to bring solid experience to his new business based on the competencies he gained as a 30 years self-employed film producer, his large network, and his ease in connecting with people on his plans. What was more difficult for Mr. Klok was his lack of willingness to start from a beginning point because he was used to working within large organizations, large budgets and support teams. For example, he had to learn how to work with the Internet and completing tasks that used to be carried out by others.

Fears and difficult decisions. Mr. Klok feels that his long career experience granted him a degree of comfort that can only come with time. As well, fears were minimized by his level of financial independence, thus he did not face many of the typical restrictions or difficulties during the start-up of his company.

Initial learning points. Initially, he was able to realize that learning from negative situations is an important tool. And Mr. Klok's decision to stay within the film industry was reconfirmed by his early experiences with his business.

Case specific experiences. Mr. Klok finds that his interaction with people in the USA provided inspiration for his work. He believes that society develops because of different types of impulses other than simply financial or business driven factors. In his approach to understanding his business, Mr. Klok stresses that embracing a sustainability perspective helps to view problems or questions in a broader framework and this can produce more sustainable business in the long run.

Message to new entrepreneurs. To new entrepreneurs, Mr. Klok says that it is important to seek out your place in the bigger framework of things. In his own experience, he became an entrepreneur at an older than average age yet has been able to combine his interests (philosophy, politics and culture) within the framework of his business. That has confirmed for him the importance of a sustainable approach to business in order to realize a greater degree of success on all levels.

Entrepreneurship and Spirituality

Role of intuition. For Mr. Klok, intuition is an influence below the surface of his decision-making and not something that he considers as a dominant factor.

Societal contribution. Although the local market is his starting point, Mr. Klok wants to give European popular culture a place through his financing approach to the production of films. He works from a European context and bases his business operations on The Treaty of Maastricht. And, Mr. Klok believes Europe can produce high quality European films. Spirituality and care for others and the community are important values for Mr. Klok. He thinks the term is modern, and has to do with your own basics values. Spirituality is the basis for you actions, in his opinion, and in his daily life he takes time for reflection. He believes in karma and feels that it is you own personal baggage that forms who you are. Entrepreneurship is a must in society, and your mentality and beliefs influence how things develop in an entrepreneurial form. It is good to have a self knowledge.

Summary Profile Hans Klok

Current venture	Marmont Film Financing
Other ventures	1993 FilmNet Television Europe
Place of business	Brussel – Amsterdam – Paris
Founding year	2003
Involvement	2003 to the present
Business sector	Services
Venture activity	Financial, commercial, investment advice in the film business
Customers	Marmont advises European film producers on the financial and commercial aspects of their film projects using all financial constructions that various European governments offer to promote the film industry. Marmont is advisor to companies who invest in film projects and helps them to maximize their financial and commercial success. National and international companies who can use the medium of film in their marketing activities.
International activities	Offices in Belgium, France, The Netherlands, shortly in the UK and Germany as well.
Company strengths	Expertise in film production, film finance and film marketing.
Company weaknesses	Undercapitalized New combination of expertise both a strength and a weakness! The film business is inward oriented

14.4   Jurrian te Gussinklo Ohmann, Bedaux Management Consultants

Although the plan was to take over my father's, then 80 year old, button producing factory, after working there for six months I left for a position at Bedaux Nederland NV where I worked for three years. That company employed 35 consultants and specialized in compensation and merit pay systems. At one point the demand for these services diminished and the business closed. Without work I decided to start my own consultancy under the name Marcad in 1969, and 10 years later I sold the venture to a colleague. In the days that followed I continued with freelance work, and among other things founded a venture in Australia. Upon my return I accepted a project from the colleague to whom I sold my company, and was exposed to working with the Kaizen concept. There were similarities with the method I used at Bedaux, which led to a motivation to start a new consultancy using the name Bedaux. It feel as if I learn every day and I get a lot of satisfaction out of my work.

Company Profile

Company size indicators. Turnover is less than 1 million euro annually, and the company was profitable last year with a stable employee base and increasing turnover. When Mr. Te Gussinklo Ohmann started the company there were two fulltime employees, today there are six and the last three years showed positive financial results.

Company development. The firm is very professional and growth is stable. In the beginning the company was formed as a limited company and the decision was taken to reform as a partnership. Slowly over time Mr. Te Gussinklo Ohmann has focused on a niche in the market and has experienced a fluctuation in the familiarity of the company within the marketplace. At times this has led to accidentally meeting new customers.

Defining Opportunities

Evaluation criteria. Evaluating why or why not a new opportunity developed is Mr. Te Gussinklo Ohmann approach. His evaluation criteria focus on considering whether the company has the right competencies, will they benefit as a company, and is the proposed project interesting.

Opportunity evaluation techniques. Reading, discussions, visiting seminars and simply just trying new things are part of his creative process for the company. Specifically with his employees, he considers in-house conferences a valuable technique for generating new insights. Most often the outcomes of this process include the redesign and re-differentiation of products or services and regular market re-segmentation.

Experiences

Remarkable initial experiences. He took big steps when he started in 1969, hiring employees even though it was always a difficult matter to secure enough work for all the employees. Looking back, Mr. Te Gussinklo Ohmann noticed that he was perhaps too quick in hiring personnel in the initial phase of the business. He stresses that he enjoys his work very much. The satisfaction he gets from it grows every day and it feels as if the "pieces of the puzzle" are falling into place.

Fears and difficult decisions. When he first started Bedaux in 1994, he experienced resistance in hiring personnel due to his earlier experiences in 1964. Some of the most difficult decisions for him have been dismissing personnel when it was necessary. Today, Mr. Te Gussinklo Ohmann works with a network of freelancers that he can hire temporarily for projects, avoiding permanent contracts.

Initial learning points. "When you start you don't really have an overview were it will lead to. And sometimes you have to fight to survive" says Mr. Te Gussinklo Ohmann. Most important, Mr. Te Gussinklo Ohmann has learned what his own capabilities are, and experienced what was successful and what was not successful. Over time, it became clear to him what his strengths and weaknesses were.

Case specific experiences. The connection between Kaizen and Bedaux, and later the founding of the business based on these concepts was an experience in innovation for Mr. Te Gussinklo Ohmann. Kaizen is a method developed in Japan about 45 years ago, and he used this as a basis for a method suitable for application within the business of Bedaux. In his projects, familiarity with the working operations is key to understanding the human side and the human drive to work. Every project is unique and therefore challenging.

Message to new entrepreneurs. According to Mr. Te Gussinklo Ohmann, people laugh too little and everyone is very serious. Often, Mr. Te Gussinklo Ohmann observes too little respect at places where work is done, the so called working floor. Being aware of the gap between people doing the work and people thinking about the work is of great importance, says Mr. Te Gussinklo Ohmann.

Entrepreneurship and Spirituality

Role of intuition. For Mr. Te Gussinklo Ohmann, intuition is an important feeling and he estimates he uses his own intuition nearly 80% when taking decisions.

Societal contribution. Spirituality and care for others and community are important values for Mr. Te Gussinklo Ohmann. He believes that everything is related to each other.

Summary Profile Jurrian te Gussinklo Ohmann

Current venture	Bedaux Management Consultants
Other ventures	Botany International Foods Pty in Australia, on assignment from one of his clients. Marcad, founded in 1969, sale in 1979
Place of business	Nunspeet, The Netherlands
Founding year	1994
Involvement	1994 to the present
Business sector	Services
Venture activity	Consultancy, training and project management for process improvement in professional organizations
Customers	Automotive OEM's and their suppliers Distribution for supermarket chains Semi-governmental, employment creation and housing foundations
International activities	Europe, many years in Australia
Company strengths	Innovation, flexibility, branch know-how, reliability, client friendly
Company weaknesses	Lack of business rigor, toughness, sales drive Too easily satisfied

14.5 Marco van Schaik, Greentel Telecom

Immediately after graduation I saw various opportunities in the market and I was motivated to launch Greentel. My thesis work was an opportunity to study a start-up company and this experience served as an introduction to the start-up processes. My family also supported my entrepreneurial aspirations as my father owned an accountancy company where I was able to share office space. I also looked within my own network for help and used borrowed capital to fund the start-up.

Company Profile

Company size indicators. Mr. Van Schaik's company was profitable over the last three years, with an increase in the number of employees and turnover. He started the firm on his own and he left when it had nine employees.

Company development. After the initial start-up phase, the venture hired technical personnel and other personnel were also hired on a contract basis for specific project needs. In this time, the organization changed structure and was established as a corporation. During the first year of operations the focus was on realizing growth. Mr. Van Schaik cooperated with larger companies, making cross-selling to customers a new possibility. Consequently, marketing costs were low. In the second and third year of business, the focus on growth was maintained yet more effort was invested towards the market. When Mr. Van Schaik started, he was a small player in a big market but had many advantages yet on the technical side. Competing with bigger players with large media campaigns was difficult. After four years, part of the company was sold and a part died as the market collapsed.

Defining Opportunities

Evaluation criteria. Marketing criteria were defined in advance when pursuing opportunities. The most important criteria to Mr. Van Schaik was assessing the life cycle stage of the market, the current players and potential new companies. In addition, understanding what investments were required, what the expected return on investment could be, what the expected increase in company valuation could be and support from existing contacts were also crucial.

Opportunity evaluation techniques. Mr. Van Schaik focused on maintaining a list of opportunities for further evaluation. At the company level informal sessions were held off-site, and these social in nature meetings generated many new ideas to keep the company current in relation to market opportunities. Resulting new ideas included product re-designs initiated monthly, quarterly market re-segmentation, and quarterly analyzed overlapping market boundaries.

Experiences

Remarkable initial experiences. As the market Greentel is part of is very capital intensive and he did not have the capital access of other big players, Mr. Van Schaik's intention has not been to become a big player. Yet his start-up experience was supported by the fact that he could rent office space from his father, and his possibility to focus his thesis project on a model of a start-up effort. Selling the business concept to banks and hardware suppliers was the biggest challenge, because both ask for guarantees that are difficult to ensure as a start-up.

Fears and difficult decisions. Uncertainty was the most difficult factor to deal with for Mr. Van Schaik, particularly getting suppliers and buyers. Perhaps even more significant was the on-going challenge of encouraging the market to believe in the business concept. And starting a new business alone was difficult.

Initial learning points. "As a starter you do not have enough money. You cannot afford making mistakes because that can lead to failures. Thus, starters need more drive to survive and they will subsequently become more creative. You have to have guts. Go for it. Call them and make appointments, try to get a meeting" says Mr. Van Schaik. Collaboration with bigger players saved marketing costs and made marketing easier. If he would start again, Mr. Van Schaik would evaluate the up-front financial investments more closely with the intention of creating better forecasts. Entrepreneurs need to focus on details from the beginning, and he learned that you need to be a jack of all trades to answer questions from others and to ask good questions of yourself. "When you succeed, you share your success, but when you fail it is only your own mistake," summarizes Mr. Van Schaik.

Case specific experiences. Mr. Van Schaik introduced himself to different large telecom companies to talk about his concept. Through these discussions he was able to learn from those companies and sometimes even sell his products to their customers. In his view, the small size of his company posed no real threat for the big parties and they were open to his contact and contribution to their customers.

Message to new entrepreneurs. "Do what you like, and after some 10 years you will see there is a connecting thread in the steps you made in your career," says Mr. Van Schaik. He also feels that as a starter it is normal to hesitate to make concrete demands of your suppliers, yet he learned that it is a necessity to do so otherwise the deals will not be yours. "Make decisions with your heart and your soul and do not worry about it afterwards," believes Mr. Van Schaik.

Entrepreneurship and Spirituality

Role of intuition. "Ask for second opinions when decisions are difficult. Intuition always plays a role. When you start it is the money you make that counts. But as you become mature yourself you see that other things in life count too."

Societal contribution. The company has created job opportunities. "As a starter you are too busy, there are too many things to manage to do more for society. Maybe as you grow you have more time for societal contributions."

Summary Profile Marco van Schaik

Previous venture	Greentel Telecom
Other ventures	Apoldro-Media B.V.
Place of business	Apeldoorn, The Netherlands
Founding year	1999
Involvement	1999 – 2002
Business sector	Telecommunications
Venture activity	Connections supplier for telecommunications and ASP-services
Customers	Small and medium size companies
Company strengths	Very innovative, pro-active, good contacts with large firms
Company weaknesses	Insufficient investment capital

14.6 Roel Wolbrink, New Tailor

I started New Tailor with Hans van Goch, with whom I had studied previously. I started a firm named Experience the Economy in 2005. Van Goch started New Tailor in 1997 and two months later I joined him. Pure, personal drive was my motivation to start the business. I was certain that I did not want to become an employee, largely due to my lack of patience. Independence and proving to myself that I could set-up something on my own were both important motivators for me. Also it is important to be able to act on what I think I should do and maintain my own point of view. And, not only was my aim to establish a new venture, I also wanted to leave a lasting reminder of something during my career, namely a successful business venture.

Company Profile

Company size indicators. In the last three years New Tailor was not profitable after taxes, yet turnover grew close to 2 million euro and staff to six persons.

Company development. The company maintains a staff of very practically oriented and not highly educated employees, and there is no defined organizational structure. Mr. Wolbrink and Mr. van Goch believe the company's approach is unique as is a niche-player with a high quality focus. Strong competition in the clothing sector forces their company to focus on lower market segments as well.

Seizing Opportunities

Evaluation criteria. Mr. Wolbrink indicates that before he pursues a market opportunity he first defines the criteria with which to evaluate the opportunity. The most important criteria for him are looking at the expected growth of the market, the number of competitors and their strengths.

Opportunity evaluation techniques. Mr. Wolbrink employs a systematic approach within his company to evaluate the business. Primarily he uses the redesign of products, re-differentiation of products, re-segmentation of products and development of competencies aimed at creating competitive advantages as techniques.

Experiences

Remarkable initial experiences. Mr. Wolbrink mentions he always wanted to be an entrepreneur, and dealing directly with customers is something that he likes; yet he admits that it was never a dream of his to start a company in the clothing business. Looking at their start-up experience, Mr. Wolbrink and Mr. Van Goch found it was easy to gather information. There were also other factors that contributed to their start-up decision; they had no family responsibilities and could afford to take risk, and they were certain there was room in the market for innovation and things for them to do. In their partnership, Mr. Wolbrink labels himself as a starter and Mr. Van Goch as the finisher. When starting, mastering the art of persuasion in communication with suppliers was a difficult experience due to lack of knowledge about the industry and money issues.

Fears and difficult decisions. While some things were simpler than others, Mr. Wolbrink couldn't list any fears that he experienced. Among the difficulties they experienced, letting an employee go ranks among the highest. Yet, Mr. Wolbrink also feels that most of the time you base decisions on intuition and it is not always possible to know if you are taking the right decision. And when it isn't possible to know the priorities of suppliers or when logistics don't work well; then real difficulties can occur.

Initial learning points. Initially, they were the dominant player in this segment and Mr. Wolbrink regrets that they did not have more money at that time to grow faster to obtain market leadership. Also, Mr. Wolbrink believes that they sold the tailored suits too cheap in the beginning. In retrospect, he also realizes that more customer information was needed by the tailor and therefore more preparation for every single order.

Case specific experiences. A noteworthy project was the joint promotion with Saab. They prepared 100 bespoke suits for Saab drivers in 1999 and 250 for re-sellers of made to measure insurance products in 2002. In 2006 they will make 100 suits for mortgage advisors. The management and logistic processes were very exciting. Another unique experience was the production of suits for musical productions, calling for a high degree of creativity to design historically accurate suits for the actors. Another observation of Mr. Wolbrink is that in the clothing sector, customer expectation management is key. People who are not familiar with tailored suits are more likely to opt for a ready to wear suit, and it is not always easy to break down barriers to reach these potential customers.

Message to new entrepreneurs. "When there are problems, just begin to solve them. Set priorities and delegate because you have to take decisions in a short pe-riod. Therefore, don't wait too long. Entrepreneurship is fun" says Mr. Wolbrink.

Entrepreneurship and Spirituality

Role of intuition. For Mr. Wolbrink, intuition plays a significant role and accounts for 80% of his decision-making experience.

Societal contribution. Mr. Wolbrink is involved in social activities, and believes this is not only interesting but more important than just making money and obtain-ing social status. Seeking a balance between family and business is also very im-portant to him. His community involvement activities include publishing books, being politically active, thinking about different societal issues and, voluntary work for the Chamber of Commerce.

Summary Profile Roel Wolbrink

Current venture	New Tailor
Other ventures	Experience the Economy
Place of business	Utrecht / Amsterdam, The Netherlands
Founding Year	Experience the Economy founded in 2005, New Tailor in 1997
Involvement	1998-present
Business sector	Tailored clothing / advise and training
Venture activity	Tailored suits and shirts
Customers	Up market customers willing to pay at least 700 euro for a suit
Company strengths	High commitment and loyalty from customers and employees, good product Customers expectations are being managed well
Company weaknesses	The production process is very labor-intensive. The market is small, terms of delivery are a challenge be-cause the suits are produced on demand, and there is no economy of scale.

14.7 Bart Zieleman, Idea Vending

I studied in the USA, worked for one year for a company and then became an entre-preneur. I started a venture in Hungary in 1998 at the time that the eastern part of Europe was opening to the rest of Europe. The business was an arcade with amuse-ment vending machines and an acquaintance asked if I wanted to start-up in Hun-gary. I saw an opportunity and experiencing Eastern Europe seemed challenging. Shortly afterwards I started another venture, a wholesale company in vending ma-chines. I also participates in the family business of my parents with my sister, which is a sauna and beauty centre with a total of 55 employees, founded in 1981.

Company Profile

Company size indicators. During the last three years the company, Idea Vending BV, achieved positive financial results as turnover and employee numbers in-creased. Turnover is in the range of 2-5 million euro and has five staff.

Company development. Since 2003, turnover doubled and since 2004 there is no outside capital in the venture. As well, the structure changed from a solo venture to a business encompassing different positions like purchasing, sales and logistics. Since 2002, new products were launched and their market position shifted from follower to market innovator. Another change occurred as well, from ad hoc sales to established distributor. The company now has more strategic partnerships.

Defining Opportunities

Evaluation criteria. When Mr. Zieleman pursues a market opportunity he defines criteria in advance, and during the process adjusts criteria and afterwards evaluates them. Most often Mr. Zieleman looks at the match with current products, the match with current customers and the possibilities to invest in new ideas.

Opportunity evaluation techniques. Mr. Zieleman focuses on the creative processes within his company, and the team supports this both conceptually and financially when it comes to trying new products. One technique he uses is re-segmenting or redefining the market, crossing established boundaries. Finally, he continuously develops new competencies to increase their competitive advantage.

Experiences

Remarkable initial experiences. Hungary was a big step for Mr. Zieleman as he did not know anyone in the country, and he also quickly realized that the Western European way of doing business was new to most people there. For example, the corruption (paying extra for realizing contracts), drinking of alcohol early in the morning and rules and regulations that did not work were constantly amazing to him. On the positive side, he had the finance for a good start and on the negative side he had to give up a certain degree of job security.

Fears and difficult decisions. When he was already busy with the business he frequently asked himself if he was going to succeed. The most difficult situations Mr. Zieleman encountered were negotiations with municipalities about permits. The most difficult decision was to divest the venture. Gambling machines were forbidden, and other game vending machines were less popular and therefore less profitable. As a result, his business partner left the venture and Mr. Zieleman went on to develop a second venture as a wholesaler in vending machines.

Initial learning points. Among key learning, Mr. Zieleman learned to take quick decisions, and to judge advantages and disadvantages whenever possible. He also became expert in managing the concerns of a small company. He believes that it is possible to realize success through focusing on your activities and target markets.

Case specific experiences. Mr. Zieleman's activities changed over time due to developments in the market. In the beginning he concentrated on amusement vending machines in Eastern Europe and later moved towards the sale of vending machines suitable for children in Western Europe. Looking back, Mr. Zieleman is happy with the transition because gambling machines were forbidden in Eastern

Europe, and therefore there was no market for it anymore. This situation encouraged the business to change products and target markets.

Message to new entrepreneurs. For Mr. Zieleman it is important to work thoroughly and with a lot of energy, always trusting intuition. The willingness to spend efforts in order to see things in a broader perspective is also very important. In Mr. Zieleman's opinion, understanding financial figures and the interaction between the market and products plays an important role and can even bring luck.

Entrepreneurship and Spirituality

Role of intuition. While he might have initially relied on intuition, today Mr. Zieleman feels he balances experience, logic and intuition more closely.

Societal contribution. Although he does not perceive that his business directly affects society, he is conscious of societal issues and concerns. For example if there was a fit with the aims of the business he would hire a disabled person. He has been always busy with norms and values and believes that this must be a logical part of who you are, it is not something you seek in theories. And Mr. Zieleman feels that being responsible for your actions is important.

Summary Profile Bart Zieleman

Current venture	Idea Vending B.V. Sauna & Beauty Centrum Soesterberg (with his family)
Other ventures	1998: Playsafe Monitoring Systems Netherlands B.V., which was bankrupt in 2003
Place of business	Amersfoort, The Netherlands
Founding year	1990: Idea Vending B.V. 1981: Sauna & Beauty Centrum
Involvement	1990 to present
Business sector	Idea Vending: Wholesale
Venture activity	Wholesale in vending machines for example for sweets and toys Lighting products and gadgets
Customers	Licensees of toy and vending machines Wholesale Hotel and catering industry installation industry
International activities	Europe by direct delivery, through distributors and agents
Company strengths	Service, products with high quality, innovative
Company weaknesses	Administrative organization Sometimes the firm sources too many products

15 Start-Ups

15.1 Introduction

In Chapter 15 we describe two profiles of start-ups. The first one of Sander Govers who set-up two firms. The second one involves the start-up of Ilco Schipper and Lex van den Hondel. Mr. Govers was asked by his sister to join the business and he found this to be a good opportunity because he was willing to find out if entrepreneurship fits him. The business enabled him to use his creativity. He thinks creativity is very important and something which he does not want to compromise on. Even though it seemed much more logical to follow a corporate career he chose to start a new venture. In both profiles it will become clear that this step of not choosing for a corporate career or leaving a corporate career was not an easy one.

Both profiles refer to start-ups because they have recently set up the firm and it is not clear how they will develop. They do not intend to stay small and growth is certainly an aim. Yet it is too early to predict this. Mr. Schipper and Mr. Van den Hondel started a firm together as well. Both were students at Nyenrode in the same year and thus they knew each other very well as was the case between Mr. Govers and his sister.

Now that Mr. Govers' sister is no longer involved in the business, he has another business partner he can brainstorm with. Working with someone else requires knowing his or her own strengths and weaknesses which is very much the case with the start-ups in this chapter.

Maybe the key characteristics for a start-up are openness towards creativity, international activities, growth and dependence on assignments from the market because they have to prove their products and services. All three participants perceived the venture as successful.

The number of start-ups in this category is too small to generalize their experiences as described in this chapter. However we may assume that the start-up entrepreneur is wide open to creativity, international orientation and growth. The main concern for the start-up is deciding on a particular focus. These cases offer examples of balanced teams: the organizer versus the creative person.

15.2 Sander Govers, Juvenis

Following my economics study I became a junior account manager in a corporate finance and strategy group. A year later my sister asked me to help her in setting up a firm. She acted as the creative partner and I was the organizer. I found the start-up process challenging and enjoyable, and after my sister was in a car accident one and a half years later, I went on to develop the company on my own.

Company Profile

Company size indicators. The company was profitable last year and both employee numbers and turnover increased. Turnover is less than 1 million euro annually and at present, the company has three full-time employees. In the last three years the financial results were positive.

Company development. In reviewing the development of the company, Mr. Govers points out that the company's employees today possess a higher level of experience and relevant knowledge than in the past. As well, turnover is annually increasing with no structural changes of note. Another significant point was the decision to increase focus on sales and raising the visibility of the company name. In three years time Mr. Govers notes that customers have gained trust in the company due to the continuity offered through the presentation of second and third collections. The customer base now includes not only retailers yet also corporate customers and private individuals.

Defining Opportunities

Evaluation criteria. It is important to Mr. Govers to define his criteria for evaluation in advance when pursuing a market opportunity.

Opportunity evaluation techniques. Mr. Govers employs a systematic approach to stimulate creative processes to uncover new opportunities by supporting those who are creative and following their ideas without discussion on compromising creativity. Therefore the intrinsic motivation is very high, stimulating all those involved in the processes. One technique Mr. Govers uses is continuously re-designing all products. Twice a year he also re-differentiates all products and redefines the market, crossing established boundaries. Finally, Mr. Govers seeks to continuously develop new competencies to increase competitive advantage.

Experiences

Remarkable initial experiences. The financial knowledge and organizational capacity, combined with the self confidence that Mr. Govers brought to the company was a good match for his sister's creativity. When he decided to join his sister he was not burdened with financial responsibilities and could afford taking a degree of financial risk, and their parents also contributed financially making it easier to approach banks for additional financing needs. Among the more memorable challenges Mr. Govers faced were dealing with the rules concerning annual financial reporting as he prefers spending time on more directly beneficial activities.

Fears and difficult decisions. Mr. Govers couldn't list any real fears, yet the decision to quit his job was a difficult one. At the moment he was considering joining his sister, it looked more logical to follow a corporate career as a financial expert. While he chose entrepreneurship with some uncertainty, Mr. Govers remains happy with his choice.

Initial learning points. Mr. Govers actually did not dream of starting his own business yet believes that his family played a role in influencing his decision. His father was a manager in a large textile company and Mr. Govers is certain that played an influential role in his ultimate decision. Starting the first business was also a great learning experience that contributed to the start of Juvenis. With the second company Mr. Govers went about things differently, realizing how important it was to work with a creative person.

Case specific experiences. Mr. Govers is convinced that it isn't feasible to compromise on creativity. He supports the creative ideas of his business partner Jorm de Geus, without criticizing him, and in the clothing industry this is especially important. The result is a collection that is very unique, down to every last detail.

Message to new entrepreneurs. In short, Mr. Govers encourages new entrepreneurs to try to identify their distinguishing characteristics and learn to understand what other people can contribute to your thinking.

Entrepreneurship and Spirituality

Role of intuition. In his experience, the most important decisions are based on intuition.

Societal contribution. Mr. Govers seeks to offer opportunities by creating new jobs and the company sends sample collections to charity organizations. According to him, the meaning of life is simple – whether you make something out of it or not, it all depends on you and you are responsible for your own happiness.

Summary Profile Sander Govers

Current venture	Juvenis
Other ventures	A-tex B.V. (1994)
Place of business	Mijdrecht / Ophemert, The Netherlands
Founding year	2003
Involvement	2003 to present
Business sector	The top segment of men's wear
Venture activity	Design and supply of own collection of men's clothes with the brand name Juvenis
Customers	Retailers in the top segment of men's clothing under the brand name Juvenis Companies for corporate clothing Private clients visit the company showroom in the Castle of Ophemert
International activities	Not yet: plans for Germany and Belgium
Company strengths	Creativity, originality, very high quality of products and services
Company weaknesses	Not yet known according to Mr. Govers

Entrepreneurship and Spirituality

Role of intuition. Although intuition admittedly plays a role in business, Mr. Aardewerk feels that he relies on his experience more than his intuition.

Societal contribution. Spirituality and care for others and community are important values for Mr. Aardewerk. He has observed that people share common interests and concerns less and less these days, and in some cases people do not care at all for the community interest. Through positive thinking and integrity in dealing with others and community it is still possible to make a contribution. He also feels that it is important to be very careful and considerate in relationships with others.

Summary Profile Abraham Aardewerk

Current venture	A. Aardewerk, Antiquair B.V.
Place of business	The Hague, The Netherlands
Founding Year	1970
Involvement	From 1970 to the present
Business sector	Retailer in antiques, especially silver
Venture activity	Antiques
Customers	Various
International activities	The Western Hemisphere, especially for purchases and incidentally for sales
Company strengths	Reliability, discretion, professional skills, and decency Does not employ personnel Customers visit the collection by appointment Mr. Aardewerk appears on a regular basis in the media, for instance on TV, as an expert
Company weaknesses	The company is very dependent on the entrepreneur

16.3 Marlene Gunning-Ho, Linking Pin

During four years at the former ING Bank, I held positions as Purchaser Housing, Employee of Business Development and Chief of Staff Purchase and Advice. And when I became pregnant I was faced with the question of 'how to guide my own career with motherhood'. After my son was born, I took care of him full-time for 10 months, and then felt it was time to get a job again. Yet the vacancies were scarce, especially in purchasing, and I didn't want to go back to the clothing industry and thus the idea was born to start a business. While working for the bank I gained experience in the purchase of company clothing with special company logos, and while that was the easiest starting point I started a business called Linking Pin in 1994. However, I never worked for the clothing industry again. In 1996 my husband joined Linking Pin. This new business opportunity also created a situation that me and my husband could be our own bosses, and combine our careers with raising our children.

Company Profile

Company size indicators. During the last year, the company was profitable with a turnover of less than 1 million euro per year. Ms. Gunning-Ho has no employees.

Company development. Ms. Gunning-Ho was always an entrepreneur without personnel. While the company changed from a solo-operator into a limited partnership, no other big changes occurred from the start-up to present.

Defining Opportunities

Evaluation criteria. Ms. Gunning-Ho mentions that when she pursues a market opportunity she defines the evaluation criteria in advance. The most important consideration for her is understanding what the chance of success is, what the turnover is, what the distance from home to work is, and how attractive or interesting the project is.

Opportunity evaluation techniques. To stimulate the creative processes, Ms. Gunning-Ho organizes brain storming sessions with her business partner. Through evaluating and brainstorming she forms ideas for new products and services.

Experiences

Fears and difficult decisions. Initially, Ms. Gunning-Ho did not have fears although acquisition of new projects during the start-up stage was challenging. The most difficult decision for her was choosing between staying with a salaried position or to employ her self through starting a business.

Initial learning points. In retrospect, she dreamed of being involved in this type of work yet not as an entrepreneur. According to Ms. Gunning-Ho, you must do what is close to you, and what you really like to do. And it is also important to focus on helping customers and to have fun doing the projects. Part of this realization included the decision not to work with personnel.

Case specific experiences. Within Linking Pin, Ms. Gunning-Ho works with her husband on a project basis and the projects are most often focused on change management or interim management tasks. A unique feature of this work is the fact that Ms. Gunning-Ho and her husband are running a business and a household together and things are progressing very well. They see this combination as a mutual responsibility. When projects and home activities cannot be combined they put their priorities together which means that some times Ms. Gunning-Ho will stay at home and other times her husband stays at home.

Message to new entrepreneurs. When asked what her message to new entrepreneurs is, Ms. Gunning-Ho emphasizes that it is necessary to try to find out what type of work you enjoy and how you can combine that work with your private life. And perhaps most importantly, you must be honest with yourself and follow your heart.

Entrepreneurship and Spirituality

Role of intuition. From Ms. Gunning-Ho's perspective, intuition plays a big role in creating a business. In her personal experience, she feels that nearly 70% of her business decisions are based on her intuition.

Societal contribution. Spirituality and care for others and community are important values for Ms. Gunning-Ho. In practice, this means that you should let your heart speak. Be honest and open, showing your feelings without causing conflicts; always take time for reflection and enjoy what you are doing.

Summary Profile Marlene Gunning-Ho

Current venture	Linking Pin
Other ventures	Business compass
Place of business	Haarlem, The Netherlands
Founding year	1994
Involvement	1994 to the present
Business sector	Services
Venture activity	Interim management, consultancy, change management, organise back offices for companies
Customers	Financial and business service providers
Company strengths	Flexibility and independence
Company weaknesses	Turnover is dependent on human efforts

16.4 Milly ter Heege, Profile Management Executive Search

After my MBA study I worked as a product manager, with corporate relations at a company and in career services at Thunderbird University USA. In 1987, I started my present company and in 1991 I made the transition to the Amsterdam Business Center, a building that provides offices to companies. The drive to start a business on my own was based on my need to create a greater degree of career independence. The experience I gained in developing a career services project for Nyenrode enabled my to identify a business opportunity and through this I became familiar with matching demand and supply.

Company Profile

Company size indicators. In the last three years, the company maintained profitability with a turnover of less than 1 million euro per year. Five years ago, Ms. Ter Heege began working with a business partner, Mr. Joost Nijhuis, whom she knew from Nyenrode. Ms. Ter Heege does not have any employees and her business relies exclusively on her personal and professional expertise.

Company development. Turnover is growing now that she has a business partner and the market position is improving. Other than that, there have been no big changes since the start of the company.

Defining Opportunities

Evaluation criteria. Ms. Ter Heege does not define criteria in advance but during the process itself. Among the key criteria she uses to evaluate opportunities, she feels that the quality of the customer and the type of assignment are the most important.

Experiences

Remarkable initial experiences. Starting from a home office, Ms. Ter Heege wanted to initially test the soundness and feasibility of her business concept before committing to overhead costs. With this strategy, Ms. Ter Heege did not require any capital to start her business, "All I needed was a telephone, a chair and bank account plus a good network", she says. The first projects came from people she knew from Nyenrode from her prior career services position. All things considered, the start-up process for Ms. Ter Heege was not really difficult. Perhaps one of the biggest challenges was being a relatively young professional within that business sector.

Fears and difficult decisions. Ms. Ter Heege couldn't identify specific fears or difficult experiences, as she made a decision to start simple and see how the business would grow; her level of exposure was minimal.

Initial learning points. When Ms. Ter Heege decided to have a professional office, she could not find one that matched her expectations. In creating the kind of office she wanted for herself, a second business, the Amsterdam Business Center (a business that offers office space to companies) was created. Her current career fits to the dreams she had.

Case specific experiences. Ms. Ter Heege mentioned that it has been a reasoned decision to keep her business small even though she knows this also makes her firm vulnerable. She therefore maintains an integrative approach to her business and every business process is guided by either her or by her business partner. As an example, business research, consultancy, the search for candidates, interviews, and meetings with clients are all activities that she integrates. From Ms. Ter Heege's perspective, this approach represents a strength that predicts the quality of the matching process. In addition, she knows her business partner very well and trusts his professional judgments and he also knows her style and approach to business.

Message to new entrepreneurs. Her message to new entrepreneurs is one of depending on oneself to learn and gain experience. Ms. Ter Heege says, 'As an entrepreneur you face several rules and regulations and fiscal aspects which you are not familiar with. These are things you only learn by doing it yourself.'

Entrepreneurship and Spirituality

Role of intuition. In evaluating her approach to her business, Ms. Ter Heege feels that she makes little use of intuition. Her actions are more reasoned, and she routinely attempts to quantify qualitative matters as well.

Societal contribution. By finding the best fit between executives and companies, Ms. Ter Heege feels she makes a difference through her high quality matching process.

Summary Profile W.L. Ter Heege

Current venture	Profile Management Executive Search B.V.
Other ventures	Amsterdam Business Center
Place of business	Amsterdam, The Netherlands
Founding year	1987
Involvement	From 1987 to present
Business Sector	Services
Venture activity	Executive search
Customers	Supervisory Boards and CEO's in a variety of sectors
International activities	Sometimes in UK, Belgium and USA
Company strengths	Quality, keeping appointments, obligation to book results, valuable network of contacts
Company weaknesses	It is small

16.5   Roeland van Straten, Seyst Finance & Strategy Advisors

I was a controller at KPN Telecom, and also worked as an acquisition advisor and investment manager. Working in a situation where I am my own boss is an idea that is important to me. A conflict with an earlier boss resulted in the loss of my job and therefore I was forced to find another job. At that time, people around me encouraged me to start a business for myself. In addition to my company, I also works on a temporary basis teaching at Nyenrode.

Company Profile

Company size indicators. Mr. Van Straten is a solo entrepreneur, his company was profitable last year and employee headcount remained stable while turnover increased. His company turnover is less than 1 million euro annually and in the last three years there were positive financial results.

Company development. With turnover growing since the start-up and no changes in the organisational structure, Mr. Van Straten shifted his focus towards bigger companies. His strategy is based on the thinking that larger companies can afford paying for his services easier when compared to the directors of smaller firms.

Defining Opportunities

Evaluation criteria. When Mr. Van Straten pursues a market opportunity he evaluates it in advance, using time in comparison with the potential benefits as his primary criteria. He also looks closely at structural gains for the future.

Opportunity evaluation techniques. Mr. Van Straten does not employ a systematic approach to stimulate the creative processes, yet one technique he uses for the company is the re-design and the re-differentiation of all products or services to improve them.

Experiences

Remarkable initial experiences. When he started his company on 1 April 2004, he had only the name of his firm and a telephone. From this point, Mr. Van Straten started making telephone calls to companies and visiting consultants. These two actions were critical in the start-up phase of his company, and the severance package he received for a short time after leaving his previous job was also helpful. What Mr. Van Straten found perhaps less simple was realising that as a solo entrepreneur you have to motivate yourself to stay in the working rhythm, and to keep active while not working on a specific project for a client.

Fears and difficult decisions. An important realisation after attempting to work with other consultancies, was understanding that he could venture out on his own. At that point, he took a decision to give himself a half year to try working on his own. In terms of fears, Mr. Van Straten couldn't say that he felt real fear in the beginning because he received a severance package. This source of finance ensured that he did not need to make an initial investment in his company.

Initial learning points. One surprising thing was winning assignments from companies he did not expect. From this, Mr. Van Straten learned that through his own marketing efforts he was able to create new customer relationships and secure projects. And although he didn't dream of his current career, he always knew that being an employee was not for him.

Case specific experiences. Mr. Van Straten noticed that many business activities and decisions are based on logical thinking and not necessarily prior experience.

With these conclusions, he decided it wasn't possible to work for anyone again and that by being his own boss he can follow his own vision.

Message to new entrepreneurs. The main reason for becoming an entrepreneur must be the drive to do things independently. When money is the main driving factor, you will not make it.

Entrepreneurship and Spirituality

Role of intuition. Intuition is an important part of how Mr. Van Straten approaches his work. When dealing with important decisions he estimates that intuition accounts for nearly 35% of his decision-making process. And, as an entrepreneur he feels that by trusting your intuition you gain valuable experience.

Societal contribution. According to Mr. Van Straten, in offering his clients solutions to stressful issues, he seeks to make a positive contribution to his customers' interests. Also of importance is religion and believing in something as a member of society, says Mr. Van Straten.

Summary Profile Roeland van Straten

Current venture	Seyst Finance & Strategy Advisors
Place of business	Zeist, The Netherlands
Founding year	2002
Involvement	2002 to the present
Business sector	Organizational consulting
Venture activity	Advice on financial, strategic and corporate finance
Customers	Division directors of big companies such as Nuon, KPN, NIB CEOs of small and medium sized companies, informal investor's, venture capitalists and Eneco
International activities	None
Company strengths	For small companies: pragmatic advice, fast, low costs, high benefits For corporate companies: simplifying highly complex problems
Company weaknesses	As a solo entrepreneur Mr. Van Straten does not have a 'big name'. He noticed that corporate firms usually work only with 'preferred suppliers" therefore he often has to work with an intermediary.

16.6 Wiebeke Vuursteen, Tailormade Events

I was born in the Netherlands, completed my BBA at the European University of Antwerp and a MBA at Nyenrode. I have worked in different countries for Philips, KPN, Pepsi and Nestle. As a corporate type working in Asia, I was asked to move to Europe where I started working as a senior manager. In my new position I dealt with buyers of products from Nestle. Knowing that I was not familiar with the English market, together with an English colleague I designed a marketing research effort in Oxford. With this new knowledge, we decided to start our own business. Even though we shared the same interests, we found that working together was not what we had expected and my partner accepted my offer to buy her share of the business after two and a half years. Today, my key activities are: presenting unique ideas for an event (preparing three ideas for each customer, rather than one), and working with the customer to reach an agreement that I will manage the entire project and all related activities.

Company Profile

Company size indicators. The last three years Tailormade events realized profits and in 2004 turnover grew to a level less than 1 million euro, yet with less employees on the payroll. Ms. Vuursteen started the business with a former colleague from her job at Nestle in Britain. In 2004, she bought out her partner and continued on her own. The company has no permanent employees and works with temporary contracts only. Each event is different and she hires personnel for each event. As an example, for a big event for 1,000 people Ms. Vuursteen hires around 200 people, and her network is based on people she knows well.

Company development. In the last two years, the turnover of the company has doubled. Ms. Vuursteen hires personnel for specific events and also gets temporary help for administration. In the beginning, Ms. Vuursteen would attempt to do every event she could, today the firm is more goal and strategically oriented. Now she concentrates on certain big events and works more with repeat customers for whom she coordinates multiple events each year. Ms. Vuursteen believes that a big challenge to the development of the company is the location. London is a difficult market, and nobody knew the company. Launching just before 9/11 there followed a downturn in the event planning market. Ms. Vuursteen believes that she got through that period quite well due to the small size of the company. Very few parties or conferences were planned at that time. In the last two years the situation changed; companies are spending money on events once again, and Tailor-Made events are gaining a good reputation in the market.

Defining Opportunities

Evaluation criteria. When Ms. Vuursteen pursues a market opportunity she first defines the criteria. For her, the most important considerations include the quality of service, the competition, the added value and the client relationship.

Opportunity evaluation techniques. Looking at her personal approach to stimulating a creative process for herself, Ms. Vuursteen makes notes about an idea immediately, and after a few days she approaches it again and works the concept out further. Once the idea has taken shape, she talks it over with people that are not familiar with the business sector. This process has led Ms. Vuursteen to identify a number of strategies that include the redesign of her products in 2004, the re-differentiation of her products in 2004, the re-segmentation of products on a yearly basis and developing competencies aimed at creating competitive advantages.

Experiences

Remarkable initial experiences. Beginning the business involved a low level of exposure, and they launched the company with a computer and a mobile telephone. The opening of an office was soon to follow, and through friends they discovered who the potential management level customers were and also contact information for secretaries within large companies. Quickly, Ms. Vuursteen noticed the importance of building good relationships with secretaries, and leveraging on these relationships to gain entry to new event planning opportunities within the companies. In most cases, the secretaries were the key contact persons and also the people responsible for advising their managers on event planning. Ms. Vuursteen identified that relationships with potential customers and unique ideas for events were the main drivers behind their decision to start the business. Still, there were challenges that they faced, among them the market situation after 9/11 which occurred five months after their business launch. In addition, establishing their reputation took time and patience.

Fears and difficult decisions. "Yes, there were fears, absolutely! In a big company and in a corporate career, you have more security…things are presented on a golden platter for you" says Ms. Vuursteen. She was on an international career path, with nearly predictable progression up the career ladder. She also liked the positions she was responsible for and it was difficult to walk away from that. Yet, after much consideration she took the decision to take a risk, hoping that she could manage the challenges and realize success. After the first six months she hadn't earned any income, and it was a difficult time for Ms. Vuursteen. Looking back, Ms. Vuursteen says "…I had to persevere. I saw big firms fall down and that medium size firms had a lot of difficulties and at that time I focused on talking with people and potential customers."

Initial learning points. Although she had considered going into business for herself and knew she was interested in owning a hotel, Ms. Vuursteen didn't dream of starting her current company. It was during her BBA that she gained insight into some of the career questions she had, and later while completing her MBA she learned even more about herself. At that point, she knew she was good in organizing things and that she was a customer oriented person. Perhaps the most difficult thing was taking the first step to start knocking on doors to get an appointment. Yet, after taking that first step, she experienced that most of the people reacted very positively and were willing to schedule an appointment to discuss opportunities further. Also, Ms. Vuursteen learned that running your own business offers little security in comparison with a corporate career, yet it is much more fun because you can be very creative. In addition, perseverance is very, very important and Ms. Vuursteen emphasizes that you can not say no to yourself, and that you must just go on with the work. Part of this perseverance includes daring to call important people at the top of the business world, striving to be available for others, continuing to take contact with potential customers and regular clients, and maintaining relationships you have already built. And Ms. Vuursteen also noted that taking risks pays.

Case specific experiences. The personalized approach is something that Ms. Vuursteen maintains is critical to her business; visiting companies and building client relations and not just sending letters is what works. Ms. Vuursteen also targets key clients at the 'top' level as opposed to many small firms in London. Another factor that differentiates her approach to the market is the fact that she does not focus on sales meetings or attempt to be involved in every conference; rather Ms. Vuursteen targets the top level of the business world and seeks to plan unique events for her clients.

For one client she was hired to plan an event in Italy where she was not familiar with the location or local resources. Her first step was to visit the location, meet with local people and gain a clearer vision of what her client was requesting for the event. During a second visit to the location she was able to hire local people for the event and at the same time contract a Dutch band from the Netherlands for the music. For Ms. Vuursteen this experience was valuable in understanding that from her London base she could organize events throughout Europe. She also learned that visiting the location, exploring unique places and ideas and meeting with local resources is crucial to successfully planning an event abroad.

Ms. Vuursteen also stresses that her decision to specialize at the top of the market can put her in a position where she must turn away project opportunities. In one case it was an offer to coordinate a conference, in another a request to organize tickets for various events – yet neither of these possibilities fit within her defined business mission. While she does not believe in saying 'no' to a client, Ms. Vuursteen will instead offer referrals to other event planners. Her key activity is focusing on tailor made events for multinationals and also for celebrities, and Ms. Vuursteen has learned that these customers like the feeling that she works exclusively for them. Maintaining a specialized focus keeps the business interesting and challenging for Ms. Vuursteen.

As well, Ms. Vuursteen does not work with agencies to hire the expertise she needs for events. Her network is composed of a unique group of people that can provide the skills she needs for planning and conducting an event. And in her opinion, Ms. Vuursteen feels that the most talented and creative people won't be found within these agencies.

Message to new entrepreneurs. Ms. Vuursteen's message to new entrepreneurs is "Dare to take risks and be proud of becoming an entrepreneur."

Entrepreneurship and Spirituality

Role of intuition. Although she thinks and considers a lot in her work, Ms. Vuursteen does rely on a balance between reason and intuition. Trying to think like your customers brings valuable insight into the planning of an event, and is something that helps Ms. Vuursteen create successful results for her clients.

Societal contribution. Ms. Vuursteen volunteers her services along with some of her suppliers to charities to organize special events. And along with creating a good feeling for all involved, she hopes that volunteering her event planning services can contribute to many children-focused charities.

Summary Profile Wiebeke Vuursteen

Current venture	Tailormade Events
Place of business	London, UK
Founding year	2001
Involvement	2001 to the present
Business sector	Event management
Venture activity	She organizes parties, product launches, diners, conferences for companies and private individuals
Customers	Multinationals and private persons
International activities	Great Britain, The Netherlands and Italy
Company strengths	It is a small, innovative, and creative business with a strong customer relationship. The business is entrepreneurial, highly ambitious and location is good.
Company weaknesses	Ms. Vuursteen works with a small group of people and therefore is limited in the number of events that she can organize simultaneously. With a bigger team she could do events in other countries where the markets are still open.

16.7 Refke Wormmeester, RefHan Productions

I wanted to become an entrepreneur in a later stage of my career and always had an affinity with film. When I stopped working at Unilever due to RSI (Repetitive Strain Injury) complaints, the opportunity to become an entrepreneur presented it- self much earlier than expected. I joined the business my husband founded. From the start I was involved in the business informally and after three years I became a managing partner.

Company Profile

Company size indicators. The business turnover is less than 1 million euro, and the company does not employ personnel yet works with freelancers. Since the launch of the business, positive financial results have been achieved and turnover has increased.

Company development. Since Ms. Wormmeester joined the company, turnover increased in part because of her influence to shift the business strategy to building sustainable relations with clients and striving to take on fewer ad hoc projects, combined with her sales and marketing background. As a result, the company developed into an Audio Visual Office for company films and not only is there a greater variety of clients, the venture also evolved from a solo entrepreneurship to a Limited Partnership.

Defining Opportunities

Evaluation criteria. When Ms. Wormmeester pursues an opportunity she begins by defining criteria and makes adjustments both during and after the process to evaluate if the criteria were appropriate. Her key criteria include questioning if the potential project suits the core-business, if it is an exciting assignment, and if it is financially responsible to undertake the project.

Opportunity evaluation techniques. Ms. Wormmeester has a systematic approach to stimulating the creative processes by continuously updating herself on developments in the sector and seeking out different sources of new information. This includes watching company films, and talking with business partners, friends, and colleagues about the films she is producing. Specifically with the business, she focuses on continuously redesigning products, re-differentiating products and reading trade literature on a weekly basis. On a monthly basis she invests in reading material and has an annual training budget.

Experiences

Remarkable initial experiences. The business started in a relaxed manner due in part to the fact that as partners they had previous business experience, established networks, and they were familiar as individuals as well. They also both shared experience in Fast Moving Consumer Goods. Listing the factors that hindered the start-up process, Ms. Wormmeester notes that in the early stages, it was difficult to make trade-offs with regards to assignments, since she was very conscious of adhering to quality over quantity. In addition, the combination of work with care of her children was a challenge.

Fears and difficult decisions. In comparison with working for multinationals, everything was new and Ms. Wormmeester had to deal with uncertainty in various areas. Initially, she was socially and economically somewhat insecure as she was now working from an office in her house. The greatest challenge was the pressure to grow while not wanting to hire employees.

Initial learning points. Ms. Wormmeester emphatically points out "what an enormous pleasure having your own firm is," and that perhaps growing up in an entrepreneurial family helps to cope with the challenges of following in those footsteps.

In her case, both she and her partner came from entrepreneurial families. As well, the conscious choice to maintain a home office was important to Ms. Wormmeester so she could provide care for her children.

Case specific experiences. From her previous work experience, Ms. Wormmeester noticed that a valuable learning point was anticipating when to intervene creatively in an on-going process.

Message to new entrepreneurs. Reflecting on her own past, Ms. Wormmeester thinks it is worthwhile to obtain corporate working experience before starting out as an entrepreneur.

Entrepreneurship and Spirituality

Role of intuition. With respect to intuition, Ms. Wormmeester estimates she uses at least 60% intuition in her approach to work.

Societal contribution. Based on the decision to not maintain regular employees, having the ability to work with and employ freelancers is Ms. Wormmeester's contribution to creative people seeking project work.

Summary Profile Refke Wormmeester

Current venture	RefHan Productions
Place of business	Barendrecht, The Netherlands
Founding year	1999
Involvement	1999-2002 as "sparring" partner Since 2003 as managing partner
Business sector	Audio visual services
Venture activity	Multi-media film and video for internal and external communication
Customers	Producers of Fast-moving Consumer Goods & Durables, Industry, Government, Financial Sector & Advertising Agencies
International activities	Filming abroad for Dutch based clients
Company strengths	The company maintains a good balance of professionalism and creativity; and a personal approach supported by a positive price quality ratio
Company weaknesses	Because of their small size, there sometimes is a limit to the amount of interesting assignments that they can take on.

17 Nyenrode – The Entrepreneurial University

17.1 A Brief History of Nyenrode

The Netherlands Educational Institute for Overseas Service (Nederlands Opleidings Instituut voor het Buitenland; NOIB), was founded in 1946. That same year the institute moved into its new home at the Nyenrode Castle estate in Breukelen on the banks of the scenic river Vecht, Province of Utrecht, The Netherlands. By the way, Brooklyn in New York was named after Breukelen. Emmering (2006) reports in her work on the early years of Nyenrode history, that as a Castle it already displayed early signs of entrepreneurship in the 13th century. At that time, so it is told, Lord Gerard Splinter van Ruwiel built a castle, which he called Nyenrode. Later his son Gijsbrecht allegedly adopted the name of the Castle. The location was well chosen; a sandy ridge, capable of supporting the heavy construction, surrounded by peat morass, which made it possible in times of danger to use water for defense of the Castle. In addition to the security of the estate (here is the historical entrepreneurial perspective), the direct vicinity of the river Vecht was a source of income as the passing ships could be made to pay a toll for their passage. Over the centuries, Nyenrode has been known by many different names. In captions for illustrations, paintings and brass etchings, you will come across names like Nyenroy, Nienroode, Nijenroden, Niewenrode en Nieurode. The spelling 'Nyenrode' is the name of the Van Nyenrode family, as it is found on the family graves in the old church of Breukelen.

Soon after its foundation, this post-secondary private educational institute became commonly known by the name of the estate as Nyenrode. Albert Plesman, an aviation pioneer, the founder of KLM and a powerhouse in Dutch business circles before, during and after WWII laid the foundations for creating an institution specifically aimed at educating people for promoting Dutch interests overseas after the devastation of the war. Plesman was convinced that after WWII international business activities would be critical for rebuilding The Netherlands economy and increased international trading activities. Traditionally, in those days, universities in The Netherlands were not preparing for international business and service, Plesman thus built broad support for starting this private, internationally oriented school to build a cadre of talented young professionals for the future. Plesman foresaw that these graduates would have to be equipped to effectively represent the interests of The Netherlands overseas and promote its exports. "This graduating young talent would have the drive to create a living overseas and posses an entrepreneurial and trader spirit." Together with colleagues from a large number of Dutch internationally active companies such as Philips, Unilever, Heineken, AKZO, Royal Dutch Shell, and ABN and with support from The Netherlands government, this plan was realized in 1946. Nyenrode's birth as an internationally and entrepreneurially oriented academy became a reality.

From 1946 through 1970 Nyenrode offered a two-year college level NOIB diploma. From that year onwards, the program was lengthened and offered a full-fledged BBA degree. The CT program was added later as a one year program for technically trained students to learn about business. The IBP (International Business Program) on the other hand allowed students from outside The Netherlands, to spend one year at Nyenrode. The BBA was discontinued after the class of 1991 graduated in 1993. The reason was the withdrawal of funding support for Nyenrode by the Dutch Government. The Ministry of Education determined at that time that public funding could not be used for private, selectively admitting, educational institutions; or, as it was called in Dutch, "selectie aan de poort" (selective admission at the gate of the university). In the traditional system in The Netherlands, those with the right secondary school education were automatically qualified to enter state universities. In entrepreneurial language, this funding withdrawal created a "fatal flaw" in the opportunity of Nyenrode's education market. The economic viability of Nyenrode's largest degree program, also the major source of revenue of the university was thus destroyed. It further dramatically changed the economic health and history of Nyenrode as the majority of the alumni community at that time saw their beloved programs which were popular from 1946 till 1993, that is for 47 years, disappear. This commenced a period of friction between the university and one of its major stakeholders and sources of support, the Nyenrode Alumni Association (VCV).

Entrepreneurially oriented and in response to the loss of the BBA program, Nyenrode designed and started at short notice the Master of Science in Management program (MSc) in 1990. It proved initially very successful, even if unsubsidized, and continues to this date. However, when a few years later state universities were also allowed by the government to enter this market which Nyenrode had pioneered, competition from public university sponsored programs at significantly lower tuition rates strongly affected enrolments in this innovative MSc in Management. The program is also offered as a Part Time MSc for the working young professional.

In response to increasing demand for executive education, Nyenrode launched its Nyenrode Executive MBA program (NEMBA) in 1986. When the University of Rochester and Nyenrode agreed to move Rochester's Executive MBA program from Rotterdam to Nyenrode in 1994, NEMBA was discontinued and RNEMBA, the Rochester Nyenrode Executive MBA program was started. In 2003 this partnership was discontinued.

In 1999 Nyenrode had initiated a part-time MBA for young executives in cooperation with the Kellogg School of Management, Northwestern University in the USA and later Stellenbosch University in South Africa. This innovative program allowed young executives to complete the requirements of a fully-fledged accredited MBA program in two years with six residency-based, two week long modules at Nyenrode, Kellogg and Stellenbosch and this program continues to attract substantial enrolments. It allows companies to retain and educate promising young executives and the students to develop themselves without the loss of income normally encountered during a full-time MBA program. A major additional benefit for both the sponsoring corporations and the students in this program is the fact that the curriculum is structured so that assignments and issues from work can be taken into the program for purposes of benchmarking, study and potential resolution. The Nyenrode Deloitte Public Governance MBA was started in 1999 in response to the need for executive and management education in the public sector in The Netherlands.

Table 17.1 Nyenrode program history 1946 – 2006

Program	Dates
NOIB	1946-1970
CT	1954-1992
IBP	1956-1993
BBA	1971-1993
NEMBA	1986-1994
PhD	1988-to date
REMBA	1994-2003
IMBA	1982-to date
MSc	1991-to date
Part time MSc	1996-to date
PTMBA	2000-to date
PGMBA	1999-to date
EMDC (executive program)	1982-to date
Nivra-Nyenrode	1994-to date
MBA-FSI	1999-to date
NYVU Executive MBA	1999-to date
Research	
Management Research Center	1990-1997
Nyenrode Forum for Economic Research (NYFER)	1995-to 2003
Nyenrode Research Group	2005-to date

17.2 Entrepreneurship Education at Nyenrode

In Chapter 2 we discussed the rather disproportionate impact of entrepreneurial or new venture activity, in society in terms of job creation, innovation and wealth generation in society. Entrepreneurship education too has become more prevalent in the business school curricula. True to the intentions of the founders of Nyenrode, the university was one of, or possibly the first, academic institutions in Europe when in 1991 it made entrepreneurship a core course requirement in its graduate and undergraduate business programs. We found that among the top 33 European MBA programs (http://www.careerdynamo/mba_ft_rank_2001.html), seven business schools have to date included Entrepreneurship as a core MBA requirement.

Table 17.2 European business schools with entrepreneurship as core MBA program (2006)

European Business Schools	
Nyenrode	The Netherlands
Instituto de Empressa	Spain
IESE	Spain
IMD	Switzerland
ESADE	France
Cranfield	Great Britain
Bath	Great Britain

In the USA the situation can be summarized as follows, as recently compiled by researchers at the University of Illinois, Urbana-Champain. Of the 824 institutions that offer graduate business education, 77 or 9.3% include entrepreneurship as a core requirement in their MBA programs. Among the private business schools in the USA this includes the institutions listed below. Somewhat surprising, such top rated USA business schools as Wharton, Stern (NYU), UCLA, Stanford, Kellogg, Cornell, Columbia and Chicago are not included in this category, though all of these do offer entrepreneurship electives.

Table 17.3 Some US business schools with entrepreneurship as core MBA program

US Business Schools	
Rensselaer Polytechnic University	Troy, New York
University of Denver	Denver, Colorado
Harvard University	Cambridge, Massachusetts
Dartmouth College	Hanover, New Hampshire
Concordia University	Portland, Oregon
Babson College	Babson Park, Massachusetts

This information was supplied to us in a communication from researchers Paul Magelli and Cynthia A. Kehoe at the Academy for Entrepreneurial Leadership, University of Illinois at Urbana-Champaign.

17.3 Executive Program at Nyenrode

The Nyenrode Executive Program designs tailor made in-company learning processes where transfer of knowledge in management is linked to the manager's own reality and personal effectiveness. The Executive Program also offers open programs such as Foundations of Management, Young Management Program, Advanced Management Program (AMP), The Director Program for members of statutory boards, Master Classes in a number of functional areas and additionally a wide variety of tailor made programs for companies and organizations in The Netherlands.

- *Nyenrode-VU Executive MBA.* The Nyenrode-VU (NyVU) Executive MBA program was specifically founded for managers at the Rabobank Group, including local Rabobanks. In comparison with other MBA programs this program pays more attention to the practical aspects of management. As in the other MBA programs, it has also an accreditation from AMBA and EQUIS. It is exclusively pays focused on management of cooperative business structures.

- *Nivra-Nyenrode.* The joint venture with the public accountancy organization in The Netherlands, Royal NIVRA, started in 1994. It has since grown into the independent Nivra-Nyenrode School of Accountancy and Controlling at Nyenrode. The school offers BSc and MSc degrees in Accountancy and Controlling and the Registered Accountant (RA) certification as well as an Executive Masters degree in Finance and Control. Executive education with in-company programs is in the start-up phase.

- *MBA-FSI.* Vlerick Leuven Gent Management School, University of St. Gallen and Nyenrode jointly designed and offer a MBA in Financial Services and Insurance. When new financial groups with substantial insurance and banking activities were emerging at the turn of the century leading to new competitive forces, this required reassessment of business strategies and adaptation of internal organizations; this MBA program addresses these needs.

17.4 Research and External Relations at Nyenrode

Research activities were started in the nineties with the foundation of MRC, the Management Research Center. From 1997 onwards, research at Nyenrode was concentrated in competence centers to also create more opportunities for conducting contract research from an academic perspective. Another research initiative was the foundation of NYFER (Nyenrode Forum for Economic Research) in 1995.

Business research is currently growing. The Nyenrode Research Group (NRG-pronounced as "energy") consists of researchers from Nyenrode Business Universiteit and INHOLLAND, within the domain of Management and Business Administration. NRG is responsible for improving research infrastructure by allocating and monitoring additional research funding. NRG has identified four themes in which research activities need to be focused and stimulated within Nyenrode. They are: Business Innovation and Business Excellence, Business Leadership, Public and Corporate Governance and Accountability, and Sustainable Entrepreneurship.

NRG aims to stimulate the design and execution of high-quality research. To accomplish this goal it will strengthen and upgrade the research potential of current Nyenrode and INHOLLAND faculty. The long-term goal is to become one of the key players in the Dutch market for research in business administration and management by 2010. This will be achieved by establishing a reputation for delivering independent, rigorous and applicable research in the target areas.

Part of Nyenrode's role in society is to recognize and encourage outstanding performance in business and contributions to society at large. Nyenrode has, since receiving university status, honored a number of individuals with honorary doctorates by Nyenrode in the past. Table 17.4 presents a list of the honorary doctorates.

Table 17.4 Honorary doctorates Nyenrode Business University

Honorary Doctorate	Promoter
Dr. Albert Heijn 14/09/1992	Prof. Ph. Naert
Dr. Samuel Johnson 14/09/1992	Prof. M. Punch
ZKH Prins Bernhard der Nederlanden 11/09/1995	Prof. Ph. Naert
Dr. Nelson Mandela 05/11/1996	Prof. J. Palm
Dr. Bill Gates 05/11/1996	Prof. A. van der Zwan
Prof. Dr. Richard T. De George 05/11/1996	Prof. H.J.L. van Luijk
Prof. Dr. Donald P. Jacobs 22/01/1999	Prof. J. Palm
Dr. Aad G. Jacobs 22/01/1999	Prof. E. Bomhoff
Prof. Dr. Geert Hofstede 03/09/2001	Prof. K. Van Miert
Dr. Martijn Sanders 18/11/2002	Prof. E. Bomhoff
Prof. Dr. Robert Pitofsky 18/11/2002	Prof. K. Van Miert
Dr. Wim Kok 02/09/2003	Prof. K. Van Miert

17.5 Entrepreneurial Management of Nyenrode – A Mini Case Study

As students, teachers and researchers of entrepreneurship, we may now ask the following honest, but also quite difficult, question, "How entrepreneurial in nature has the management of Nyenrode been in practice during the last 60 years?" That is to say "Have we, an educational institution, practiced what we preached?"

In the history of Nyenrode we list in Table 17.5, the management teams and their leaders with varying titles from Dean to Chair of the Management Board to President.

Table 17.5 Nyenrode CEOs: 1946 to date

Team Name	Period	Title
Habbema	1946-1950	Dean
Postma	1950-1980	Dean, later, Chair Management Board
Schijff	1980-1991	Chair Management Board
Kroes	1991-2000	President
Van Miert	2000-2003	President
Bruggink	2003-to date	President

The next question then presents itself, "How would we evaluate the answer to this question about entrepreneurial leadership effectiveness at Nyenrode?" It is not our intent here to produce an in-depth academic study of Nyenrode's management periods. That would be a study by itself. Yet, we did want to highlight the entrepreneurship models as discussed in Chapters 3 and 4 and do this here in brief by using the example of entrepreneurship at Nyenrode during three of the longest of these management periods, i.e. the Postma, Schijff and Kroes management eras.

For a review of the start-up period of Nyenrode (Habbema) we refer to Emmering who recently completed an in-depth historical study of this period (2006). The key concepts in entrepreneurship, at the organizational level, are grouped around the management of resources, opportunity and people. We used a qualitative research methodology and designed a short questionnaire around these items and invited a small number of people from among the major stakeholders of the university, such as alumni, faculty and staff from these periods, to comment on these areas. Additionally, we used the Nyenrode archives for papers and speeches from the executive officers in question during the period from 1950 until 2000 to obtain insight into their intentions and activities.

- *Resource Management:* (1) Assets such as land, buildings, equipment, library, proprietary rights; (2) Fund raising, money management; and (3) External relations

- *People Management:* (1) Leadership; (2) Management and team development for staff and faculty; and (3) Student affairs and communication

- *Opportunity Identification and Management:* (1) New ideas and pursuit of educational services, products and programs; (2) Partnerships, alliances, marketing; and (3) Other innovations in other aspects of managing the institution

External relations activities, part of Resource Management in this model, have always been a crucial part of the creation and growth of Nyenrode. Thus, we have for discussion purposes given this category a separate mention in the following reviews of the Nyenrode management periods.

Our analysis, evaluation and comments concern the entrepreneurial management processes during the periods 1950-1980 Postma Management Team, 1980-1991 Schijff Management Team and 1991-2000 Kroes Management Team. As we had insufficient access to the history of the internal team dynamics in each of these three cases, our comments specifically address the management teams *as a whole* in terms of the dynamic leadership processes during the periods reviewed.

17.5.1 Postma Management Team: 1950-1980

Resource Management

During the Postma period two new buildings were completed to accommodate required new student housing as the enrolments had accelerated significantly since the founding of Nyenrode. The library was also expanded. In the early days of this period, facilities still remained inadequate. In addition to the educational goal of Nyenrode, Postma was also deeply involved in the details of managing the physical estate. Fundraising, as the only private college and later university in The Netherlands, remained an on-going concern. Some of the Dutch multinational companies such as Philips, AKZO, etc, were regularly solicited for funding, especially on capital projects. There was no fundraising manager yet Dr. Postma, the longest serving head of Nyenrode, was very effective in building support of key figures from industry to assist in matters of resources. In the early days, the purely entrepreneurial content of the curriculum was rather minimal as the focus was on broader fields such as, international companies, international relations, law, economics, languages, philosophy and physical exercise (1986).

External Relations

The captains of industry and managers visited the Nyenrode campus regularly as guest speakers and for other events. Dr. Postma was described as the quintessential relationship builder and this paid off handsomely in terms of the required state certification as a college, enabling the certification to award masters degrees. Involvement in alumni relations and estate maintenance was also one of the strengths of this management period. During this period Nyenrode was also ahead among European business schools in building exchange relationships with universities in North America, the most important of which was with the University of Oregon. There were no external relations or career services staff members in the early part of the Postma period.

People Management

Dr. Postma was seen as a strong, if not autocratic, leader of a committed faculty and staff as well as a stern, fair and bright headmaster and scholar. The faculty and staff and the entire Nyenrode community were committed to his leadership. Department Head meetings only commenced after 1980. He excelled in involving all stakeholders in Nyenrode to make things happen in terms of resources and government relationships.

> *"... I prefer an eager colleague who considers the goals of the university or those of the faculty, including the wellbeing of the students, a key value to which he will use his capacities to contribute. Rather than a hyper gifted ego-tripper who primarily (and secondarily) works for his own glory ..."*
> *(Postma, 1980)*

Opportunity Management

After the original program (NOIB) with which Nyenrode started, two new programs were created during this period. Those were the CT program for students who already had a technical background as well as the IBP program which brought many college level business students from abroad to Nyenrode for one year. At the same time Nyenrode students, selected for academic excellence were offered the opportunity to spend one year in the US. Many so completed their BBA degrees even before Nyenrode itself instituted that degree program in 1971. As from September 1, 1972 women participated at Nyenrode that was 25 years after its foundation.

From an entrepreneurial point of view, given the nature of this venture which had started in 1946, the Postma era could be seen as the successful take-off after the Habbema Management start-up period. There was a clear mission, vision and direction established and managed while resource development as well as team management and additionally educational innovations were achieved. In terms of the Adizes life-cycle model, Nyenrode had passed from the Go-Go through the Adolescence into the Prime stage where, given a stable management structure and a continuing entrepreneurial outlook, the stage was set for further innovation and stable growth.

17.5.2 Schijff Management Team: 1980-1991

Resource Management

During this period a comprehensive construction plan was implemented including a major new student housing complex on campus, campus restaurant, gymnasium and a library. Additionally, the existing Plesman building was remodeled into a campus hotel and a former dormitory was rebuilt into a faculty building. In a breakthrough development for The Netherlands, where all universities were essentially state-funded institutions, Nyenrode as a private foundation, was granted university status by the government in 1982. Through the university status and from then onwards until 1991, an annually approved and government funded budget for the academic activities reduced the funding challenges of the past. Though the facilities were dramatically improved, the university remained in fact, as it still is today, a relatively small but unique business school located on a large historical estate with Nyenrode Castle in the center of The Netherlands. Research methodology and curriculum development needed to be addressed and introduced systematically. Private funding was required for the Nyenrode Executive Management Center (EMDC) as that non-degree educational activity was not covered by the government funding facility. Nyenrode remained primarily a teaching institution (1986).

External Relations

An external relations department was established which built networks for Nyenrode in The Netherlands and abroad and Nyenrode became part of the young European Foundation for Management Development (EFMD) association, the European counterpart of the AACSB in North America. Marketing for the EMDC was informal and carried out on a personal basis by the management; the use of formal marketing tools was limited.

People Management

It was at the beginning of this management period that the personnel department was established at Nyenrode. Also, regular staff and managers meeting were initiated, increased professionalism of management functions developed when Nyenrode became a university in 1982, there were only three full professors, the remainder of the academic staff were lecturers and assistants and these numbers increased significantly thereafter. In terms of academics, course curriculum development needed and received formalization. Nyenrode management supported the formalization of the academic process in the degree programs. The faculty was less motivated to do so. Tension existed at times between the academic and the executive education groups of the university.

> *"... It will have to be our approach to teach our students to arrive at a responsible reduction of complexity with the goal of gaining insight into management processes and become better leaders. Some would say that creativity is only destroyed in formal education. Even more important is our challenge to teach our students to see what often remains hidden. That has much to do with art and culture, with invention and discovery, with experimentation and playing, with curiosity and with a never ending drive to venturing. To creatively embrace complexity demands knowledge and ability ..."*
> *(Schijff, 1987)*

Opportunity Management

A program for business practitioners, the weekend MBA (WEMBA), was designed and eventually this became the Nyenrode Executive MBA (NEMBA). This program was created with governmental seed funding to promote business practitioner education opportunities in The Netherlands. NEMBA included a module at the Kellogg School of Management, Northwestern University in the USA. The Management Research Center was founded at Nyenrode and did not really take off, maybe due to insufficient market research. Yet the Nyenrode International MBA did take off in international enrolments. International MBA exchange agreements with IESE in Barcelona, the University of Florida and Emory University in Atlanta offered more options to students. The first Nyenrode PhD was awarded in 1988. Remarkably, President Schijff predicted already in 1988 that Europe would eventually also convert to the Anglo-Saxon university structure of university organization in terms of undergraduate and graduate divisions.

This management team period was characterized by producing significant growth as well innovative incursions into new areas of education programs such as executive education. Nyenrode was granted university status which opened up new possibilities as well as funding and moved Nyenrode to the beginning of the organizational stage described in the Adizes model as Maturity.

17.5.3 Kroes Management Team: 1991-2000

Resource Management

The decision by the Dutch Government in 1991 to cancel their financial support for Nyenrode created a funding crisis of major proportions for the university leading ultimately to the decision to terminate the BBA program which had been in place since 1971. During the period of her presidency Ms. Kroes brought a very active dedication to resource development to Nyenrode. The first stage of a major campus accommodation upgrade was completed and a new campus hotel added. Renovation of the De Rooij building accommodating NIVRA / Nyenrode housing and the renovation off the Gerrit Jeelof Hall in the Castle were completed. The planning and construction of the Albert Heijn building to house faculty offices, lecture halls and the Pfizer Auditorium was started during this period. Substantial amounts of money were raised for building, campus development, academic chairs and research. However, no permanent endowment remained. Room for improvement of library and computer services remained. In terms of funding and finance this was a dramatic, dynamic and at times difficult period for Nyenrode. The campus remained a very special location. The trend towards an increased level of academic research by faculty continued steadily.

*"... The year of Nijenrode's 1991/1992 anniversary was for everyone con-
cerned a turbulent year. Nijenrode's idiosyncrasy was tested intensely. The
admirable esprit de corps of Nijenrodians – at home and abroad – mani-
fested itself in a struggle for the continuity of tradition, and attitude and
way of life worthy of defending. I understood the reactions. But, I freely
admit, I underestimated how deeply the feelings ran ..." (Kroes, 1992)*

External Relations

The International Advisory Board established by President Kroes added an important network to Nyenrode as well as a funding resource. Over this period of this
management team and, for that matter, thereafter, this board remained underutilized.
The partnership with Rochester was continued and relations with Kellogg were
strengthened through the establishment of the Nyenrode PTMBA program. Following the cancellation of the BBA program, relations with alumni and the VCV, Nyenrode Alumni Association, were challenging and stressed. Intermittently staffed career services for graduate programs were only one example of this stress.

People Management

Inspiring and quick, offering opportunities as well as taking chances, occasionally
ad hoc in nature, can best describe Nyenrode during these days. In terms of leadership, initially clear choices were made between undergraduate and graduate education, the international market was emphasized over home markets leading to the
hiring of a number of international faculty members. Later, there was also a shift
to support for full-time and part-time domestic MSc programs. Relatively high
turnover in Deans and Associate Deans was also an issue.

Opportunity Management

Open to new ideas! Nyenrode experienced innovative development of the IDP program, later renamed the MSc program in response to the BBA cancellation. These
new programs further led to the successful development and effective marketing of
the new PTMBA, which was international in nature. Active international marketing
and promotional efforts for International MBA in a very competitive environment
were also on the agenda. At the same time, there was limited marketing of executive
development. Distance learning was investigated but not deemed successful and
daily pressures competed with attention to creativity and innovation.

In this management team period the severe crisis in the loss of funding forced
Nyenrode to dramatically cut back expenses and look for new alternatives to gen-
erate resources and develop a new business model. This process was complicated
by the perceived need to seek fast solutions for new business models, frequent
management turnover and undermined stakeholder support from the Nyenrode
Alumni Association.

17.6 Entrepreneurial Activity Among Nyenrode Alumni

To investigate the entrepreneurial activity among Nyenrode alumni, we carried out a unique research project in 2003 on the entrepreneurial spirit of Nyenrode alumni to assess their participation rate in entrepreneurial activities. Some 8,000 alumni on record were approached with a questionnaire and 725 responses were received.

We faced one difficulty in view of the existence of several definitions of the term 'entrepreneur'. Thus, half of the questionnaire consisted of definitional questions. About 38% of those who responded were entrepreneurs, 7% were former entrepreneurs[2], 2% were sole proprietors, and almost 6% were only upper level managers in a company and almost 9% were nascent entrepreneurs[3]. The rest were non-entrepreneurs.

We checked how representative our sample in the 2003-study was. As entrepreneurs were overrepresented in our sample in comparison with the Nyenrode population we corrected for this in the findings. We did not have information about the nascent entrepreneurs in the population therefore we could not check how representative the finding is for this particular group.

We used the GEM index referring to the Netherlands. In our study we applied the same questions as in the GEM for defining the nascent entrepreneurs, the young companies and the established companies. When compared with the Dutch population as a whole this represents a high rate of entrepreneurial activity among Nyenrode alumni.

In 2003 the nascent entrepreneurial rate for the Netherlands was 1.7. This means that 1.7% of the Dutch population between 18-65 years were nascent entrepreneurs; the index for our Nyenrode alumni was much higher with a rate of 8.8% (see table 17.6).

The index for the owners of young firms according to GEM was 1.9% for the Netherlands (GEM 2003). Based on our data, the index for Nyenrode alumni is 3.5. The GEM adds these two indexes and labels the total entrepreneurial activity (TEA); in this case it amounted to 3.6 for the Netherlands (1.7 + 1.9). Based on our data, the Nyenrode alumni rate is 12.3 (8.8+3.5).

For the longer established firms the GEM uses a different index. The Entrepreneurial rate of established firms (based on ownership of businesses older than 42 months) is 3.8. In our study this rate among Nyenrode alumni is much higher, 10.

From these findings we may conclude that among Nyenrode alumni there exists a much higher entrepreneurial activity than in the population of the Netherlands (5.7 versus 13.5).

---

[2] Criteria: Founders or owners and upper level managers in the company.

[3] Criteria: Nascent entrepreneurs are defined as being involved in setting up an own company in the past three months, or intent to found an own company between now and a period of one year and expect favourable opportunities over the next six months for founding a company and expect to be able to obtain financial resources necessary for founding the own company.

Table 17.6 Entrepreneurial activity

Groups	Netherlands[4]	Nyenrode
Nascent entrepreneurs	1.7	8.8
Young companies (up to 42 months)	1.9	3.5
TEA index	3.6	12.3
Older ventures	3.8	10.0
Young and older ventures	5.7	13.5

To the question if there are more entrepreneurs among Nyenrode's alumni in comparison with the population of The Netherlands in general, we can thus respond positively.

The next question being raised in the research was "Does the Nyenrode education contribute to the high entrepreneurial activity or is there a selection in advance?" In the first place Nyenrode is associated more with managers than with entrepreneurs, although in recent communications we stressed the entrepreneurial spirit due to the fact that the subject entrepreneurship has been obligatory in the curriculum for the past six years in the MSc and since 1991 in the MBA programs. The entrepreneurs and former-entrepreneurs were asked in the questionnaire to tell us how Nyenrode contributed to their entrepreneurship. Most of the answers could be categorized into the following five Nyenrode contributions: (1) Provided a broad picture / general knowledge / some basics; (2) Contributed to networks / contacts; (3) Developed our skills in management and several social skills; (4) Contributed to our personality / mentality / characteristics such as initiative courage, self-confidence, critical view, competitiveness; and (5) Contributed because of the practical focus of the education.

Academic research on the effect of education on entrepreneurs is scarce. Van der Sluis, van Praag and Vijverberg (2004) have conducted a meta-analysis based on 299 observations, mainly resulting in the conclusion that this field of research is scarce and contains various definition issues which make comparison of results of studies not reliable and therefore weak. One overall conclusion they draw is that selection of entrepreneurs is not affected by the level of education (measured as college graduate and years of schooling). However, performance (measured as survival, duration or growth) has a positive relationship with education pursued. The relationship gets stronger if performance is measured by earnings. The link between education and performance seems to be higher for the US than elsewhere. This might be due to a schooling system that is more oriented towards entrepreneurship and knowledge, or to better business conditions that predominantly benefit the more highly educated. The authors who conducted the research conclude by saying that if education is so positively related to performance in the employees and even in en-

---

[4] The Global Entrepreneurship Monitor (GEM) prepares an annual comparison between countries. The index for The Netherlands 2003 was used for the purposes of this comparison.

trepreneurship, it is worthwhile to invest in human capital through schooling. In the case of entrepreneurship as profession we can therefore assume that schooling related to specific skills needed, will improve entrepreneurship performances more.

17.7 Conclusion

With the input from a number of members of the Nyenrode community representing students, alumni, staff, faculty and management we summarized the 3 management periods in terms of entrepreneurial activities and performance. We also consulted papers and speeches from the Nyenrode archives for input on the intent and evaluation by the management teams in these periods. In terms of process this represents a limited qualitative research approach at looking back at the entrepreneurial management history of Nyenrode. What can be gleaned from this brief history for the future of the university?

Table 17.7 Summary comparison of Nyenrode MT performance on entrepreneurial factors

	Resources	External Relations	People	Opportunity
1950-1980: Postma team	++	+++	++	+
1980-1991: Schijff team	+++	++	++	+
1991-2000: Kroes team	++	++	+	+

Following the entrepreneurial model we used, it appears from Table 7 that especially the opportunity identification, verification, design and implementation processes would benefit from a more, organization-wide, systematic approach. As a private business school with an entrepreneurial history and a 60 year track record, opportunities themselves would appear, as in the past, continue to be abundant. The issue would be to attend to systematic and long-term oriented opportunity management in terms of identification, evaluation, and selection and management processes of new programs, ventures and strategic relationships. The second area of attention flowing from this small research effort is, as can be seen in Table 17.7, related to people and relationship management. What can even anecdotally be seen from successful business schools, such as Kellogg, Wharton, or London and Insead in Europe, just to name a few, is that long-term opportunity and charismatic people management leads to success.

Based on research we also conclude that alumni from Nyenrode are much more entrepreneurial in comparison with the Dutch population. There was no data available from other university for comparison. Other Dutch Universities do not have the tradition of building strong ties with alumni, and in this sense Nyenrode can be viewed as a best practice in the Dutch context because of the high level of entrepreneurs within its' alumni community, the strong ties with alumni and the core character of the entrepreneurship course.

Appendix 1: Executives and Entrepreneurs Identification

Business Sector	Name	Company Name	Study Year
8 Executives			
Foods / consumer products	Anthony Burgmans	Chairman Unilever N.V.	1969
Live entertainment	Tanja Dik	Director / Joop van den Enden Theater productions / stage entertainment	1993
Pharmaceuticals	Lodewijk de Vink	Former CEO Warner-Lambert	1967
Pharmaceutical industry	Edwin van Houten	CEO Organon Mexicana SA de CV	1985
Wholesale	Arnold Koomen	CEO / Koninklijke Jongeneel B.V.	1987
Retail	John Schollink	CEO / Etam Retail Services B.V.	1996
Foods	Thomas Versterre	CEO / SMITS Vuren BV, GCM Ltd. (Sobel N.V.)	2002
NGO	Rudolf Deutekom	Retired Director, UNICEF Private Sector Division	1963
Public services	Harjan van Dam	CEO / B.V. Sport Leeuwarden	1997
Public services / government	Wim Kok	Former Prime Minister	1958
9 Venturers			
Consultancy and interim management	Gerard Boskma	Boer & Croon Strategy and Management Group / interim group	1964
Steel industry	Lex Entrop	Intal	1949
Management en training	Jan de Jong	Management Advice and Training Center Holland	1953
Consultancy and services	Erik Maassen	Full*Finance Consultants	1982
Management consultancy	Michael Pullens	Strategic Development Group	1988
Food industry	Bert Reeders	General Cocoa Company Holland	1954
Interim management	Philip van Rooijen	C2Results	1995
Wholesale in leaf tobacco	Ger Sterken	Interleaf B.V.	1954

10 Re-launchers

Shipbuilding industry	Britt Blomsma	GeuzenBoats	2002
Publishing / media	Erik Brink	WeerOnline B.V.	1996
Education & training	Dick Houtman	Gooiconsult Advies & Training	1994
Wholesale, import, export	Wim de Knoop	Amcom	1963
Household goods trading	Michael Moore	Merison Group B.V.	1993
Industrial construction	Peter Ruigrok	H2R Invest B.V.	1994
Stationery publishing	Marjon Velthuis	SRT International B.V.	1982
Wholesale	Evert Versluis	Van Egmond Mechanisch Transport	1965

11 Trend Entrepreneurs

Cosmetics	Ariane Inden	Ariane Inden Cosmetics	1988
Consultancy and services	Carel Jongbloed	Base Group AG	1975
Wood trading	Christian Mayorga	Globex International	2003
Wholesale, import, export	Jack Spoorenberg	Spoorenberg International B.V.	1972
Environmental technology	John Verstraaten	Environmental Concepts Inc.	1973
Waste handling, recycling	Han Ypes	Industrial Shredders B.V.	2003

12 Family Business Entrepreneurs

Shipbuilding	Annelies Damen	Damen Shipyards Group	1991
Packaging materials	Annemarie Dekker	Remmert Dekker Printing	1989
Health Care	Christel Hodes	Hodes Verenigde Bedrijven Ltd.	1998
Professional services for governments	Jorrit van Kraaikamp	MB-All B.V.	1993

13 Significant Business Entrepreneurs

Drugstore products	Arnolf de Wolf	Wolco Holland B.V.	1958
Import / wholesale	Bruce Kindler	Kinco International	1969
Wholesale in textile	Norbert Mutsaerts	Noppies Inc	1985
Internet services	Arnold Tuinenburg	Apcare B.V.	2002
Entertainment	Rob van Rozendaal	The Music Marketeers B.V.	1987
Retail foods	Hans van Well	Foodwell B.V.	1979
Shoes	Frank van Wezel	Hi-Tec Sport PLC	1960
Methanol	Deo van Wijk	Saturn Methanol Conversion Company	1974
Telecommunication services	Edmée Vitzthum von Eckstadt	Switchtrax Telecom Limited	1986
Chemical industry	Walter Westendorp	TLP International B.V.	1959

14 Small Business Entrepreneurs

Metal industry	Jaap Bellingwout	Robelco B.V.	1949
Consultancy and services	Hans Klok	Marmont Film Financing	1963
Consultancy and services	Jurrian te Gussinklo Ohmann	Bedaux Management Consultants	1965
Telecommunications	Marco van Schaik	Greentel Telecom	1998
Clothing	Roel Wolbrink	New Tailor	1995
Wholesale	Bart Zieleman	Idea Vending B.V.	1986

15 Start-ups

Clothing	Sander Govers	Juvenis	1989
Telecommunication Services	Lex van den Hondel and Ilco Schipper	TrendCall Services Ltd.	2004 2004

16 Enterprising Persons

Retailer in antiques	Bram Aardewerk	A. Aardewerk, Antiquair B.V.	1956
Consultancy and services	Marlene Gunning-Ho	Linking Pin	1988
Executive search	Milly ter Heege	Profile Management Executive Search	1979
Consultancy and services	Roeland van Straten	Seyst Finance & Strategy Advisors	1994
Events management	Wiebeke Vuursteen	Tailormade Events	1996
Audio visual services	Refke Wormmeester	RefHan Productions	1992

Appendix 2: Questionnaire

The following questions were asked of each person interviewed:

- Background knowledge:
    1. What was your motivation to start a venture?
    2. Was there a specific reason at that particular time?
- Knowledge of entrepreneurial processes:
    1. What were remarkable experiences?
    2. Which conditions or factors stimulated the start-up?
    3. Which conditions or factors disturbed the start-up?
    4. If you think back, was it something you dreamt about?
    5. What were your fears at the moment you started the venture?
    6. Did you take difficult decisions, which and how did you cope with them?
    7. What are the learning points? Are there things you would approach differently after you current experiences?
    8. What was a unique experience in your entrepreneurial career that worked out positively? Describe the situation, the approach and learning points.
    9. What was a unique experience in your entrepreneurial career that worked out negatively? Describe the situation, the approach and learning points.
- Data and dynamics about the firm:
    1. Describe the firm results in terms of turnover, headcount, founding year, turnover growth for the past three years or the last three years of involvement?
    2. Describe the firm development in terms of change in educational level of personnel; finance, organization, strategy, market position, type of customers or markets?
    3. What are strong points and what is a weak point of the firm?
    4. Judgment of success?
    5. What are your criteria concerning opportunity pursuit?
    6. Do you stimulate creativity in yourself, in your company and how?
    7. What techniques have you been using for developing the firm?

- Relationship with the community:
  1. What is the attitude towards current trends of spirituality?
  2. What is the contribution of the venture to the society?
- Psychological background assessment:
  1. Promotion and prevention orientation which is related to the process of decision making in terms of achieving rewards or avoiding punishments / negative outcomes.
  2. Action and state orientation which is related to the initiate behavioural actions needed in dealing with challenges or even setbacks.
  3. Mental fitness which related to coping with challenges and setbacks.
  4. Behavioral attributes are related to a general personality profile.

Appendix 3: Measurement Information

Promotion Prevention Orientation

The concept of promotion and prevention can be measured through a validated scale originally developed by Higgins (2000) and translated and validated in Dutch including 12 items. The Cronbach's alpha in our small sample was .92 for the prevention orientation and for the promotion orientation the alpha was .65 which is reasonably high. Of course the English speaking participants received the original items.

Action-State Orientation

All respondents of our case studies were asked to fill in the Action Control Scale. This scale was developed by Kuhl (1994). For psychometric details of the scale please review Chapter 2 of the book "Volition and personality: action versus state orientation". For Dutch respondents, we used the Dutch version of this scale validated by Otten et al. (1994) and for non-Dutch we used the English version. Both the failure related action orientation scale (AOF) and the prospective action orientation scale (AOD) exists of 12 items. In our small sample, the AOF scale resulted in a Cronbach's alpha of .60 and the AOD scale resulted in a Cronbach's alpha of .67. Within our research only nine people could be labeled as more state oriented persons. The cut-off score was 18 and the minimum score of these 9 people varied from 13 to 18; this means that the participants of the case studies are not extremely state oriented focused.

Mental Fitness of Moods

Participants of the case studies were asked to fill in a questionnaire dealing with the five concepts: self-confidence, energy, alertness, tension and satisfaction. We used a ten point scale for each item, and in total there were 30 items. Factor analyses were conducted on a dataset of 275 respondents, mainly sportsmen, which revealed the five factors. Each factor resulted in good Cronbach's alpha scores, a method used for assessing reliabilities that vary from .60 to .88. In our small sample, we also found good reliability scores. For self confidence .81, for energy .79, for tension .83, for alertness .84, and for satisfaction .80.

Behavioral Attributes

Within the case studies the seven attributes from the EBAI scale are included. Each attribute shows reliable Cronbach's alpha scores with a minimum of .60 and a maximum of .75.

Postscript

The Essence of Entrepreneurship at Nyenrode

Throughout this book we have focused on the 60 entrepreneurs and entrepreneurial executives in our study and the environments in which they are, or were active. As an academic entrepreneurial venture, we designed this study with multiple objectives in mind. Of course, the main purpose was to study the process of entrepreneurship, primarily from a human and social perspective, as that side of enterprise appears relatively underexposed, both in practice as well as in academic research. As such, our emphasis was exploratory and qualitative in nature. Once again, from an entrepreneurial point of view, we saw an opportunity, be it a challenging one, to write about creative and venturing behavior not only as an academic exercise yet also to address other entrepreneurial aspects of the Nyenrode community. As mentioned in the Preface, we targeted our study and thus this book, at entrepreneurs, business professionals, students of entrepreneurs as well as at researchers. This book was additionally written for the Nyenrode community at large with all the case studies concerning Nyenrode graduates from 1946, when the institute was founded by a number of leading international Dutch corporations as the first business school in The Netherlands, until present day. In this last chapter we offer the following concluding observations.

Profit is the Main Indicator to Pursue and Evaluate Opportunities

In their search for opportunities, entrepreneurs and entrepreneurial executives from Nyenrode use several profit related criteria. Criteria related to results include added value, effect on margins, gross margin, profit, return-on-investment, turnover increase and financially speaking, "good deals". Power-based, profit-related criteria refer to, for instance, market size, ownership, competitor strengths and market growth. Resource-based, profit-related criteria refer to required expenditure. Related to the market, entrepreneurs use relevant criteria such as a good fit with the other products of the business and competitive positioning.

The Human Factor is a Main Driver in Entrepreneurship

Although the profit-related criteria appear to be the most relevant, in the start-up process, the human factor seems to dominate. Approaching entrepreneurial processes from a human perspective provides new insights. For instance, this perspective can bring new understanding to the interactive processes that occur within the individual, between individuals and in response to the bigger framework in which entrepreneurs function.

The case studies showed that the entrepreneurial team as a whole, in terms of relevant experiences, relevant personalities and the quality of their match were the positive drivers for starting a venture. Factors that had a negative impact in the start-up phase were also related to these types of team issues. These factors might especially be applicable to Nyenrode alumni as the core curriculum pays a significant amount of attention to the development of soft skills.

Entrepreneurship Is About Attitudes and Skills

Our research confirmed that the human factor is of importance. Our primary conclusion is therefore that entrepreneurship is about attitudes and skills. The good news is that attitudes can be influenced and skills can be acquired and empowering people to pursue entrepreneurship means creating a climate for entrepreneurship.

Entrepreneurial Climates Encourage True Entrepreneurship

A productive entrepreneurial climate is fostered by:

- Offering tools for stimulating creativity continuously to see or to imagine opportunities;

- A focus on skills that offer a sense of control, especially in times of uncertainty;

- Building and maintaining a positive image of entrepreneurship by offering role models;

- Creating learning materials based on failures, difficulties and setbacks;

- Coaching and mentoring support;

- Recognition of the various types of entrepreneurs and understanding individual drivers related to entrepreneurial activities;

- Thinking in terms of the fit between a person and an opportunity because not every opportunity fits everyone;

- Recognition that the social domain can also gain from entrepreneurial attitudes, skills and tools;

- Awareness that innovation needs nurturing and time and that it will flourish in the case of teams characterized by diversity;

- An opportunity based attitude can be learned by reinforcing the behaviors expressed through achievement drive, creativity, dominance, and taking risks;

- Partnerships between high-tech potential and business oriented potential might lead to the growth of innovation.

As in sports, very few people have the mixture of talent, courage and stimulation to reach the top. Also in entrepreneurship, very few will actually reach the top. It would be an illusion to think that encouraging entrepreneurship makes society highly innovative in the short-term. Instead, it is a process that needs time and nurturing. Of course, a part of entrepreneurship remains a black box that means that it is not totally predictable.

As for other human behaviors, in entrepreneurship the nurture and nature debate also formulates the question of which part can be learned and which part cannot. Entrepreneurial attitudes in terms of starting a firm, acting from a winning perspective and taking initiatives can be encouraged. Skills such as presentation, selling, negotiation can be trained. Creativity can be stimulated. Knowledge about market strategies, valuation, accounting and other business topics can be taught.

For several professions, selection based on certain defined skills, knowledge and behavioral requirement seems to work. The different types of entrepreneurs can be approached as distinct professions which create the possibility of selecting entrepreneurial profiles in deciding who is more and who is less suitable for a certain profile. Active entrepreneurial career counseling might help to find a good fit between the person and an entrepreneurial activity.

From the research, both in theory and practice, it is clear which human factors may positively influence entrepreneurial activities. Measuring these factors can thus provide predictability.

And, governments as well as businesses can play a role in encouraging entrepreneurship and successful venturing outcomes. Through education students can be prepared for various types of entrepreneurial activities.

Nyenrode and the Entrepreneurial Climate

Nyenrode is one of the examples where several skills relevant for entrepreneurial activities are a normal part of the admission procedure, such as presentation, and building a team in addition to other regular cognitive capacities. It is also important to note that as a private university, the institution itself has to work entrepreneurially in order to survive competition. The university has to practice what it preaches!

Entrepreneurial Training

Training in venturing skills are a big part of the curriculum. The education aims to find a good balance between soft skills and cognitive knowledge in order to prepare students for work in an entrepreneurial environment.

More Entrepreneurs Among Nyenrode Alumni

We have observed that alumni from Nyenrode are, in comparison with the Dutch population, considerably more entrepreneurial. The Nyenrode alumni rate of participation as assessed by the Total Entrepreneurship Activity rate (TEA index from the Global Entrepreneurship Monitor) is three times higher than the general entrepreneurial population. Most universities in The Netherlands do not have a tradition of building durable communities with their alumni. Nyenrode has an up to date alumni database which, as among North American business schools, is a resource which can help support entrepreneurial attitudes in the community.

Entrepreneurship as a Core Curriculum Requirement

At Nyenrode, as documented in this study as is true for a small number of other European business schools, entrepreneurship is a core requirement in MBA and MSc Management programs. In Europe, among the top 33 European MBA programs, only seven business schools have included Entrepreneurship as a core MBA requirement. In the USA, among 824 institutions which offer graduate business education, 77 include entrepreneurship as a core MBA requirement while, as in Europe, many offer electives in this field.

Nyenrode Entrepreneurs Have a High Change Propensity

Entrepreneurs profiled in the case studies were willing to vary their strategies for the evaluation of on-going opportunities, indicating a high level of willingness to change. Re-designing products or services, and periodic re-segmentation of products, services and markets are important techniques to identify ever developing new opportunities.

Developing Creativity and Competence as Part of Empowerment

The entrepreneurs in the case studies stimulated creativity and developed their competences to evaluate on-going opportunities. It was found that entrepreneurs who stimulate their own creativity were more capable of dealing with setbacks; and they experienced greater feelings of control. Those who were better prepared for setbacks (high score on hardiness) seemed to be better prepared for seeking opportunities as well. And, those entrepreneurs defined their search criteria in advance. This confirms that good preparation does indeed have benefits.

Finally, for Nyenrode, entrepreneurship is a logical theme. The university has always offered the academic climate to encourage entrepreneurship. Among the graduates it is possible to find various types of entrepreneurs, from solo business people to high growth entrepreneurs. Because of this entrepreneurial climate, Nyenrode alumni tend to use different tools to encourage creativity and transformational leadership in their business practices and many have reached prestigious positions in the business community.

We conclude this study with two quotes of well known entrepreneurs from both sides of the Atlantic.

"The educational process is critical. European universities must play a key role in promoting entrepreneurship and innovation, helping students learn not just how to start, but also how to grow, enterprises and across national boundaries."

Bert Twaalfhoven, Founder of Indivers and EFER (European Foundation of Entrepreneurship Research)[5]

"It's quite simple. The success of Ben & Jerry's from the very beginning had to do with really caring for all aspects of the business – our people, our customers, our shareholders, the communities we live in and serve and, of course, the Earth. The reality is that these are really inseparable. That and truly great ice cream, have continued to attract customers, increase shareholder value and nurture creativity.

Ben Cohen, Co-founder of Ben & Jerry's

---

[5] Between 1960 and 2000, Twaalfhoven was a driving force in fifty start-ups in ten countries. He is quick to point out as well that seventeen of those ventures did not survive with him at the helm, a part of the entrepreneurial process he puts into perspective by referring to an ancient Chinese proverb, "The learning that comes from failure is the basis for future success".

References

Adizes I (1979) Organizational Passages, Diagnosing and Treating Lifecycle problems of Organizations. Organizational Dynamics

Ajzen I (1989) Attitudes, structure and behaviour. In: AR Pratkanis, SJ Breckler and AG Greenwald (eds) Attitude, structure and function. Hillsdale, NJ: Lawrence Erlbaum Associates

Ajzen I, Fishbein M (1980) Understanding attitude and predicting social. Prentice-Hall, Inc, Englewood Cliffs, New Jersey

Ajzen I, Madden TJ (1986) Prediction of Goal-directed: attitudes, intentions, and perceived al control. Journal of Experimental Social Psychology 22: 453-474

Aldrich HE, Zimmer C (1986) Entrepreneurship through Social Networks. In: Sexton DL Smilor EW (eds) The Art and Science of Entrepreneurship. Cambridge, MA Ballinger: 3-23

Anderson RC (1998) Mid-Course correction

Ashcraft MH (1998) Fundamentals of cognition. Addison-Wesley Educational Publishers Inc

Bandura A (1991) Social Cognitive Theory of Self-Regulation. Organizational Behavior & Human Decision Processes 50: 248

Barlow N (2000) Batteries Included, Creating Legendary Service, Random House, London

Baron RA (1998) Cognitive mechanism in entrepreneurship: why and when entrepreneurs think differently than other people. Journal of Business Venturing, 13: 275-294

Barrett R (1998) Liberating the Corporate Soul, Building a Visionary Organization. Butterworth Heinemann, Boston

Begley TM, Boyd DP (1987) Psychological Characteristics associated with Performance in Entrepreneurial Firms and Smaller Businesses. Journal of Business Venturing 2: 79-93

Bhidé A (2000) The origin and evolution of new businesses. Oxford University Press

Birch DL (1989) Change, Innovation and Job Generation. Journal of Labor Research 10:33-38

Bird BJ, Jelinek M (1988). The operation of Entrepreneurial Intentions. Entrepreneurship Theory and Practice 13: 21-29

Bosma N, Wennekers S (2004) Global entrepreneurship Monitor (GEM). Entrepreneurial attitudes versus entrepreneurial activities. GEM 2003. The Netherlands. EIM, Zoetermeer, The Netherlands

Brockhaus RH Sr (1982) The psychology of the entrepreneur. In: C Kent, D Sexton, K Vesper (eds) The entrepreneur: encyclopedia of entrepreneurship. Englewood Cliffs, NJ: Prentice-Hall, pp 39-57

Brown L (2006) Plan B 2.0 Rescuing a Planet under Stress and a Civilization in Trouble, W.W. Norton & Company

Business Week (2005) China at a Cross Roads, November 8

CEEDR, Middlesex University, final report. Ethnic minority entrepreneurs http://europe.eu.int/comm/enterprise/entrepreneurship/craft/craft-studies/documents/recommendations.pdf

Chaiken S, Stangor C (1987) Attitudes and attitude change. Annual Review of Psychology, 38: 575-630

Chappell T (1999) The Seven Intentions of Values-centered Leadership, Managing Upside Down. William Morrow and Company Inc., New York

Chell EH, Brearly S (1991). The entrepreneurial Personality. Concepts, cases and categories. Routledge, London

Chrisman JJ, Bauerschmidt A, Hofer CW (1999) The Determinants of New Venture Performance: An Extended Model. Entrepreneurship Theory and Practice, pp 5-22

Chrisman JJ, McMullan WE (2000) A preliminary assessment of outsider assistance as a knowledge resource: The longer-term impact of new venture counselling. Entrepreneurship Theory and Practice, 24: 37-53

Clawson JG (1996) Mentoring in the information aged. Leadership and Organizational Development Journal, pp 6-15

Commission of the European communities. Green paper entrepreneurship in Europe. Brussels 21.1.2003

Csikszentmihalyi M, (2003) Flow in zaken, (About Flow in Business) Boom, Amsterdam

Da Silva D (2006) UK ethnic minorities lead on entrepreneurship. ABi

Deutsch C (2005) New York Times, November 22

Devins D, Johnson, S (2001) Can start-up support increase the chances of new business survival? An empirical analysis of 100 programme participants, Paper presented at the 2001 small business and enterprise development conference, march 29-30th, the university of Leicester, UK

Directorate Enterprise and Industry of the European Commission (2006) http://ec.europa.eu/enterprise/entrepreneurship/craft/craft-minorities/minorities.htm

Economisch Instituut voor Midden – en Kleinbedrijf (EIM) en Ministerie van Economische Zaken (EZ) (1997) Entrepreneurship in the Netherlands: Ambitious entrepreneurs: the driving force for the next millennium. Zoetermeer

EIM (2003) Immigrant entrepreneurship in the Netherlands. Demographic determinants of entrepreneurship of immigrants from non-western countries. Zoetermeer, The Netherlands

Eisenhouwer JG (1995) The entrepreneurial decision: economic theory and empirical evidence

Emmering H (2006) Nederlands Instituut voor het Buitenland, Oprichting en Ontwikkeling van de eerste Business School in Nederland, 1946-1950. Nyenrode Press (forthcoming)

Ewing Marion Kaufman Foundation, (2006) Kaufman Index of Entrepreneurial Activity, http://www.kauffman.org/entrepreneurship.cfm?topic=economic_development&itemID=665

Fishbein M, Ajzen I (1975) Belief, Attitude, Intention and Behavior. Reading, Addison-Wesley

Flanagan JC (1954) The critical incident technique. Psychological Bulletin, 51: 327-355

Gartner WB (1988) Who Is an Entrepreneur? Is the Wrong Question. American Journal of Small Business 12: 11-32

Gartner WB (2001) Is There an Elephant in Entrepreneurship? Blind Assumptions in Theory Development, Entrepreneurship Theory and Practice, pp 27-39

Gartner WB, Bird BJ, Starr JA (1992) Acting as if: differentiating entrepreneurial from organizational behaviour. Entrepreneurship theory and practice, pp 13-31

Global Entrepreneurship Monitor (2002) http://www.gemconsortium.org/

Global Entrepreneurship Monitor (2004)

Global Entrepreneurship Monitor (2006) GEM Global Executive Report 2005.

Gross JJ (1999) Emotion and emotion regulation. In: LA Pervin and OP J (eds). Handbook of personality. Theory and Research. New York Guilford Press

Harding G (1968) The Tragedy of the Commons Science/162, December 13: 1243-1248

Hawken P, Lovins A, Lovins LH (2000) Natural Capitalism, Little Brown and Company

Hazel H (1995) Paradigms in Progress, Berrett-Koehler Publishers

Higgins ET (1998) Promotion and Prevention: regulatory focus as a motivational principle. Advances in experimental social psychology, 30: 1-46

Higgins ET (2000) Making a good decision: value from fit. American Psychologist, pp 1217-1230

Hollender J (2004) What Matters Most: How a Small Group of Pioneers is Teaching Social Responsibility to Big Business and Why Big Business is Listening. Basic Books, Persus Book Group

Intergovernmental Panel on Climate Change (2001) Synthesis Report

International Monetary Fund (2005), IMF Annual Report

Isaak R (2004) The Making of the Ecoentrepreneur. Greener Management International, The Journal of Corporate Environmental Strategy and Practice and Environmental Entrepreneurship pp 38

Jankowicz AD (2000) Business Research Projects. Business Press Thomson Learning

Keizer WAJ, Vooren I (2006) Mentale fitheid als bron van prestatie (About Mental Fitness a source of Performance) Publication of Keizer Prestatie Consultancy, Amsterdam

Kroes Drs. N (1992) Opening of the academic Year 1992-1993 and conferring of Honorary Degrees

Kuhl J (1994) Action versus state orientation: Psychometric properties of the action control scale (ACS-90) In: J Kuhl, J Beckmann (eds) Volition and personality: Action versus state orientation pp 47-59

Kuhl J, Beckmann J (1994) Volition and personality: Action versus state orientation. Seattle, WA: Hogrefe and Huber

Low MB (2001) The adolescence of entrepreneurship research: specification of purpose. Entrepreneurship Theory and Practice 25: 17-26

Low MB, MacMillan IC (1988) Entrepreneurship: past research and future challenges. Journal of Management 14: 139-161

Manstead ASR, Fischer AH (2001) Commentaries: Emotion Regulation in Full

McClelland DC (1961) The achieving Society, Princeton, NY: van Nostrand

McClelland DC (1965) Need achievement and entrepreneurship: a longitudinal study. Journal of Personality and Social Psychology. 1: 389-392

McCrae RR, Costa PT Jr, Hrebickova M, Urbanie T, Marin, TA, Oryol, VE, Rukavishnikov, AA, Senin IG (2004) Age differences in personality traits across cultures: Self-report and observer perspective, European Journal of Personality 18: 143-157

McGrath R, MacMillan I (2000) The Entrepreneurial Mindset, Strategies for Creating Opportunity in an Age of Uncertainty, Harvard Business School Press

Miner JB (1999) A psychological typology of Successful Entrepreneurs. Quorum Books. London

Mitchell RK, Busenitz, L, Lant, T, McDougall PP, Morse EA, Smith JB (2002) Toward a theory of entrepreneurial cognition: Rethinking the People Side of Entrepreneurship Research. Entrepreneurship Theory and Practice, pp 93-104

Nandram SS (2002) Attributes of Entrepreneurial Success and failures. New Perspectives gained from the Critical Incident Technique. In: Conference Proceedings The 2002 small Business and Entrepreneurship Development Conference. 15-16 April, The University of Nottingham, UK

Nandram SS (2002-2004) Entrepreneur of Year studies Netherlands. Confidential reports

Nandram SS (2003) Predicting Entrepreneurial growth: The role of decisiveness and opportunity perception," paper presented at the Small Business and Entrepreneurship Development Conference 3-4 April 2003 Guilford, U.K

Nandram SS, Samsom KJ (2000) (Personality and successful entrepreneurship) Persoonlijkheid en ondernemerssucces. Economische Statistische Berichten, pp 717-719

Nandram SS, Samsom KJ (2001) Het Onderzoek: Hoe Ondernemend is Nederland?" In De Succesvolle Ondernemer, Ondernemers vertellen over succes en falen. Ministerie van Economische Zaken en NVP

Nandram SS, Samsom KJ (2005) Hoe wordt Nederland ondernemender. *Management Team*, October 7. (How can The Netherlands become more entrepreneurial?)

Nandram, SS, van Dijk, G (2003) Groeien is meer dan groter worden. BDO Accountants and Advisors

New Scientist.com (2006) Special Report On Key Topics in Science and Technology. Climate Change

Nijenrode (1986) Nijenrode, de ontwikkeling van een toekomst. Van 1946 tot 1986 en daarna. Nijenrode Press

OECD working paper no 239 (23-April-2002) The role of policy and institutions for productivity and firm dynamics: evidence from micro and industry data

Otten R, Boekaerts M, Seegers G (1994) Handelingsvaardigheden in het onderwijs (action control at school). Tijdschrift voor onderwijsresearch, 19: 343-355

Palich LE, Bagby DR (1995) Using cognitive theory to explain entrepreneurial risk-taking. Challenging conventional wisdom. Journal of Business Venturing 10: 425-438

Postma EBJ (1980) Rede gehouden bij het aftreden als voorzitter van het College van Bestuur van de Stichting Nijenrode, Instituut voor Bedrijfskunde te Bre

Ray P (2004) Rx for Green Market Place Growth. Lohas Journal. Volume 5, Issue 1

Reeve J (2001) Understanding motivation and emotion Harcourt, Orlando.

Roberts BW, Robins, RW, Trzesnieuwski KH, Caspi A (2003) Personality trait development in adulthood, In: The Handbook of the Life Course. J.T. Mortimer and M.J. Shanahan (eds.). (pp 579-595). New York: Kluwer Plenum

Roberts BW, Robins RW (2004) "Person-environment fit and its implications for personality development: A longitudinal study," Journal of Personality, 72: 89-110.

Roberts P (2004) The End of Oil, Houghton Mifflin Company

Robinson PB, Stimpson DV, Huefner JC, Hunt HK (1991) An Attitude approach to the prediction of entrepreneurship. Entrepreneurship Theory and Practice pp 13-31

Robson PJA, Bennett RJ (2000) The influence of business advice on SME growth, Paper presented at the 2000 small business and enterprise development conference, April 10-11th, The university of Manchester, UK

Samsom KJ (2005) Duurzaam entrepreneurship-uitdaging en kans! In: W Burggraaf, RH Floren, JMV Kunst (eds) Ondernemerschap en ondernemen, de ondernemer centraal. Netwerkpers

Samsom KJ (1999) The Case for Entrepreneurship in a Cost-externalizing Economy Nyenrode Press

Sarasvathy SD (2004) Making it happen: beyond theories of the firm to theories of firm design. Entrepreneurship Theory and practice pp 519-531

Schijf Ir FJ (1986) Rede gehouden ter gelegenheid van de opening va het academisch jaar 1986-1987

Shane S, Venkataraman S (2000) The promise of entrepreneurship as a field of research. Academy of Management Review 25: 217-226

Stevenson H (2000) The six dimensions of entrepreneurship, In: Mastering Entrepreneurship, (eds) S Birley DF Muzyka, Pearson Education Ltd

Stockly S (2000) Building and maintaining the entrepreneurial team -a critical competence for venture growth. In: S Birley & DF Muzyka (eds) Mastering Entrepreneurship, Person Education Ltd

Sullivan R (2000) Entrepreneurial Learning and Mentoring, International Journal of Entrepreneurial Behaviour & Research, 6: 160-175

Timmons J (1978) Characteristics and role demands of entrepreneurship. American Journal of Small Business 3: 5-17

Timmons JA (1998) New Venture Creation. Homewood, IL: Irwin

Timmons JA, Spinelli S (2004) New Venture Creation, Entrepreneurship for the 21st Century. McGraw Hill

Ucbasaran D, Westhead P, Wright M (2001) The Focus of Entrepreneurial Research: Contextual and Process Issues. Entrepreneurship Theory and Practice pp 57-80

Valdez Z (2002) Beyond Ethnic Entrepreneurship: Ethnicity and the Economy in Enterprise. University of California, Working Paper, wrkg63

Van der Sluis J, Van Praag M, Vijverberg W (2004) Education and Entrepreneurship in Industrialized Countries: A Meta analysis of the Role of Education. University of Amsterdam

Van Praag M (1996) Determinants of Successful Entrepreneurship. Tinbergen Institute Research Series, Dissertation

Venkataram S (1997) The distinctive domain of entrepreneurship research: an editor's perspective Advances in Entrepreneurship, Firm Emergence, and growth 3: 119-138 Greenwich, CT: JAI Press

Walton J (1998) Mentoring in mainland Europe and the republic of Ireland. www.enterprise-ireland.com

Westhead P, Wright M (1998) Novice, portfolio, and serial founders: Are they different? Journal of Business Venturing, 13: 173-204

Wickham PA (2004) Strategic Entrepreneurship: A Decision-Making Strategic Approach to New Venture Creation and Management, Pearson Education Limited, Harlow, England

Zhao H, Seibert SE (2006) The big five personality dimensions and entrepreneurial status: a meta-analytical review. Journal of Applied Psychology, 91: 259-271

Subject Index

Printing: Krips bv, Meppel
Binding: Stürtz, Würzburg